First Japanese Reader for Beginners
Beginner Elementary (A1 A2)

Miku Ono

First Japanese Reader for Beginners
Bilingual for Speakers of English
Beginner Elementary (A1 A2)

First Japanese Reader for Beginners

by Miku Ono

Audio tracks www.audiolego.com/Japanese/

Homepage www.lppbooks.com

Graphics: Audiolego Design

Copyright © 2015 2016 2021 Language Practice Publishing

Copyright © 2016 2021 Audiolego

This book is in copyright. Subject to statutory exception and to the provisions of relevant collective licensing agreements, no reproduction of any part may take place without the written permission of Language Practice Publishing.

目次
Table of contents

How to control the playing speed 7
Pronunciation 8
Beginner Course 11
Chapter 1 Robert has a dog 12
Chapter 2 They live in San Francisco (the USA) 17
Chapter 3 Are they Germans? 22
Chapter 4 Can you help, please? 29
Chapter 5 Robert lives in the USA now 37
Chapter 6 Robert has many friends 44
Chapter 7 David buys a bike 51
Chapter 8 Linda wants to buy a new DVD 56
Chapter 9 Paul listens to German songs 61
Chapter 10 Paul buys textbooks on design 68
Chapter 11 Robert wants to earn some money (Part 1) 74
Chapter 12 Robert wants to earn some money (Part 2) 81
Elementary Course 87
Chapter 13 ホテルの名前 88
Chapter 14 アスピリン（鎮痛剤）.. 94
Chapter 15 ナンシーとカンガルー 101
Chapter 16 パラシュート 108
Chapter 17 ガスを消して！！ 119
Chapter 18 職業紹介所 127
Chapter 19 デイビッドとロバートはトラックを洗います（パート１）...... 136
Chapter 20 デイビッドとロバートはトラックを洗います（パート２）...... 144
Chapter 21 授業 153
Chapter 22 ポールは出版社で働きます 160
Chapter 23 猫のルール 169

- Chapter 24 チームワーク 176
- Chapter 25 ロバートとデイビッドは新しい仕事を探しています 185
- Chapter 26 サンフランシスコニュースへ応募 197
- Chapter 27 警察パトロール（パート１） 206
- Chapter 28 警察パトロール（パート２） 220
- Chapter 29 留学生の学校とオペア 233
- 日英辞書 Japanese-English dictionary 243
- 英日辞書 English-Japanese dictionary 259
- Recommended reading 275

How to control the playing speed

The book is equipped with the audio tracks. The address of the home page of the book on the Internet, where audio files are available for listening and downloading, is listed at the beginning of the book on the bibliographic description page before the copyright notice. With the help of QR codes, you can call up an audio file in no time, without typing a web address manually. Simply hold your smartphone with camera app on over the QR code. Your smartphone will scan the code and will offer you to follow the scanned audio file link.

We recommend using free **VLC media player** to control the playing speed. You can control the playing speed by decreasing or increasing the speed value on the button of the VLC media player's interface.

Android users: After installing VLC media player, click an audio track at the top of a chapter or on the home page of the book if you read a paper book. When prompted choose "Open with VLC". If you experience difficulties opening audio tracks with VLC, change default app for music player. Go to Settings→Apps, choose VLC and click "Open by default" or "Set default".

Kindle Fire users: After installing VLC media player, click an audio track at the top of a chapter or on the home page of the book if you read a paper book. Complete action using →VLC.

iOS users: After installing VLC media player, copy the link to an audio track at the top of a chapter or on the home page of the book if you read a paper book. Paste it into Downloads section of VLC media player. After the download is complete, go to All Files section and start the downloaded audio track.

Windows users: After installing VLC media player, right-click an audio track at the top of a chapter or on the home page of the book if you read a paper book. Choose "Open with→VLC media player".

MacOS users: After installing VLC media player, right-click an audio track at the top of a chapter or on the home page of the book if you read a paper book, then download it. Right-click the downloaded audio track and choose "Get info". Then in the "Open with" section choose VLC media player. You can enable "Change all" to apply this change to all audio tracks.

Pronunciation

Hiragana	Katakana	Romaji	Hiragana	Katakana	Romaji
あ	ア	a	そ	ソ	so
い	イ	i	しゃ	シャ	sha/sya
う	ウ	u	しゅ	シュ	shu/syu
え	エ	e	しょ	ショ	sho/syo
お	オ	o	た	タ	ta
や	ヤ	ya	ち	チ	chi/ti
ゆ	ユ	yu	つ	ツ	tsu/tu
よ	ヨ	yo	て	テ	te
か	カ	ka	と	ト	to
き	キ	ki	ちゃ	チャ	cha/tya
く	ク	ku	ちゅ	チュ	chu/tyu
け	ケ	ke	ちょ	チョ	cho/tyo
こ	コ	ko	な	ナ	na
きゃ	キャ	kya	に	ニ	ni
きゅ	キュ	kyu	ぬ	ヌ	nu
きょ	キョ	kyo	ね	ネ	ne
さ	サ	sa	の	ノ	no
し	シ	shi/si	にゃ	ニャ	nya
す	ス	su	にゅ	ニュ	nyu
せ	セ	se	にょ	ニョ	nyo

Hiragana	Katakana	Romaji	Hiragana	Katakana	Romaji
は	ハ	ha	る	ル	ru
ひ	ヒ	hi	れ	レ	re
ふ	フ	fu/hu	ろ	ロ	ro
へ	ヘ	he	りゃ	リャ	rya
ほ	ホ	ho	りゅ	リュ	ryu
ひゃ	ヒャ	hya	りょ	リョ	ryo
ひゅ	ヒュ	hyu	わ	ワ	wa
ひょ	ヒョ	hyo	ゐ	ヰ	i/wi/i
ま	マ	ma	ゑ	ヱ	e/we/e
み	ミ	mi	を	ヲ	o/wo/o
む	ム	mu	ん	ン	n-n'(m) /n-n'
め	メ	me	が	ガ	ga
も	モ	mo	ぎ	ギ	gi
みゃ	ミャ	mya	ぐ	グ	gu
みゅ	ミュ	myu	げ	ゲ	ge
みょ	ミョ	myo	ご	ゴ	go
や	ヤ	ya	ぎゃ	ギャ	gya
ゆ	ユ	yu	ぎゅ	ギュ	gyu
よ	ヨ	yo	ぎょ	ギョ	gyo
ら	ラ	ra	ざ	ザ	za
り	リ	ri	じ	ジ	ji/zi

Hiragana	Katakana	Romaji	Hiragana	Katakana	Romaji
ず	ズ	zu	び	ビ	bi
ぜ	ゼ	ze	ぶ	ブ	bu
ぞ	ゾ	zo	べ	ベ	be
じゃ	ジャ	ja/zya	ぼ	ボ	bo
じゅ	ジュ	ju/zyu	びゃ	ビャ	bya
じょ	ジョ	jo/zyo	びゅ	ビュ	byu
だ	ダ	da	びょ	ビョ	byo
ぢ	ヂ	ji/di/zi	ぱ	パ	pa
づ	ヅ	zu/du/zu	ぴ	ピ	pi
で	デ	de	ぷ	プ	pu
ど	ド	do	ぺ	ペ	pe
ぢゃ	ヂャ	ja/dya/zya	ぽ	ポ	po
ぢゅ	ヂュ	ju/dyu/zyu	ぴゃ	ピャ	pya
ぢょ	ヂョ	jo/dyo/zyo	ぴゅ	ピュ	pyu
ば	バ	ba	ぴょ	ピョ	pyo

Beginner Course

1

Audio

ろば と いぬ か
ロバートは 犬 を飼っています

Robert has a dog

A

たんご
単 語
Words

1. 4つ [yottsu] - four
2. お店 [o mise] - shop
3. お店（複数）[o mise （fukusuu）] - shops
4. これ、この；この本 [kore, kono ; kono hon] - this, this book
5. それ、あれ [sore, are] - that
6. それら、あれら（複数）[sorera, are ra （fukusuu）] - these, those
7. たくさんの、多くの [takusan no, ooku no] - many, much
8. テーブル、机 [teーburu, tsukue] - table
9. テーブル、机（複数）[teーburu, tsukue （fukusuu）] - tables

10. ではない [de wa nai] - not
11. と [to] - and
12. ノート [no—to] - notebook
13. ノート（複数）[no—to（fukusuu）] - notebooks
14. ひとつ [hitotsu] - one
15. ベッド [beddo] - bed
16. ベッド（複数）[beddo（fukusuu）] - beds
17. ペン [pen] - pen
18. ペン（複数）[pen（fukusuu）] - pens
19. ホテル [hoteru] - hotel
20. ホテル（複数）[hoteru（fukusuu）] - hotels
21. わたしの、自分の [watashi no, jibun no] - my
22. わたしは [watashi wa] - I
23. 公園 [kouen] - park
24. 公園（複数）[kouen（fukusuu）] - parks
25. 単語、言葉 [tango, kotoba] - word
26. 単語、言葉（複数）[tango, kotoba（fukusuu）] - words
27. 同じく、〜も [onajiku, 〜mo] - too
28. 夢 [yume] - dream
29. 大きい [ookii] - big
30. 少しの、小さな [sukoshi no, chiisana] - little
31. 彼の；彼のベッド [kare no ; kare no beddo] - his, his bed
32. 彼は [kare wa] - he
33. 彼らは [karera wa] - they
34. 持っている、飼っている、ある；彼／彼女／それは持っている；彼は本を持っている [mo tte iru, ka tte iru, aru ; kare／kanojo／sore wa mo tte iru ; kare wa hon wo mo tte iru] - have, he/she/it has, he has a book.
35. 教科書、本文 [kyoukasho, honbun] - text
36. 新しい [atarashii] - new
37. 星 [hoshi] - star
38. 本 [hon] - book
39. 犬 [inu] - dog
40. 猫 [neko] - cat
41. 生徒、学生 [seito, gakusei] - student
42. 生徒達、学生達（複数）[seito tachi, gakusei tachi（fukusuu）] - students
43. 目 [me] - eye
44. 目（複数）[me（fukusuu）] - eyes
45. 窓 [mado] - window
46. 窓（複数）[mado（fukusuu）] - windows
47. 素敵な、優しい、素晴らしい [suteki na, yasashii, subarashii] - nice
48. 緑の [midori no] - green
49. 自転車 [jitensha] - bike
50. 通り、道 [toori, michi] - street

51. 通り、道（複数）[toori, michi（fukusuu）] - streets
52. 部屋 [heya] - room
53. 部屋（複数）[heya（fukusuu）] - rooms
54. 青い [aoi] - blue
55. 黒い [kuroi] - black
56. 鼻 [hana] - nose

B

ロバートは 犬 を飼っています
roba—to wa inu wo ka tte i masu

Robert has a dog

1. この学生は本を持っています。 2. 彼はぺんも持っています。 ichi. kono gakusei wa hon wo mo tte i masu. ni. kare wa pen mo mo tte i masu.

1. This student has a book.
2. He has a pen too.

3. さんふらんしすこにはたくさんの通りと公園があります。 4. この通りには、新しいほてるとお店があります。 5. このほてるは四つ星です。 6. このほてるには、たくさんの素敵で大きな部屋があります。 san. sanfuranshisuko ni wa takusan no toori to kouen ga ari masu. yon. kono toori ni wa, atarashii hoteru to o mise ga ari masu. go. kono hoteru wa yotsu boshi desu. roku. kono hoteru ni wa, takusan no suteki de ookina heya ga ari masu.

3. San Francisco has many streets and parks. 4. This street has new hotels and shops.
5. This hotel has four stars.
6. This hotel has many nice big rooms.

7. あの部屋にはたくさんの窓があります。 8. そしてこれらの部屋には、たくさんの窓はありません。 9. これらの部屋には、4つのべっどがありま

7. That room has many windows. 8. And these rooms do not have many windows.
9. These rooms have four beds.
10. And those rooms have one

す。10. そしてそれらの部屋には、べっどがひとつあります。11. あの部屋にはてーぶるがたくさんありません。12. そしてそれらの部屋には、大きなてーぶるがたくさんあります。 nana. ano heya ni wa takusan no mado ga ari masu. hachi. soshite korera no heya ni wa, takusan no mado wa ari mase n. kyuu. korera no heya ni wa, yottsu no beddo ga ari masu. juu. soshite sorera no heya ni wa, beddo ga hitotsu ari masu. juuichi. ano heya ni wa te—buru ga takusan ari mase n. juu ni. soshite sorera no heya ni wa, ookina te—buru ga takusan ari masu.

bed. 11. That room does not have many tables. 12. And those rooms have many big tables.

13. この通りにはほてるがありません。14. あの大きなお店には窓がたくさんあります。 juusan. kono toori ni wa hoteru ga ari mase n. juuyon. ano ookina o mise ni wa mado ga takusan ari masu.

13. This street does not have hotels. 14. That big shop has many windows.

15. 生徒達はのーとを持っています。16. 彼らはぺんも持っています。17. ろばーとは小さな黒いのーとをひとつ持っています。18. ぽーるは新しい緑ののーとを4冊持っています。 juugo. seito tachi wa no—to wo mo tte i masu. juuroku. karera wa pen mo mo tte i masu. juunana. roba—to wa chiisana kuroi no—to wo hitotsu mo tte i masu. juu hachi. po—ru wa atarashii midori no no—to wo yon satsu mo tte i masu.

15. These students have notebooks. 16. They have pens too. 17. Robert has one little black notebook. 18. Paul has four new green notebooks.

19. この生徒は自転車を持っています。20. 彼は新しい青い自転車を持っています。21. でいびっども自転車を持っています。22. 彼は素敵な黒い自転車を持っていま

19. This student has a bike. 20. He has a new blue bike. 21. David has a bike too. 22. He has a nice black bike.

す。juu kyuu. kono seito wa jitensha wo mo tte i masu. ni juu. kare wa atarashii aoi jitensha wo mo tte i masu. ni juu ichi. deibiddo mo jitensha wo mo tte i masu. ni juu ni. kare wa suteki na kuroi jitensha wo mo tte i masu.

23. ぽーるには 夢 があります。24. わたしにも 夢 があります。ni juu san. po─ru ni wa yume ga ari masu. ni juu yon. watashi ni mo yume ga ari masu.

23. Paul has a dream. 24. I have a dream too.

25. わたしは 犬 を飼っていません。26. わたしは 猫 を飼っています。27. わたしの 猫 には、素敵な 緑 の目があります。28. ろばーとは 猫 を飼っていません。29. 彼 は 犬 を飼っています。 30. 彼の犬は小さな黒い鼻があります。ni juu go. watashi wa inu wo ka tte i mase n. ni juu roku. watashi wa neko wo ka tte i masu. Ni juu nana. watashi no neko ni wa, suteki na midori no me ga ari masu. ni juu hachi. roba─to wa neko wo ka tte i mase n. ni juu kyuu. kare wa inu wo ka tte i masu. san juu. kare no inu wa chiisana kuroi hana ga ari masu.

25. I do not have a dog. 26. I have a cat. 27. My cat has nice green eyes. 28. Robert does not have a cat. 29. He has a dog.

30. His dog has a little black nose.

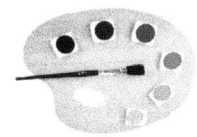

2

Audio

かれ　　　さんふらんしすこ　す　　　　　　　あめりか
彼らはサンフランシスコに住んでいます（アメリカ）

They live in San Francisco (the USA)

A

たんご
単語
Words

1. 〜に、〜で [~ ni, ~ de] - in
2. あなたは [anata wa] - you
3. アメリカ [amerika] - USA
4. アメリカ人 [amerika jin] - American
5. お腹がすいている；わたしはお腹がすいています [onaka ga sui te iru ; watashi wa onaka ga sui te i masu] - hungry; I am hungry
6. カナダ [kanada] - Canada
7. カナダ人 [kanada jin] - Canadian
8. から、出身；アメリカ出身 [kara, shusshin ; amerika shusshin] - from; from the USA

9. サンドイッチ [sandoicchi] - sandwich
10. スーパー [su―pa―] - supermarket
11. ドイツ人 [doitsu jin] - German
12. ふたつ [futatsu] - two
13. わたしたちは [watashi tachi wa] - we
14. 今、現在 [ima, genzai] - now
15. 住んでいる [sun de iru] - live
16. 兄、弟 [ani, otouto] - brother
17. 大きな、大きい [ookina, ookii] - big
18. 姉、妹 [ane, imouto] - sister
19. 彼女は [kanojo wa] - she
20. 母、お母さん [haha, okaasan] - mother
21. 街、市 [machi, shi] - city
22. 買う [kau] - buy

B

彼らはサンフランシスコに住んでいます
(アメリカ)

karera wa sanfuranshisuko ni sun de i masu
(ame rika)

They live in San Francisco (the USA)

1. さんふらんしすこは大きな街です。2. さんふらんしすこはあめりかにあります。ichi. sanfuranshisuko wa ookina machi desu. ni. sanfuranshisuko wa amerika ni ari masu.

1. San Francisco is a big city.
2. San Francisco is in the USA.

3. こちらはろばーとです。4. ろばーとは学生です。5. 彼は今さんふらんしすこにいます。6. ろばーとはどいつ出身です。7. ろばーとはどいつ人です。8. ろばーとには、母、父、兄（又は弟）、姉（又は妹）がいます。9. 彼らはどいつに住んで

3. This is Robert. 4. Robert is a student. 5. He is in San Francisco now. 6. Robert is from Germany. 7. He is German. 8. Robert has a mother, a father, a brother and a sister. 9. They live in Germany.

います。san. kochira wa roba—to desu. yon. roba—to wa gakusei desu. go. kare ha ima sanfuranshisuko ni i masu. roku. roba—to ha doitsu shusshin desu. nana. roba—to wa doitsu jin desu. hachi. roba—to ni wa, haha, chichi, ani（matawa otouto）, ane（matawa imouto）ga i masu. kyuu. karera wa doitsu ni sun de i masu.

10. こちらはぽーるです。11. ぽーるも学生です。12. 彼はかなだ出身です。13. 彼はかなだ人です。14. ぽーるには、母、父、そしてふたりの姉（又は妹）がいます。15. 彼らはかなだに住んでいます。juu. kochira wa po—ru desu. juu ichi. po—ru mo gakusei desu. juu ni. kare wa kanada shusshin desu. juu san. kare wa kanada jin desu. juu yon. po—ru ni wa, haha, chichi, soshite futari no ane（matawa imouto）ga i masu. juu go. karera wa kanada ni sun de i masu.

10. This is Paul. 11. Paul is a student too. 12. He is from Canada. 13. He is Canadian. 14. Paul has a mother, a father and two sisters. 15. They live in Canada.

16. ろばーととぽーるは今、すーぱーにいます。17. 彼らはお腹がすいています。18. 彼らはさんどいっちを買います。juu roku. roba—to to po—ru wa ima, su—pa— ni i masu. juu nana. karera wa onaka ga sui te i masu. juu hachi. karera wa sandoicchi wo kai masu.

16. Robert and Paul are in a supermarket now. 17. They are hungry. 18. They buy sandwiches.

19. こちらはりんだです。20. りんだはあめりか人です。21. りんだもさんふらんしすこに住んでいます。22. 彼女は学生ではありません。juu kyuu. kochira wa rinda desu. nijuu. rinda wa amerika jin desu. ni juu ichi. rinda mo sanfuranshisuko ni sun de i masu. ni juu ni. kanojo wa gakusei de wa ari mase n.

19. This is Linda. 20. Linda is American. 21. Linda lives in San Francisco too. 22. She is not a student.

23. わたしは 学生 です。 24. わたしはどいつ 出身 です。 25. わたしは 今 さんふらんしすこにいます。 26. わたしはお腹 がすいていません。 ni juu san. watashi wa gakusei desu. ni juu yon. watashi wa doitsu shusshin desu. ni juu go. watashi wa ima sanfuranshisuko ni i masu. ni juu roku. watashi wa onaka ga sui te i mase n.

23. I am a student. 24. I am from Germany. 25. I am in San Francisco now. 26. I am not hungry.

27. あなたは 学生 です。 28. あなたはどいつ人 です。 29. あなたは 今 どいつにいません。 30. あなたは 今 あめりかにいます。 ni juu nana. anata wa gakusei desu. ni juu hachi. anata wa doitsu jin desu. ni juu kyuu. anata wa ima doitsu ni i mase n. san juu. anata wa ima amerika ni i masu.

27. You are a student. 28. You are German. 29. You are not in Germany now. 30. You are in the USA.

31. わたしたちは 学生 です。 32. わたしたちは 今 あめりかにいます。 san juu ichi. watashi tachi wa gakusei desu. san juu ni. watashi tachi wa ima amerika ni i masu.

31. We are students. 32. We are in the USA now.

33. これは 自転車 です。 34. この 自転車 は 青 いです。 35. この 自転車 は 新 しくありません。 san juu san. kore wa jitensha desu. san juu yon. kono jitensha wa aoi desu. san juu go. kono jitensha wa atarashiku ari mase n.

33. This is a bike. 34. The bike is blue. 35. The bike is not new.

36. これは 犬 です。 37. この 犬 は 黒 いです。 38. この 犬 は 大 きくありません。 san juu roku. kore wa inu desu. san juu nana. kono inu wa kuroi desu. san juu hachi. kono inu wa ookiku ari mase n.

36. This is a dog. 37. The dog is black. 38. The dog is not big.

39. これらはお店 です。 40. これらのお店 は

39. These are shops. 40. The

大きくありません。41.それらは小さいです。42.あのお店は窓がたくさんあります。43.あれらの店は窓がたくさんありません。san juu kyuu. korera wa o mise desu. yon juu. korera no o mise wa ookiku ari mase n. yon juu ichi. sorera wa chiisai desu. yon juu ni. ano o mise wa mado ga takusan ari masu. yon juu san. arerano mise wa mado ga takusan ari mase n.

shops are not big. 41. They are little. 42. That shop has many windows. 43. Those shops do not have many windows.

44.あの猫は部屋にいます。45.あれらの猫は部屋にいません。yon juu yon. ano neko wa heya ni i masu. yon juu go. arerano neko wa heya ni i mase n.

44. That cat is in the room.
45. Those cats are not in the room.

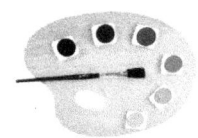

3

Audio

かれ　　　どいつじん
彼らはドイツ人？

Are they Germans?

A

たんご
単語
Words

1. CDプレーヤー [shi— di— pure—ya—] - CD player
2. あなた [anata] - you
3. いいえ、ちがいます [iie, chigai masu] - no
4. カフェ [kafe] - café
5. スペイン人の、スペイン語の [supein jin no, supein go no] - Spanish
6. すべての、全部の [subete no, zenbu no] - all
7. それ [sore] - it
8. で、にて [de, nite] - at

9. どう [dou] - how
10. どこ、どちら [doko, dochira] - where
11. の上に、ついて [no ue ni, tsui te] - on
12. はい、そうです [hai, sou desu] - yes
13. わたしたちの [watashi tachi no] - our
14. 動物 [doubutsu] - animal
15. 地図 [chizu] - map
16. 女性 [josei] - woman
17. 家 [ie] - house
18. 彼女の ; 彼女の本 [kanojo no ; kanojo no hon] - her; her book
19. 男の子 [otokonoko] - boy
20. 男性、人 [dansei, hito] - man

B

彼らはドイツ人？
karera wa doitsu jin?

1

-ぼくは男の子です。ぼくは部屋にいます。
-あなたはあめりか人ですか？
-いいえ、違います。わたしはどいつ人です。
-あなたは学生ですか？
-はい、わたしは学生です。

ichi
- boku wa otokonoko desu. boku wa heya ni i masu.
- anata wa amerika jin desu ka?
- iie, chigai masu. watashi wa doitsu jin desu.
- anata wa gakusei desu ka?
- hai, watashi wa gakusei desu.

2

-こちらは女性です。女性も部屋にいます。

Are they Germans?

1

- I am a boy. I am in the room.

- Are you American?

- No, I am not. I am German.

- Are you a student?

- Yes, I am. I am a student.

2

- This is a woman. The woman is in the room too.

23

- 彼女はどいつ人ですか？
- いいえ、違います。彼女はあめりか人です。
- 彼女は学生ですか？
- いいえ、違います。彼女は学生ではありません。
- こちらは男性です。彼はてーぶるにいます。
- 彼はあめりか人ですか？
- はい、そうです。彼はあめりか人です。

ni
- kochira wa josei desu. josei mo heya ni i masu.
- kanojo wa doitsu jin desu ka?
- iie, chigai masu. kanojo wa amerika jin desu.
- kanojo wa gakusei desu ka?
- iie, chigai masu. kanojo wa gakusei de wa ari mase n.
- kochira wa dansei desu. kare wa te一buru ni i masu.
- kare wa amerika jin desu ka?
- hai, sou desu. kare wa amerika jin desu.

- Is she German?
- No, she is not. She is American.
- Is she a student?
- No, she is not. She is not a student.
- This is a man. He is at the table.
- Is he American?
- Yes, he is. He is American.

3

- これらは学生です。彼らは公園にいます。
- 彼らは全員あめりか人ですか？
- いいえ、違います。彼らは、どいつ、あめりか、そしてかなだ出身です。

san
- korera wa gakusei desu. karera wa kouen ni i masu.

3

- These are students. They are in the park.
- Are they all Americans?
- No, they are not. They are from Germany, the USA and Canada.

- karera wa zen'in amerika jin desu ka?
- iie, chigai masu. karera wa, doitsu, amerika, soshite kanada shusshin desu.

4

―これはてーぶるです。それは大きいです。

―それは新しいですか？

―はい、そうです。それは新しいです。

yon

- kore wa te―buru desu. sore wa ookii desu.
- sore wa atarashii desu ka?
- hai, sou desu. sore wa atarashii desu.

5

―これは猫です。部屋の中にいます。

―それは黒いですか？

―はい、そうです。それは黒く、素敵です。

go

- kore wa neko desu. heya no naka ni i masu.
- sore wa kuroi desu ka?
- hai, sou desu. sore wa kuroku, suteki desu.

6

―これらは自転車です。それらは家にあります。

―それらは黒いですか？

―はい、そうです。それらは黒いです。

roku

- korera wa jitensha desu. sorera wa ie ni ari masu.
- sorera wa kuroi desu ka?
- hai, sou desu. sorera wa kuroi desu.

4

- This is a table. It is big.
- Is it new?
- Yes, it is. It is new.

5

- This is a cat. It is in the room.
- Is it black?
- Yes, it is. It is black and nice.

6

- These are bikes. They are at the house.
- Are they black?
- Yes, they are. They are black.

7

- あなたはのーとを持っていますか？
- はい、持っています。
- あなたはのーとを何冊持っていますか？
- わたしは2冊ののーとを持っています。

nana
- anata wa noーto wo mo tte i masu ka?
- hai, mo tte i masu.
- anata wa noーto wo nan satsu mo tte i masu ka?
- watashi wa ni satsu no noーto wo mo tte i masu.

- Do you have a notebook?
- Yes, I do.
- How many notebooks do you have?
- I have two notebooks.

8

- 彼はぺんを持っていますか？
- はい、持っています。
- 彼はぺんを何本持っていますか？
- 彼は1本のぺんを持っています。

hachi
- kare wa pen wo mo tte i masu ka?
- hai, mo tte i masu.
- kare wa pen wo nan hon mo tte i masu ka?
- kare wa ippon no pen wo mo tte i masu.

- Does he have a pen?
- Yes, he does.
- How many pens does he have?
- He has one pen.

9

- 彼女は自転車を持っていますか？ －はい、持っています。
- 彼女の自転車は青いですか？
- いいえ、違います。彼女の自転車は青く

- Does she have a bike?
- Yes, she does.
- Is her bike blue?
- No, it is not. Her bike is not blue. It is green.

ないです。緑です。

kyuu
- kanojo wa jitensha wo mo tte i masu ka?
- hai, mo tte i masu.
- kanojo no jitensha wa aoi desu ka?
- iie, chigai masu. kanojo no jitensha wa aoku nai desu. midori desu.

10
-あなたはすぺいん語の本を持っていますか?
-いいえ。わたしはすぺいん語の本を持っていません。本は全く持っていません。

juu
- anata wa supein go no hon wo mo tte i masu ka?
- iie. watashi wa supein go no hon wo mo tte i mase n. hon wa mattaku mo tte i mase n.

10

- Do you have a Spanish book?

- No, I do not. I do not have a Spanish book. I have no books.

11
- 彼女は猫を飼っていますか?
-いいえ。彼女は猫を飼っていません。彼女は動物を全く飼っていません。

juu ichi
- kanojo wa neko wo ka tte i masu ka?
- iie. kanojo wa neko wo ka tte i mase n. kanojo wa doubutsu wo mattaku ka tte i mase n.

11

- Does she have a cat?

- No, she does not. She does not have a cat. She has no animal.

12
-あなたたちはCD ぷれーやーを持っていますか?
-いいえ。私たちはCD ぷれーやーを持っていません。

juu ni

12

- Do you have a CD player?

- No, we do not. We do not have a CD player.

- anata tachi wa shi―di―pure―ya― wo mo tte i masu ka?
- iie. watashi tachi wa shi―di―pure―ya― wo mo tte i mase n.

13

-わたしたちの地図はどこですか？
-わたしたちの地図は部屋にあります。
-それはて―ぶるの上ですか？
-はい、そうです。

juu san
- watashi tachi no chizu wa doko desu ka?
- watashi tachi no chizu wa heya ni ari masu.
- sore wa te―buru no ue desu ka?
- hai, sou desu.

14

-男の子達はどこですか？
-彼らはかふぇにいます。
-自転車はどこですか？
-それらはかふぇにあります。
-ぽ―るはどこですか？
-彼もかふぇにいます。

juu yon
- otokonoko tachi wa doko desu ka?
- karera wa kafe ni i masu.
- jitensha wa doko desu ka?
- sorera wa kafe ni ari masu.
- po―ru wa doko desu ka?
- kare mo kafe ni i masu.

13

- *Where is our map?*
- *Our map is in the room.*
- *Is it on the table?*
- *Yes, it is.*

14

- *Where are the boys?*
- *They are in the café.*
- *Where are the bikes?*
- *They are at the café.*
- *Where is Paul?*
- *He is in the café too.*

4

Audio

<ruby>助<rt>たす</rt></ruby>けてもらえませんか、お<ruby>願<rt>ねが</rt></ruby>いします

Can you help, please?

A

<ruby>単語<rt>たんご</rt></ruby>
Words

1. 住所 [juusho] - address
2. お願いします [onegai shi masu] - please
3. かもしれない、許可する・される [kamo shire nai, kyoka suru. sa reru] - may
4. してはいけない [shi te ha ike nai] - must not
5. しなければならない；わたしは行かなければならない [shi nakere ba nara nai ; watashi ha ika nakere ba nara nai] - must; I must go
6. することができる；わたしは読むことができる [suru koto ga dekiru ; watashi ha yomu koto ga dekiru] - can; I can read

7. ために [tame ni] - for
8. でも、しかし [demo, shikashi] - but
9. とる、使う、持って行く、食べる、飲む [toru, tsukau, mo tte iku, taberu, nomu] - take
10. 助ける、手伝う；助けるために、手伝うために [tasukeru, tetsudau ; tasukeru tame ni, tetsudau tame ni] - help; to help
11. 学ぶ、習う [manabu, narau] - learn
12. 座る [suwaru] - sit
13. 感謝する；ありがとうございます、ありがとう [kansha suru; arigatou gozai masu, arigatou] - thank; thank you, thanks
14. 書く [kaku] - write
15. 置く、場所 [oku, basho] - place
16. 行く；銀行へ行く [iku ; ginkou e iku] - go; I go to the bank
17. 話す [hanasu] - speak
18. 読む [yomu] - read
19. 遊ぶ、する [asobu, suru] - play
20. 銀行 [ginkou] - bank

B

助(たす)けてもらえませんか、お願(ねが)いします

tasuke te morae mase n ka, onegai shi masu

1

-手伝(てつだ)ってもらえませんか、お願(ねが)いします。
-はい、いいですよ。
-わたしは英語(えいご)で住所(じゅうしょ)を書(か)くことができません。わたしのために書(か)いてもらえませんか？
-はい、いいですよ。
-ありがとうございます

ichi

- tetsuda tte morae mase n ka, onegai shi masu.
- hai, ii desu yo.
- watashi wa eigo de juusho wo kaku koto ga deki

Can you help, please?

1

- Can you help me, please?

- Yes, I can.

- I cannot write the address in English. Can you write it for me?

- Yes, I can.

- Thank you.

mase n. watashi no tame ni kai te morae mase n ka?
- hai, ii desu yo.
- arigatou gozai masu.

2

-あなたはてにすができますか？

-いいえ、できません。でも、学(まな)べます。学(まな)ぶのを手伝(てつだ)ってもらえませんか？

-はい、いいですよ。あなたがてにすを学(まな)ぶのを手伝(てつだ)えます。

-ありがとうございます。

- anata wa tenisu ga deki masu ka?
- iie, deki mase n. demo, manabe masu. manabu no wo tetsuda tte morae mase n ka?
- hai, ii desu yo. anata ga tenisu wo manabu no wo tetsudae masu.
- arigatou gozai masu.

3

-あなたは英語(えいご)を話(はな)すことができますか？

-わたしは英語(えいご)を話(はな)すことと、読(よ)むことができますが、書(か)くことができません。

-あなたはどいつ語(ご)を話(はな)せますか？

-私(わたし)はどいつ語(ご)を話(はな)すこと、読(よ)むこと、そして書(か)くことができます。

-りんだもどいつ語(ご)を話(はな)すことができますか？

2

- Can you play tennis?

- No, I cannot. But I can learn. Can you help me to learn?

- Yes, I can. I can help you to learn to play tennis.

- Thank you.

3

- Can you speak English?

- I can speak and read English but I cannot write.

- Can you speak German?

- I can speak, read and write German.

- Can Linda speak German too?

- No, she cannot. She is American.

-いいえ、話せません。りんだはあめりか人です。
- 彼らは英語を話すことができますか?
-はい、少し話せます。彼らは学生で、英語を学んでいます。この男の子は英語が話せません。

- Can they speak English?
- Yes, they can a little. They are students and they learn English. This boy cannot speak English.

san

- anata wa eigo wo hanasu koto ga deki masu ka?
- watashi wa eigo wo hanasu koto to, yomu koto ga deki masu ga, kaku koto ga deki mase n.
- anata wa doitsugo wo hanase masu ka?
- watashi wa doitsugo wo hanasu koto, yomu koto, soshite kaku koto ga deki masu.
- rinda mo doitsugo wo hanasu koto ga deki masu ka?
- iie, hanase mase n. rinda wa amerika jin desu.
- karera wa eigo wo hanasu koto ga deki masu ka?
- hai, sukoshi hanase masu. karera wa gakusei de, eigo wo manan de i masu. kono otokonoko wa eigo ga hanase mase n.

4

- 彼らはどこですか?
- 彼らは今てにすをしています。
-わたしたちもてにすをしてもいいですか?
-はい、いいですよ。

4

- Where are they?
- They play tennis now.
- May we play too?
- Yes, we may.

yon

- karera wa doko desu ka?
- karera wa ima tenisu wo shi te i masu.
- watashi tachi mo tenisu wo shi te mo ii desu ka?
- hai, ii desu yo.

5

- ろばーとはどこですか？
- 彼（かれ）はかふぇにいるかもしれません。

go
- roba ー to wa doko desu ka?
- kare wa kafe ni iru kamo shire mase n.

6

- このてーぶるに座（すわ）ってください。
- ありがとうございます。てーぶるの上（うえ）にわたしの本（ほん）を置（お）いてもいいですか？ -はい、いいですよ。
- ぽーるは彼（かれ）のてーぶるに座（すわ）ってもいいですか？
- はい、いいですよ。

roku
- kono te ー buru ni suwa tte kudasai.
- arigatou gozai masu. te ー buru no ue ni watashi no hon wo oi te mo ii desu ka?
- hai, ii desu yo.
- po ー ru wa kare no te ー buru ni suwa tte mo ii desu ka?
- hai, ii desu yo.

7

- わたしは彼女（かのじょ）のべっどに座（すわ）ってもいいですか？
- いいえ、座（すわ）ってはいけません。
- りんだは彼（かれ）のCDぷれーやーを使（つか）ってもいいですか？

5

- Where is Robert?
- He may be at the café.

6

- Sit at this table, please.
- Thank you. May I place my books on that table?
- Yes, you may.
- May Paul sit at his table?
- Yes, he may.

7

- May I sit on her bed?
- No, you must not.
- May Linda take his CD player?
- No. She must not take his CD

-いいえ。彼女は彼のCDぷれーやーを使ってはいけません。

nana
- watashi wa kanojo no beddo ni suwa tte mo ii desu ka?
- iie, suwa tte wa ike mase n.
- rinda wa kare no shi― di― pure―ya― wo tsuka tte mo ii desu ka?
- iie. kanojo wa kare no shi― di― pure―ya― wo tsuka tte wa ike mase n.

8
- 彼らは彼女の地図を使ってもいいですか？
-いいえ、使わないでください。

hachi
- karera wa kanojo no chizu wo tsuka tte mo ii desu ka?
- iie, tsukawa nai de kudasai.

9
-あなたは彼女のべっどの上には座ってはいけません。
- 彼女は彼のCDぷれーやーを使ってはいけません。
- 彼らはこれらののーとを使ってはいけません。

kyuu
- anata wa kanojo no beddo no ue ni wa suwa tte wa ike mase n.
- kanojo wa kare no shi― di― pure―ya― wo tsuka tte wa ike mase n.

player.

8

- *May they take her map?*
- *No, they may not.*

9

You must not sit on her bed.

She must not take his CD player.

They must not take these notebooks.

- karera wa korera no nōto wo tsuka tte wa ike mase n.

10

-わたしは銀行に行かなければいけません。
-あなたは今行かないといけないのですか？
-はい、そうです。

juu
- watashi wa ginkou ni ika nakere ba ike mase n.
- anata wa ima ika nai to ike nai no desu ka?
- hai, sou desu.

11

-あなたはどいつ語を学ばなければいけないのですか？
-わたしはどいつ語は学ぶ必要がありません。英語を学ばなければいけません。

juu ichi
- anata wa doitsugo wo manaba nakere ba ike nai no desu ka?
- watashi wa doitsugo wa manabu hitsuyou ga ari mase n. eigo wo manaba nakere ba ike mase n.

12

-彼女は銀行に行かなければいけませんか？
-いいえ。彼女は銀行に行く必要はありません。
-この自転車を使ってもいいですか？
-いいえ、この自転車は使わないでください。

10

- I must go to the bank.
- Must you go now?
- Yes, I must.

11

- Must you learn German?
- I need not learn German. I must learn English.

12

- Must she go to the bank?
- No. She need not go to the bank.
- May I take this bike?
- No, you must not take this bike.
- May we place these notebooks

-わたしたちはこれらののーとを彼女のべっどの上に置いてもいいですか？

-いいえ。あなたたちはのーとを彼女のべっどの上に置いてはいけません。

juu ni

- kanojo wa ginkou ni ika nakere ba ike mase n ka?
- iie. kanojo wa ginkou ni iku hitsuyou wa ari mase n.
- kono jitensha wo tsuka tte mo ii desu ka?
- iie, kono jitensha wa tsukawa nai de kudasai.
- watashi tachi wa korera no no―to wo kanojo no beddo no ue ni oite mo ii desu ka?
- iie. anata tachi wa no―to wo kanojo no beddo no ue ni oite wa ike mase n.

on her bed?

- No. You must not place the notebooks on her bed.

5

Audio

ろば　と　いま　あめりか　す
ロバートは 今、アメリカに住んでいます

Robert lives in the USA now

A

たんご
単 語
Words

1. 朝食 [choushoku] - breakfast
2. 3 [san] - three
3. 5 [go] - five
4. 6 [roku] - six
5. 7 [nana] - seven
6. 8 [hachi] - eight
7. いくつか [ikutsu ka] - some
8. いす [isu] - chair
9. お茶 [ocha] - tea
10. そこ [soko] - there
11. よい、おいしい、上手 [yoi, oishii, jouzu] - good, well

12. わたしは音楽を聞きます。 [watashi wa ongaku wo kiki masu.] - I listen to music.
13. 人々 [hitobito] - people
14. 女の子 [onnanoko] - girl
15. 好き、大好き [suki, daisuki] - like, love
16. 家具 [kagu] - furniture
17. 広場 [hiroba] - square
18. 必要である、必要とする [hitsuyou de aru, hitsuyou to suru] - need
19. 新聞 [shinbun] - newspaper
20. 朝食をとる [choushoku wo toru] - have breakfast
21. 欲しい、欲しがる [hoshii, hoshi garu] - want
22. 聞く、聴く [kiku, kiku] - listen
23. 農場 [noujou] - farm
24. 音楽 [ongaku] - music
25. 食べる [taberu] - eat
26. 飲む [nomu] - drink

B

ロバートは今、アメリカに住んでいます

roba—to wa ima, amerika ni sun de i masu

Robert lives in the USA now

1

りんだは英語を上手に読みます。私も英語を読みます。生徒達は公園へいきます。彼女も公園へいきます。

ichi

rinda wa eigo wo jouzu ni yomi masu. watashi mo eigo wo yomi masu. seito tachi wa kouen e iki masu. kanojo mo kouen e iki masu.

Linda reads English well. I read English too. The students go to the park. She goes to the park too.

2

わたしたちはさんふらんしすこに住んでいます。ぽーるも今はさんふらんしすこに住んでいます。彼の

We live in San Francisco. Paul lives in San Francisco now too. His father and mother live in Canada.

父と母はかなだに住んでいます。ろばーとは今、さんふらんしすこに住んでいます。彼の父と母はどいつに住んでいます。

Robert lives in San Francisco now. His father and mother live in Germany.

ni

watashi tachi wa sanfuranshisuko ni sun de i masu. po─ru mo ima wa sanfuranshisuko ni sun de i masu. kare no chichi to haha wa kanada ni sun de i masu. roba─to wa ima, sanfuranshisuko ni sun de i masu. kare no chichi to haha wa doitsu ni sun de i masu.

3

生徒達はてにすをします。ぽーるはてにすが上手です。ろばーとは上手ではありません。

The students play tennis. Paul plays well. Robert does not play well.

san

seito tachi wa tenisu wo shi masu. po─ru wa tenisu ga jouzu desu. roba─to wa jouzu de ha ari mase n.

4

わたしたちはお茶を飲みます。りんだは緑茶を飲みます。でいびっどは紅茶を飲みます。わたしも紅茶を飲みます。

We drink tea. Linda drinks green tea. David drinks black tea. I drink black tea too.

yon

watashi tachi wa ocha wo nomi masu. rinda wa ryokucha wo nomi masu. deibiddo wa koucha wo nomi masu. watashi mo koucha wo nomi masu.

5

わたしは音楽を聞きます。さらも音楽を聞きます。彼女はよい音楽を聞くのが好きです。

I listen to music. Sarah listens to music too. She likes to listen to good music.

go

watashi wa ongaku wo kiki masu. sara mo ongaku wo kiki masu. kanojo wa yoi ongaku wo kiku no ga suki desu.

6

わたしはのーとが6冊必要です。でいびっどはのーとが7冊必要です。りんだはのーとが8冊必要です。

roku

watashi wa no—to ga roku satsu hitsuyou desu. deibiddo wa no—to ga nana satsu hitsuyou desu. rinda wa no—to ga hassatsu hitsuyou desu.

7

さらは（飲み物が）飲みたいです。私も飲みたいです。ぽーるは（食べ物が）食べたいです。

nana

sara wa （nomimono ga） nomi tai desu. watashi mo nomi tai desu. po—ru wa （tabemono ga） tabe tai desu.

8

新聞がてーぶるの上にあります。ぽーるがそれをとり、読みます。彼は新聞を読むのが好きです。

hachi

shinbun ga te—buru no ue ni ari masu. po—ru ga sore wo tori, yomi masu. kare wa shinbun wo yomu no ga suki desu.

9

部屋の中にいくつかの家具があります。そこには、てーぶるが6つと、いすが6つあります。

kyuu

heya no naka ni ikutsu ka no kagu ga ari masu. soko ni wa,

6

I need six notebooks. David needs seven notebooks. Linda needs eight notebooks.

7

Sarah wants to drink. I want to drink too. Paul wants to eat.

8

There is a newspaper on the table. Paul takes it and reads. He likes to read newspapers.

9

There is some furniture in the room. There are six tables and six chairs there.

te―buru ga muttsu to, isu ga muttsu ari masu.

10
へや　なか　　おんな　こ　　にん
部屋の 中 には 女 の子が３人 います。
かのじょたち　　ちょうしょく
彼女達は 朝 食 をとっています。

juuheya no naka ni wa onnanoko ga san nin i masu. kanojo tachi wa choushoku wo to tte i masu.

11
　　　　　　　た　　　　ちゃ　の
さらはぱんを食べて、お 茶 を飲んでいます。
かのじょ　　 りょくちゃ　す
彼 女 は 緑 茶 が好きです。

juu ichi
sara wa pan wo tabe te, ocha wo non de i masu. kanojo wa ryokucha ga suki desu.

12
　　　　　うえ　なんさつ　　ほん
てーぶるの 上 に何 冊 かの 本 があります。それ
　　　 あたら　　　　　　　　　　ふる
らは 新 しくありません。 古 いです。

juu ni
te―buru no ue ni nan satsu ka no hon ga ari masu. sorera wa atarashiku ari mase n. furui desu.

13
　　　　とお　　ぎんこう
-この 通 りに 銀 行 はありますか？
　　　　　　　　　　　　　とお　　　　　ぎんこう
-はい、あります。この 通 りには、銀 行 が５つあ
　　　　　　　 ぎんこう　　おお
ります。それらの 銀 行 は 大 きくありません。

juu san
- kono toori ni ginkou wa ari masu ka?
- hai, ari masu. kono toori ni wa, ginkou ga itsutsu ari masu. sorera no ginkou wa ookiku ari mase n.

10
There are three girls in the room. They are eating breakfast.

11
Sarah is eating bread and drinking tea. She likes green tea.

12
There are some books on the table. They are not new. They are old.

13
- Is there a bank in this street?

- Yes, there is. There are five banks in this street. The banks are not big.

14

- 広場には人がいますか？
- はい、います。何人かの人が広場にいます。

juu yon
- hiroba ni wa hito ga i masu ka?
- hai, i masu. nan nin ka no hito ga hiroba ni i masu.

15

- かふぇに自転車はありますか？
- はい、あります。かふぇには自転車が4台あります。それらは新しくないです。

juu go
- kafe ni jitensha wa ari masu ka?
- hai, ari masu. kafe ni wa jitensha ga yon dai ari masu. sorera wa atarashiku nai desu.

16

- この通りにほてるはありますか？
- いいえ。この通りにはほてるはありません。

juu roku
- kono toori ni hoteru wa ari masu ka?
- iie. kono toori ni wa hoteru wa ari mase n.

17

- その通りに何か大きなお店はありますか？
- いいえ。その通りには大きなお店はありません。

juu nana
- sono toori ni nani ka ookina o mise wa ari masu ka?
- iie. sono toori ni wa ookina o mise wa ari mase n.

14

- Are there people in the square?
- Yes, there are. There are some people in the square.

15

- Are there bikes at the café?
- Yes, there are. There are four bikes at the café. They are not new.

16

- Is there a hotel in this street?
- No, there is not. There are no hotels in this street.

17

- Are there any big shops in that street?
- No, there are not. There are no big shops in that street.

18

-あめりかには 農場 がありますか？ -はい。あめりかにはたくさんの 農場 があります。

juu hachi
- amerika ni wa noujou ga ari masu ka?
- hai. amerika ni wa takusan no noujou ga ari masu.

19

-その部屋には 何か家具がありますか？ -はい。そこには、てーぶるが４つと、いくつかのいすがあります。

juu kyuu
- sono heya ni wa nani ka kagu ga ari masu ka?
- hai. soko ni wa, te―buru ga yottsu to, ikutsuka no isu ga ari masu.

18

- *Are there any farms in the USA?*
- *Yes, there are. There are many farms in the USA.*

19

- *Is there any furniture in that room?*
- *Yes, there is. There are four tables and some chairs there.*

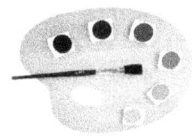

6

Audio

<ruby>ロバート<rt>ろば と</rt></ruby>にはたくさんの <ruby>友 達<rt>ともだち</rt></ruby> がいます

Robert has many friends

A

<ruby>単 語<rt>たんご</rt></ruby>
Words

1. CD [shi一 di一] - CD
2. 来る / 行く [kuru / iku] - come / go
3. コーヒー [ko一hi一] - coffee
4. コンピューター [konpyu一ta一] - computer
5. たくさん、多くの [takusan, ooku no] - much, many
6. デイビッドの本 [deibiddo no hon] - David's book
7. ドア [doa] - door
8. の下 [no shita] - under
9. パパ、お父さん [papa, otousan] - dad
10. 中へ、中に [naka e, naka ni] - into
11. 仕事 ; 職業紹介所 [shigoto ; shokugyou shoukai jo] - job; job agency
12. 仕事がたくさんある [shigoto ga takusan aru] - have a lot of work

13. 友達 [tomodachi] - friend
14. 同様に、同じく [douyou ni, onajiku] - as well
15. 知る [shiru] - know
16. 空いている [ai te iru] - free
17. 空き時間 [aki jikan] - free time
18. 紹介所、代理店 [shoukai jo, dairi ten] - agency
19. 綺麗、清潔 [kirei, seiketsu] - clean
20. 調理道具、コンロ [chouri dougu, konro] - cooker
21. 車 [kuruma] - car

B

ロバートにはたくさんの友達がいます

roba―to ni wa takusan no tomodachi ga i masu

Robert has many friends

1

ろばーとにはたくさんの友達がいます。ろばーとの友達はかふぇに行きます。彼らはこーひーを飲むのが好きです。ろばーとの友達はたくさんのこーひーを飲みます。

ichi

roba―to ni wa takusan no tomodachi ga i masu. roba―to no tomodachi wa kafe ni iki masu. karera wa ko―hi― wo nomu no ga suki desu. roba―to no tomodachi wa takusan no ko―hi― wo nomi masu.

1

Robert has many friends. Robert's friends go to the café. They like to drink coffee. Robert's friends drink a lot of coffee.

2

ぽーるのお父さんは車を持っています。お父さんの車は綺麗ですが、古いです。ぽーるのお父さんはたくさん運転します。彼は良い

2

Paul's dad has a car. The dad's car is clean but old. Paul's dad drives a lot. He has a good job and he has a

しごと　　　　　　しごと
仕事をしていて、仕事がたくさんあります。

ni

po―ru no otousan wa kuruma wo mo tte i masu. otousan no kuruma wa kirei desu ga, furui desu. po―ru no otousan wa takusan unten shi masu. kare wa yoi shigoto wo shi te i te, shigoto ga takusan ari masu.

lot of work now.

3

でいびっどはたくさんのCDを持っています。でいびっどのCDは彼のべっどの上にあります。でいびっどのCDぷれーやーも、同様に彼のべっどの上にあります。

san

deibiddo wa takusan no shi― di― wo mo tte i masu. deibiddo no shi― di― wa kare no beddo no ue ni ari masu. deibiddo no shi― di― pure―ya― mo, douyou ni kare no beddo no ue ni ari masu.

3

David has a lot of CDs. David's CDs are on his bed. David's CD player is on his bed as well.

4

ろばーとはあめりかの新聞を読みます。ろばーとの部屋のてーぶるの上にはたくさんの新聞があります。

yon

roba―to wa amerika no shinbun wo yomi masu. roba―to no heya no te―buru no ue ni wa takusan no shinbun ga ari masu.

4

Robert reads American newspapers. There are many newspapers on the table in Robert's room.

5

なんしーは猫と犬を飼っています。なんしーの猫は部屋のべっどの下にいます。なんしーの犬

5

Nancy has a cat and a dog. Nancy's cat is in the room under the bed. Nancy's dog is in the room as well.

も同じく部屋の中にいます。

go

nanshi─ wa neko to inu wo ka tte i masu. nanshi─ no neko wa heya no beddo no shita ni i masu. nanshi─ no inu mo onajiku heya no naka ni i masu.

6

この車の中に男性がいます。この男性は地図を持っています。男性の地図は大きいです。この男性はたくさん運転します。

6

There is a man in this car. This man has a map. The man's map is big. This man drives a lot.

roku

kono kuruma no naka ni dansei ga i masu. kono dansei wa chizu wo mo tte i masu. dansei no chizu wa ookii desu. kono dansei wa takusan unten shi masu.

7

わたしは学生です。わたしにはたくさんの空き時間があります。わたしは職業紹介所に行きます。わたしには良い仕事が必要です。

7

I am a student. I have a lot of free time. I go to a job agency. I need a good job.

nana

watashi wa gakusei desu. watashi ni wa takusan no aki jikan ga ari masu. watashi wa shokugyou shoukai jo ni iki masu. watashi ni wa yoi shigoto ga hitsuyou desu.

8

ぽーるとろばーとは空き時間が少ししかありません。彼らも同様に職業紹介所に行きます。ぽーるはこんぴゅーたを持っています。

8

Paul and Robert have a little free time. They go to the job agency as well. Paul

職業紹介所はぽーるに良い仕事を紹介するかも知れません。

hachi

poーru to robaーto wa aki jikan ga sukoshi shika ari mase n. karera mo douyou ni shokugyou shoukai jo ni iki masu. poーru wa konpyuーta wo mo tte i masu. shokugyou shoukai jo wa poーru ni yoi shigoto wo shoukai suru kamo shire mase n.

9

りんだは新しい調理道具を持っています。
りんだの調理道具は良いもので、綺麗です。
りんだは子供達の朝食をつくります。なんしーとでいびっどはりんだの子供達です。りんだの子供達はたくさんのお茶を飲みます。母はこーひーを少し飲みます。なんしーの母は、独単語をとても少しだけ話せます。彼女はどいつ語をほんの少しだけ話します。りんだは仕事をしています。彼女は自由時間が少しだけあります。

kyuu

rinda wa atarashii chouri dougu wo mo tte i masu. rinda no chouri dougu wa yoi mono de, kirei desu. rinda wa kodomo tachi no choushoku wo tsukuri masu. nanshiー to deibiddo wa rinda no kodomo tachi desu. rinda no kodomo tachi wa takusan no ocha wo nomi masu. haha wa koーhiー wo sukoshi nomi masu. nanshiー no haha wa, doku tango wo totemo sukoshi dake hanase masu. kanojo wa doitsugo wo honno sukoshi dake hanashi masu. rinda wa shigoto wo shi te i masu. kanojo wa jiyuu jikan ga

has a computer. The agency may give Paul a good job.

9

Linda has a new cooker. Linda's cooker is good and clean. Linda cooks breakfast for her children. Nancy and David are Linda's children. Linda's children drink a lot of tea. The mother drinks a little coffee. Nancy's mother can speak very few German words. She speaks German very little. Linda has a job. She has little free time.

sukoshi dake ari masu.

10

ろばーとは少しだけ英語を話すことができます。ろばーとは英単語をとても少しだけ知っています。わたしはたくさんの英単語を知っています。わたしは少しだけ英語を話すことができます。この女性はたくさんの英単語を知っています。彼女は英語を上手に話せます。

juuroba―to wa sukoshi dake eigo wo hanasu koto ga deki masu. roba―to wa eitango wo totemo sukoshi dake shi tte i masu. watashi wa takusan no eitango wo shi tte i masu. watashi wa sukoshi dake eigo wo hanasu koto ga deki masu. kono josei wa takusan no eitango wo shi tte i masu. kanojo wa eigo wo jouzu ni hanase masu.

10

Robert can speak English little. Robert knows very few English words. I know a lot of English words. I can speak English a little. This woman knows a lot of English words. She can speak English well.

11

じょーじは職業紹介所で働いています。この職業紹介所はさんふらんしすこにあります。じょーじは車を持っています。じょーじの車は通りにあります。じょーじにはたくさんの仕事があります。彼は紹介所に行かなければなりません。彼はそこへ運転してきます。じょーじは紹介所にきました。そこにはたくさんの学生がいます。彼らには仕事が必要です。じょーじの仕事

11

George works at a job agency. This job agency is in San Francisco. George has a car. George's car is in the street. George has a lot of work. He must go to the agency. He drives there. George comes into the agency. There are a lot of students there. They need jobs. George's job is to help the students.

は学生を助けることです。

juu ichi

jo—ji wa shokugyou shoukai jo de hatarai te i masu. kono shokugyou shoukai jo wa sanfuranshisuko ni ari masu. jo—ji wa kuruma wo mo tte i masu. jo—ji no kuruma wa toori ni ari masu. jo—ji ni wa takusan no shigoto ga ari masu. kare wa shoukai joo ni ika nakere ba nari mase n. kare wa soko e unten shi te ki masu. jo—ji wa shoukai jo ni ki mashi ta. soko ni wa takusan no gakusei ga i masu. karera ni wa shigoto ga hitsuyou desu. jo—ji no shigoto wa gakusei wo tasukeru koto desu.

12

ほてるに車があります。車のどあは綺麗ではありません。たくさんの学生達がこのほてるに住んでいます。ほてるの部屋は小さいですが、清潔です。これはろばーとの部屋です。部屋の窓は大きくて清潔です。

juu ni

hoteru ni kuruma ga ari masu. kuruma no doa wa kirei de wa ari mase n. takusan no gakusei tachi ga kono hoteru ni sun de i masu. hoteru no heya wa chiisai desu ga, seiketsu desu. kore wa roba—to no heya desu. heya no mado wa ookiku te seiketsu desu.

12

There is a car at the hotel. The doors of this car are not clean.

Many students live in this hotel. The rooms of the hotel are little but clean. This is Robert's room. The window of the room is big and clean.

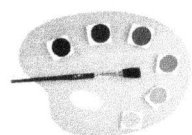

7

Audio

<ruby>デイビッド<rt>でいびっど</rt></ruby>は<ruby>自転車<rt>じてんしゃ</rt></ruby>を<ruby>買<rt>か</rt></ruby>います

David buys a bike

A

<ruby>単語<rt>たんご</rt></ruby>
Words

1. オフィス [ofisu] - office
2. おやつ、スナック [o yatsu, sunakku] - snack
3. お風呂場、お手洗い ; お風呂 [o furoba, o tearai ; o furo] - bathroom; bath
4. お風呂場のテーブル [o furoba no tēburu] - bathroom table
5. キッチン [kicchin] - kitchen
6. スポーツ; スポーツ店 [supōtsu ; supōtsu ten] - sport; sport shop
7. スポーツバイク [supōtsu baiku] - sport bike
8. そして、その後 [soshite, sonogo] - then
9. その後 [sonogo] - after that
10. と一緒に、で [to issho ni, de] - with

11. バス；バスで行く [basu ; basu de iku] - bus; go by bus
12. ひとりずつ [hitori zutsu] - one by one
13. メーカー [meーkaー] - maker
14. 中心；中心街 [chuushin ; chuushin gai] - centre; city centre
15. 今日、本日 [kyou, honjitsu] - today
16. 企業、会社 [kigyou, kaisha] - firm
17. 企業、会社（複数）[kigyou, kaisha（fukusuu）] - firms
18. 作る、料理をする [tsukuru, ryouri wo suru] - make
19. 列 [retsu] - queue
20. 土曜日 [doyoubi] - Saturday
21. 家、家庭；帰宅する、家に帰る [ie, katei ; kitaku suru, ie ni kaeru] - home; go home
22. 従業員、労働者 [juugyou in, roudou sha] - worker
23. 時間 [jikan] - time
24. 朝 [asa] - morning
25. 洗う [arau] - wash
26. 洗濯機 [sentakuki] - washer
27. 自転車で行く [jitensha de iku] - go by bike, ride a bike
28. 顔 [kao] - face

B

デイビッドは自転車を買います
deibiddo wa jitensha wo kai masu

土曜日の朝です。でいびっどはお手洗いに行きます。お手洗いは大きくありません。そこにはお風呂、洗濯機、そしてばするーむてーぶるがあります。でいびっどは顔を洗います。そして彼はきっちんへ行きます。きっちんてーぶるの上にはてぃーめーかーがあります。でいびっどは朝食を食べます。でいびっどの朝食は大きくはありません。そして彼はこーひーめーかーでこーひ

David buys a bike

It is Saturday morning. David goes to the bathroom. The bathroom is not big. There is a bath, a washer and a bathroom table there. David washes his face. Then he goes to the kitchen. There is a tea-maker on the kitchen table. David eats his breakfast. David's breakfast is not big. Then he makes some coffee

わをかしてそれを飲みます。彼は今日はすぽーつ店に行きたいのです。でいびっどは通りに出ます。彼は7番のばすに乗ります。ばすでお店まで行くのには少しの時間がかかります。

doyoubi no asa desu. deibiddo wa o tearai ni iki masu. o tearai wa ookiku ari mase n. soko ni wa o furo, sentakuki, soshite basuru—mu te—buru ga ari masu. deibiddo wa kao wo arai masu. soshite kare wa kicchin e iki masu. kicchin te—buru no ue ni wa ti— me—ka— ga ari masu. deibiddo wa choushoku wo tabe masu. deibiddo no choushoku wa ookiku wa ari mase n. soshite kare wa ko—hi— me—ka— de ko—hi— wo wakashi te sore wo nomi masu. kare wa kyou wa supo—tsu ten ni iki tai no desu. deibiddo wa toori ni de masu. kare wa nana ban no basu ni nori masu. basu de o mise made iku no ni wa sukoshi no jikan ga kakari masu.

でいびっどがお店に入ります。彼は新しいすぽーつばいくを買いたいのです。そこにはたくさんのすぽーつばいくがあります。黒、青そして緑色のばいくです。でいびっどは青いばいくが好きです。彼は青いのが買いたいのです。お店には列ができています。でいびっどがばいくを買うのには長い時間がかかります。その後、彼は通りへ出て、ばいくに乗ります。彼は中心街までばいくをこぎます。そして、彼は中心街から公園までばいくをこぎます。新しいすぽーつばいくに乗るのは本当に

with the coffee-maker and drinks it. He wants to go to a sport shop today. David goes into the street. He takes bus seven. It takes David a little time to go to the shop by bus.

David goes into the sport shop. He wants to buy a new sport bike. There are a lot of sport bikes there. They are black, blue and green. David likes blue bikes. He wants to buy a blue one. There is a queue in the shop. It takes David a lot of time to buy the bike. Then he goes to the street and rides the bike. He rides to the city centre. Then he rides from the city centre to the city park. It is so nice to

すば
素晴らしい！

deibiddo ga o mise ni hairi masu. kare wa atarashii supo─tsu baiku wo kai tai no desu. soko ni wa takusan no supo─tsu baiku ga ari masu. kuro, ao soshite midori iro no baiku desu. deibiddo wa aoi baiku ga suki desu. kare wa aoi no ga kai tai no desu. o mise ni wa retsu ga deki te i masu. deibiddo ga baiku wo kau no ni wa nagai jikan ga kakari masu. sonogo, kare wa toori e de te, baiku ni nori masu. kare wa chuushin gai made baiku wo kogi masu. soshite, kare wa chuushin gai kara kouen made baiku wo kogi masu. atarashii supo─tsu baiku ni noru no wa hontouni subarashii!

ride a new sport bike!

　　　　どようび　あさ
　　　土曜日の朝ですが、じょーじはおふぃすにいます。彼は、今日はたくさんの仕事があります。じょーじのおふぃすには列ができています。たくさんの学生達と労働者が列に並んでいます。彼らは仕事を必要としています。彼らはひとりずつじょーじの部屋へ行きます。彼らはじょーじと話をします。そして彼は企業の住所を渡します。

It is Saturday morning but George is in his office. He has a lot of work today. There is a queue to George's office. There are many students and workers in the queue. They need a job. They go one by one into George's room. They speak with George. Then he gives addresses of firms.

　　doyoubi no asa desu ga, jo─ji wa ofisu ni i masu. kare wa, kyou wa takusan no shigoto ga ari masu. jo─ji no ofisu ni wa retsu ga deki te i masu. takusan no gakusei tachi to roudou sha ga retsu ni naran de i masu. karera wa shigoto wo hitsuyou to shi te i masu. karera wa hitori zutsu jo─ji no heya e iki masu. karera wa jo─ji to hanashi wo shi masu. soshite kare wa kigyou no juusho wo watashi masu.

　　　　　　じかん
　　おやつの時間です。じょーじはこーひーめーかー

It is snack time now. George makes some coffee with the coffee maker. He

でこーひーを湧かします。彼はおやつを食べ、こーひーを飲みます。彼のおふぃすに今、列はありません。じょーじは家に帰ることができます。彼は通りに出ます。今日はとても素晴らしい日だ！じょーじは帰宅します。彼は子供達をつれて街の公園へ行きます。彼らはそこで良い時間を過ごします。o yatsu no jikan desu. jo—ji wa ko—hi— me—ka— de ko—hi— wo wakashi masu. kare wa o yatsu wo tabe, ko—hi— wo nomi masu. kare no ofisu ni ima, retsu wa ari mase n. jo—ji wa ie ni kaeru koto ga deki masu. kare wa toori ni de masu. kyou wa totemo subarashii hi da! jo—ji wa kitaku shi masu. kare wa kodomo tachi wo tsure te machi no kouen e iki masu. karera wa soko de yoi jikan wo sugoshi masu.

eats his snack and drinks some coffee. There is no queue to his office now. George can go home. He goes into the street. It is so nice today! George goes home. He takes his children and goes to the city park. They have a nice time there.

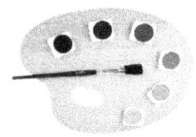

8

Audio

りんだ　あたら　　　ＤＶＤ　か
リンダは 新 しいＤＶＤが買いたいです

Linda wants to buy a new DVD

A

たんご
単 語
Words

1. 15 [juu go] - fifteen
2. 20 [ni juu] - twenty
3. DVD [DVD] - DVD
4. アドベンチャー、冒険 [adobenchaー, bouken] - adventure
5. いなくなる、消える、なくなる [i naku naru, kieru, nakunaru] - go away
6. お気に入りの、好きな [okiniiri no, suki na] - favourite
7. お気に入りの映画 [okiniiri no eiga] - favourite film
8. カップ、コップ [kappu, koppu] - cup
9. さらに、もっと、より [sarani, motto, yori] - more

10. ビデオカセット [bideokasetto] - videocassette
11. ビデオショップ [bideo shoppu] - video-shop
12. フレンドリーな [furendorī na] - friendly
13. みせる [miseru] - show
14. より；ジョージはリンダより年上です [yori ; jōji wa rinda yori toshiue desu] - than; George is older than Linda.
15. 与える、渡す [ataeru, watasu] - give, hand
16. 大きい／より大きな／一番大きい [ookii / yori ookina / ichiban ookii] - big / bigger / the biggest
17. 店員 [ten'in] - shop assistant
18. 接続詞なので訳さない；わたしはこの本が面白いことを知っています [setsuzokushi na node yakusa nai ; watashi wa kono hon ga omoshiroi koto wo shi tte i masu] - that; I know that this book is interesting.
19. 映画 [eiga] - film
20. 時間 [jikan] - hour
21. 箱、ダンボール [hako, danbōru] - box
22. 続く、かかる；映画は3時間以上かかります [tsuzuku, kakaru ; eiga wa san jikan ijou kakari masu] - last, take; The movie lasts more than three hours.
23. 興味深い、おもしろい [kyoumibukai, omoshiroi] - interesting
24. 若い、年下の [wakai, toshishita no] - young
25. 言う [iu] - say
26. 質問する、頼む、お願いする [shitsumon suru, tanomu, onegai suru] - ask
27. 長い [nagai] - long

B

リンダは 新しいＤＶＤが買いたいです
rinda wa atarashii DVD ga kai tai desu

でいびっどとなんしーはりんだの子供達です。なんしーが一番年下の子供です。彼女は５歳です。でいびっどはなんしーより、１５歳年上です。彼は２０歳です。なんしーはでい

Linda wants to buy a new DVD

David and Nancy are Linda's children. Nancy is the youngest child. She is five years old. David is fifteen years older than

びっどよりとても若いです。deibiddo to nanshī wa rinda no kodomo tachi desu. nanshī ga ichiban toshishita no kodomo desu. kanojo wa go sai desu. deibiddo wa nanshī yori, juu go sai toshiue desu. kare wa ni ju ssai desu. nanshī wa deibiddo yori totemo wakai desu.

なんしー、りんだ、でいびっどはきっちんにいます。彼らはお茶を飲みます。なんしーのこっぷは大きいです。りんだのこっぷはさらに大きいです。でいびっどのこっぷは一番大きいです。nanshī, rinda, deibiddo wa kicchin ni i masu. karera wa ocha wo nomi masu. nanshī no koppu wa ookii desu. rinda no koppu wa sarani ookii desu. deibiddo no koppu wa ichiban ookii desu.

りんだはたくさんの興味深い映画のびでおかせっととDVDを持っています。彼女はもっと新しい映画が買いたいです。彼女はびでおしょっぷに行きます。そこには、びでおかせっととDVDが入ったたくさんの箱があります。彼女は店員に助けてくれるように頼みます。店員はりんだにいくつかのかせっとを渡します。りんだはそれらの映画についてもっと知りたいのですが、店員はいなくなってしまいます。rinda wa takusan no kyoumibukai eiga no bideokasetto to DVD wo mo tte i masu. kanojo wa motto atarashii eiga ga kai tai desu. kanojo wa bideo shoppu ni iki masu. soko ni wa, bideokasetto to DVD ga hai tta takusan no hako ga ari masu. kanojo wa ten'in ni tasuke te kureru you ni tanomi masu. ten'in wa rinda ni ikutsu ka no kasetto wo watashi

Nancy. He is twenty. Nancy is much younger than David.

Nancy, Linda and David are in the kitchen. They drink tea. Nancy's cup is big. Linda's cup is bigger. David's cup is the biggest.

Linda has a lot of videocassettes and DVDs with interesting films. She wants to buy a newer film. She goes to a video-shop. There are many boxes with videocassettes and DVDs there. She asks a shop assistant to help her. The shop assistant hands Linda some cassettes. Linda wants to know more about these films but the shop assistant goes away.

masu. rinda wa sorera no eiga nitsuite motto shiri tai no desu ga, ten'in wa i naku na tte shimai masu.

店内には、もうひとりの店員がいて、彼女はよりふれんどーです。彼女はりんだに、彼女のお気に入りの映画について質問をします。りんだはろまんす映画とあどべんちゃー映画が好きです。"たいたにっく"という映画が、彼女のお気に入りです。店員は、りんだに最新のはりうっど映画の"どいつ人の友達"のDVDをみせます。それは、あめりかのある男性と若い女性の、恋愛あどべんちゃーについての映画です。tennai ni wa, mou hitori no ten'in ga i te, kanojo wa yori furendorī desu. kanojo wa rinda ni, kanojo no okiniiri no eiga nitsuite shitsumon wo shi masu. rinda wa romansu eiga to adobenchā eiga ga suki desu. "taitanikku" toiu eiga ga, kanojo no okiniiri desu. ten'in ha, rinda ni saishin no hariuddo eiga no "doitsu jin no tomodachi" no DVD wo mise masu. sore wa, amerika no aru dansei to wakai josei no, ren'ai adobenchā nitsuite no eiga desu.

彼女はりんだに"ざ・ふぁーむ"という映画のDVDもみせます。店員は、"ざ・ふぁーむ"という映画は最も面白い映画のうちのひとつだ、と言います。そして最も長い映画のうちのひとつでもあると。映画は3時間以上続きます。りんだはより長い映画が好きです。"たい

There is one more shop assistant in the shop and she is friendlier. She asks Linda about her favorite films. Linda likes romantic films and adventure films. The film "Titanic" is her favorite film. The shop assistant shows Linda a DVD with the newest Hollywood film "The German Friend". It is about romantic adventures of a man and a young woman in the USA.

She shows Linda a DVD with the film "The Firm" as well. The shop assistant says that the film "The Firm" is one of the most interesting films. And it is one of the longest films as well. It is more than three

59

たにっく"は、彼女が持っている映画の中で一番面白くて長い映画だ、と彼女は言います。りんだは"ざ・ふぁーむ"という映画のDVDを買います。彼女は店員にお礼を言い、出て行きます。kanojo wa rinda ni "za fa—mu" toiu eiga no DVD mo mise masu. ten'in wa, "za fa—mu" toiu eiga wa mottomo omoshiroi eiga no uchi no hitotsu da, to ii masu. soshite mottomo nagai eiga no uchi no hitotsu de mo aru to. eiga wa san jikan ijou tsuzuki masu. rinda wa yori nagai eiga ga suki desu. "taitanikku" wa, kanojo ga mo tte iru eiga no naka de ichiban omoshiroku te nagai eiga da, to kanojo wa ii masu. rinda wa "za fa—mu" toiu eiga no DVD wo kai masu. kanojo wa ten'in ni orei wo ii, de te iki masu.

hours long. Linda likes longer films. She says that "Titanic" is the most interesting and the longest film that she has. Linda buys a DVD with the film "The Firm". She thanks the shop assistant and goes.

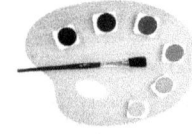

9

Audio

<ruby>ポール<rt></rt></ruby>は<ruby>ドイツ<rt>どいつ</rt></ruby>の <ruby>歌<rt>うた</rt></ruby> をききます

Paul listens to German songs

A

単語
Words

1. あたま、長、リーダー；へ向かう [atama, chou, riーdaー ; e mukau] - head; to head, to go
2. かばん [kaban] - bag
3. ジャンプする、飛び降りる、ジャンプ [janpu suru, tobioriru, janpu] - jump
4. たくさん、とても [takusan, totemo] - very
5. なぜなら、だって [nazenara, datte] - because
6. について、ほど [nitsuite, hodo] - about
7. バター [bataー] - butter
8. パン [pan] - bread

9. フレーズ、言葉 [fure—zu, kotoba] - phrase
10. 全ての、それぞれの [subete no, sorezore no] - every
11. 分 [fun] - minute
12. 前に、前は [mae ni, mae wa] - before
13. 名前、名前を挙げる、教える [namae, namae wo ageru, oshieru] - name
14. 好き；わたしはそれが好きです [suki ; watashi wa sore ga suki desu] - like; I like that.
15. 始める、始まる [hajimeru, hajimaru] - begin
16. 家族 [kazoku] - family
17. 寮 [ryou] - dorms
18. 帽子 [boushi] - hat
19. 恥じる；彼は恥ずかしがっている [hajiru ; kare wa hazukashi ga tte iru] - be ashamed; he is ashamed
20. 故障中 [koshou chuu] - out of order
21. 日 [nichi] - day
22. 歌う；歌手 [utau ; kashu] - sing; singer
23. 簡単な、単純な [kantan na, tanjun na] - simple
24. 走る、動かす [hashiru, ugokasu] - run
25. 近いこと [chikai koto] - nearness
26. 近くに、近くの、隣の [chikaku ni, chikaku no, tonari no] - near, nearby, next
27. 電話する [denwa suru] - call on the phone
28. 電話する；コールセンター [denwa suru ; ko—ru senta—] - call; call centre
29. 電話機；電話をする [denwaki ; denwa wo suru] - telephone; to telephone

B

ポールはドイツの歌をききます
po—ru wa doitsu no uta wo kiki masu

Paul listens to German songs

きゃろるは学生です。彼女は２０歳です。きゃろるはすぺいん出身です。きゃろるは学生寮に住んでいます。彼女はとてもや

Carol is a student. She is twenty years old. Carol is from Spain. She lives in the student dorms. She is a very

さしい女の子です。きゃろるは青いどれすを着ています。きゃろるは帽子をかぶっています。

kyaroru wa gakusei desu. kanojo wa ni ju ssai desu. kyaroru wa supein shusshin desu. kyaroru wa gakusei ryou ni sun de i masu. kanojo wa totemo yasashii onnanoko desu. kyaroru wa aoi doresu wo ki te i masu. kyaroru wa boushi wo kabu tte i masu.

きゃろるは今日自分の家族に電話がしたいです。彼女は自分の電話が故障中のため、こーるせんたーへ向かいます。こーるせんたーはかふぇの前です。きゃろるは自分の家族に電話をします。彼女は母と父と話します。電話は5分ほどかかりました。そして彼女は友達のあんじぇらに電話をします。この電話は3分ほどかかりました。

kyaroru wa kyou jibun no kazoku ni denwa ga shi tai desu. kanojo wa jibun no denwa ga koshou chuu no tame, ko―ru senta― e mukai masu. ko―ru senta― wa kafe no mae desu. kyaroru wa jibun no kazoku ni denwa wo shi masu. kanojo wa haha to chichi to hanashi masu. denwa wa go fun hodo kakari mashi ta. soshite kanojo wa tomodachi no anjera ni denwa wo shi masu. kono denwa wa san fun hodo kakari mashi ta.

ろばーとはすぽーつが好きです。彼は毎朝寮の近くの公園で走ります。彼は今日も走っています。彼はじゃんぷもします。彼のじゃんぷはとても長いのです。ぽーるとでぃ

nice girl. Carol has a blue dress on. There is a hat on her head.

Carol wants to telephone her family today. She heads to the call centre because her telephone is out of order. The call centre is in front of the café. Carol calls her family. She speaks with her mother and father. The call takes her about five minutes. Then she calls her friend Angela. This call takes her about three minutes.

Robert likes sport. He runs every morning in the park near the dorms. He is running today too. He jumps as well. His jumps are very

びっどはろばーとと一緒に走って、じゃんぷをしています。でいびっどのじゃんぷは、より長いじゃんぷです。ぽーるのじゃんぷは一番長いです。彼は全員の中で一番のじゃんぷをします。その後、ろばーととぽーるは寮まで走り、でいびっどは家まで走ります。roba—to wa supo—tsu ga suki desu. kare wa maiasa ryou no chikaku no kouen de hashiri masu. kare wa kyou mo hashi tte i masu. kare wa janpu mo shi masu. kare no janpu wa totemo nagai no desu. po—ru to deibiddo wa roba—to to issho ni hashi tte, janpu wo shi te i masu. deibiddo no janpu wa, yori nagai janpu desu. po—ru no janpu wa ichiban nagai desu. kare wa zen'in no naka de ichiban no janpu wo shi masu. sonogo, roba—to to po—ru wa ryou made hashiri, deibiddo wa ie made hashiri masu.

long. Paul and David are running and jumping with Robert. David's jumps are longer. Paul's jumps are the longest. He jumps best of all. Then Robert and Paul run to the dorms and David runs home.

ろばーとは自分の部屋で朝食を食べます。彼はぱんとばたーを食べます。彼はこーひーめーかーでこーひーを湧かします。そして彼はばたーをぱんに塗って食べます。roba—to wa jibun no heya de choushoku wo tabe masu. kare wa pan to bata— wo tabe masu. kare wa ko—hi— me—ka— de ko—hi— wo wakashi masu. soshite kare wa bata— wo pan ni nu tte tabe masu.

Robert has his breakfast in his room. He takes bread and butter. He makes some coffee with the coffee-maker. Then he butters the bread and eats.

ろばーとはさんふらんしすこの寮に住んでいます。彼の部屋はぽーるの部屋の近くです。ろばーとの部屋は大きくありません。ろばーとがまいにちそうじをするので、部屋は綺麗です。彼

Robert lives in the dorms in San Francisco. His room is near Paul's room. Robert's room is not big. It is clean because Robert cleans it

の部屋には、机 ひとつ、いくつかのいす、その他いくつかの家具があります。ろばーとの本とのーとは机の上にあります。彼のかばんは机の下にあります。いすはてーぶるにあります。ろばーとは何枚かのCDを手にとり、ぽーるの部屋へ向かいます。なぜならぽーるがどいつの音楽をききたがっているからです。roba—to wa sanfuranshisuko no ryou ni sun de i masu. kare no heya wa po—ru no heya no chikaku desu. roba—to no heya wa ookiku ari mase n. roba—to ga mainichi souji wo suru node, heya wa kirei desu. kare no heya ni wa, tsukue hitotsu, ikutsu ka no isu, sonota ikutsu ka no kagu ga ari masu. roba—to no hon to no—to wa tsukue no ue ni ari masu. kare no kaban wa tsukue no shita ni ari masu. isu wa te—buru ni ari masu. roba—to wa nan mai ka no CD wo te ni tori, po—ru no heya e mukai masu. nazenara po—ru ga doitsu no ongaku wo kiki ta ga tte iru kara desu.

ぽーるは彼の部屋の机にいます。彼の猫はつくえの下にいます。猫の前にぱんがあります。猫がぱんを食べます。ろばーとはCDをぽーるに渡します。CDの中には、どいつで一番の曲がはいっています。ぽーるはどいつ人歌手の名前を知りたがります。ろばーとは彼のお気に入りの歌手の名前を挙げます。彼は、Blümchen, Nena と HerbertGrönemeyer の名前を挙げます。これらの名前はぽーるにとって、新しい

every day. There is a table, a bed, some chairs and some more furniture in his room. Robert's books and notebooks are on the table. His bag is under the table. The chairs are at the table. Robert takes some CDs in his hand and heads to Paul's because Paul wants to listen to German music.

Paul is in his room at the table. His cat is under the table. There is some bread before the cat. The cat eats the bread. Robert hands the CDs to Paul. There is the best German music on the CDs. Paul wants to know the names of the German singers as well. Robert names his favorite singers. He names Blümchen, Nena and Herbert

なまえ
名前です。

　po—ru wa kare no heya no tsukue ni i masu. kare no neko wa tsukue no shita ni i masu. neko no mae ni pan ga ari masu. neko ga pan wo tabe masu. roba—to wa CD wo po—ru ni watashi masu. CD no naka ni wa, doitsu de ichiban no kyoku ga hai tte i masu. po—ru wa doitsu jin kashu no namae wo shiri ta gari masu. roba—to wa kare no okiniiri no kashu no namae wo age masu. kare wa, Blümchen, Nena to Herbert Grönemeyer no namae wo age masu. korera no namae wa po—ru nitotte, atarashii namae desu.

かれ　　　　　　　　　ご　うた　うた　はじ
　彼 はCDをきいて、どいつ語の 歌 を 歌い 始
　　　　かれ　　　　　　うた　　　　だいす
めます！彼 はこれらの 歌 がとても 大 好 きです。
　　　　　　　きょく　かし　か
ぽーるはろばーとに 曲 の歌詞を書いてくれるよう
　たの　　　　　　　　　いち　きょく　かし
に 頼 みます。ろばーとはどいつ 一 の 曲 の歌詞
　　　　　　　　　　　　か　　　　うた　たんご
をぽーるのために 書きます。ぽーるは 歌 の 単 語 を
まな　　　　　い　　　　　　　　てつだ
学 びたいと言い、ろばーとに 手 伝 ってくれるよう
　たの　　　　　　　　　　　どくたんご　まな
に 頼 みます。ろばーとはぽーるが 独 単 語 を 学
　　てつだ　　　　　　　　　えいご　じょうず
ぶのを 手 伝 います。ろばーとは英語が 上 手 に
はな　　　　　　　　　　　　じかん
話 せないので、たくさんの 時 間 がかかります。ろ
　　　は　　　　　　　　　　　かれ　かんたん
ばーとは恥ずかしがっています。彼 は 簡 単 なふ
　　い　　　　　　　　　　　　　ご
れーずも 言うことができません。その後、ろばーとは
かれ　へや　もど　　えいご　べんきょう
彼 の部屋に 戻 り、英語を 勉 強 します。

kare wa CD wo kii te, doitsugo no uta wo utai hajime masu! kare wa korera no uta ga totemo daisuki desu. po—ru wa roba—to ni kyoku no kashi wo kai te kureru you ni tanomi masu. roba—to wa doitsu ichi no kyoku no kashi wo po—ru no tame ni kaki masu. po—ru wa uta no tango wo manabi tai to ii, roba—to ni tetsuda tte

Grönemeyer. These names are new to Paul.

　He listens to the CDs and then begins to sing the German songs! He likes these songs very much. Paul asks Robert to write the words of the songs. Robert writes the words of the best German songs for Paul. Paul says that he wants to learn the words of some songs and asks Robert to help. Robert helps Paul to learn the German words. It takes a lot of time because Robert cannot speak English well. Robert is ashamed. He cannot say some simple phrases! Then Robert goes to his room and learns English.

kureru you ni tanomi masu. roba―to wa po―ru ga doku tango wo manabu no wo tetsudai masu. roba―to wa eigo ga jouzu ni hanase nai node, takusan no jikan ga kakari masu. roba―to wa hazukashi ga tte i masu. kare wa kantan na fure―zu mo iu koto ga deki mase n. sonogo, roba―to wa kare no heya ni modori, eigo wo benkyou shi masu.

10

Audio

<ruby>ポール<rt>ぽ る</rt></ruby>はデザインの教科書を買います

Paul buys textbooks on design

A

単語
Words

1. いくつかの [ikutsu ka no] - any
2. こんにちは [konnichiwa] - hello
3. さようなら、じゃあまた [sayounara, jaa mata] - bye
4. デザイン [dezain] - design
5. プログラム [puroguramu] - program
6. レッスン、授業 [ressun, jugyou] - lesson
7. 写真 [shashin] - picture
8. 勉強する [benkyou suru] - study

9. 唯一の [yuiitsu no] - only
10. 大学 [daigaku] - college
11. 彼に [kare ni] - him
12. 支払う [shiharau] - pay
13. 教科書 [kyoukasho] - textbook
14. 本当に [hontouni] - really
15. 母国語 [bokoku go] - native language
16. 種類 [shurui] - kind, type
17. 素晴らしい、良い [subarashii, yoi] - fine
18. 見る [miru] - look
19. 見る、理解する [miru, rikai suru] - see
20. 言語 [gengo] - language
21. 説明する [setsumei suru] - explain
22. 費用がかかる [hiyou ga kakaru] - cost
23. 選ぶ、決める [erabu, kimeru] - choose

B

ポールはデザインの教科書を買います

po—ru wa dezain no kyoukasho wo kai masu

ぽーるはかなだ人で、英語は彼の母国語です。彼はさんふらんしすこの大学ででざいんの勉強をしています。po—ru wa kanada jin de, eigo wa kare no bokoku go desu. kare wa sanfuranshisuko no daigaku de dezain no benkyou wo shi te i masu.

今日は土曜日でぽーるはたくさんの空き時間があります。彼は新しいでざいんの本が買いたいです。彼は近くの本屋へ行きます。彼らは、でざいんの教科書を売っているかも

Paul buys textbooks on design

Paul is Canadian and English is his native language. He studies design at college in San Francisco.

It is Saturday today and Paul has a lot of free time. He wants to buy some books on design. He goes to the nearby book shop. They may have

しれません。彼はお店に入り本棚を見ます。女性がぽーるの方へ来ます。彼女は店員です。kyou wa doyoubi de po—ru wa takusan no aki jikan ga ari masu. kare wa atarashii dezain no hon ga kai tai desu. kare wa chikaku no honya e iki masu. karera wa, dezain no kyoukasho wo u tte iru kamo shire mase n. kare wa o mise ni hairi hondana wo mi masu. josei ga po—ru no hou e ki masu. kanojo wa ten'in desu.

some textbooks on design. He comes into the shop and looks at the tables with books. A woman comes to Paul. She is a shop assistant.

"こんにちは。お手伝いしましょうか？"店員が彼にたずねます。"konnichiwa. otetsudai shi masho u ka?" ten'in ga kare ni tazune masu.

"Hello. Can I help you?" the shop assistant asks him.

"こんにちは。"ぽーるは言います。"わたしは大学ででざいんを勉強しています。わたしは教科書が必要です。でざいんについての教科書はおいていますか？"ぽーるは彼女にたずねます。"konnichiwa." po—ru wa ii masu. "watashi wa daigaku de dezain wo benkyou shi te i masu. watashi wa kyoukasho ga hitsuyou desu. dezain nitsuite no kyoukasho wa oi te i masu ka?" po—ru wa kanojo ni tazune masu.

"Hello," Paul says, "I study design at college. I need some textbooks. Do you have any textbooks on design?" Paul asks her.

"どんな種類のでざいんですか？わたしたちは家具でざいん、車でざいん、すぽーつでざいん、いんたーねっとでざいんについての教科書があります。"彼女は彼に説明します。"donna shurui no dezain desu ka? watashi tachi wa kagu dezain, kuruma dezain, supo—tsu dezain, inta—netto dezain nitsuite no kyoukasho ga ari masu." kanojo wa kare ni setsumei shi masu.

"What kind of design? We have some textbooks on furniture design, car design, sport design, internet design," she explains to him.

"家具でざいんといんたーねっとでざいんのきょうかしょをみせてもらえませんか？"ぽーるがかのじょに言います。 "kagu dezain to inta―netto dezain no kyoukasho wo mise te morae mase n ka?" po―ru ga kanojo ni ii masu.

"教科書棚から本を選べますよ。見てみてください。こちらはいたりあの家具でざいなーPalatinoの本です。このでざいなーはいたりあの家具でざいんについて説明します。彼はよーろっぱとあめりかの家具でざいんについて上手に説明をします。そこには何枚かの素晴らしい写真ものっています、"店員が説明します。 "kyoukasho dana kara hon wo erabe masu yo. mi te mi te kudasai. ko chi ra wa itaria no kagu dezaina―Palatino no hon desu. kono dezaina― wa itaria no kagu dezain nitsuite setsumei shi masu. kare wa yo―roppa to amerika no kagu dezain nitsuite jouzu ni setsumei wo shi masu. soko ni wa nan mai ka no subarashii shashin mo no tte i masu," ten'in ga setsumei shi masu.

"この本にはれっすんもいくつかのっているみたいですね。この本はとても素晴らしい。おいくらですか？"ぽーるがかのじょに質問します。 "kono hon ni wa ressun mo ikutsu ka no tte iru mitai desu ne. kono hon wa totemo subarashii. o ikura desu ka?" po―ru ga kanojo ni shitsumon shi masu.

"52どるです。そして本と一緒にCDもついて

"Can you show me some textbooks on furniture design and internet design?" Paul says to her.

"You can choose the books from the next tables. Look at them. This is a book by Italian furniture designer Palatino. This designer explains the design of Italian furniture. He explains the furniture design of Europe and the USA as well. There are some fine pictures there," the shop assistant explains.

"I see there are some lessons in the book too. This book is really fine. How much is it?" Paul asks her.

"It costs 52 dollars. And with the book you have a CD.

きます。CDには家具でざいんのこんぴゅーたーぷろぐらむがあります。"店員が彼に言います。 "go juu ni doru desu. soshite hon to issho ni shi— di— mo tsui te ki masu. shi— di— ni wa kagu dezain no konpyu—ta— puroguramu ga ari masu." ten'in ga kare ni ii masu.

"それは本当にいいですね。"ぽーるが言います。 "sore ha hontouni ii desu ne." po—ru ga ii masu.

"何冊かのいんたーねっとでざいんの教科書も、そこでみることができます。"女性が彼に説明します。"この本はまいくろそふとおふぃすのこんぴゅーたーぷろぐらむについてです。そしてこれらの本はこんぴゅーたーぷろぐらむ、ふらっしゅについてです。こちらの赤い本をみてみてください。ふらっしゅについての本で、いくつかの面白いれっすんもあります。選んでください、お願いします。" "nan satsu ka no inta—netto dezain no kyoukasho mo, soko de miru koto ga deki masu." josei ga kare ni setsumei shi masu." kono hon wa maikurosofuto ofisu no konpyu—ta— puroguramu nitsuite desu. soshite korera no hon wa konpyu—ta— puroguramu, furasshu nitsuite desu. kochira no akai hon wo mi te mi te kudasai. furasshu nitsuite no hon de, ikutsu ka no omoshiroi ressun mo ari masu. eran de kudasai, onegai shi masu."

"この赤い本はおいくらですか？"ぽーるが彼女に聞きます。"kono akai hon wa o ikura desu

There is a computer program for furniture design on the CD," the shop assistant says to him.

"I really like it," Paul says.

"You can see some textbooks on internet design there," the woman explains to him, "This book is about the computer program Microsoft Office. And these books are about the computer program Flash. Look at this red book. It is about Flash and it has some interesting lessons. Choose, please."

"How much is this red book?" Paul asks her.

ka?" po―ru ga kanojo ni kiki masu.

"この 本 はCD2 枚 がついて、たったの43 どるです" 店 員 が 彼 に 言います。 "kono hon wa shi―di― ni mai ga tsui te, tatta no yon juu san doru desu" ten'in ga kare ni ii masu.

"This book, with two CDs, costs only 43 dollars," the shop assistant says to him.

nari mase n ka?" po―ru ga tazune masu.

"わたしは、Palatino の家具でざいんについてのこの 本 と、ふらっしゅについてのこの 赤 い 本 が買いたいです。わたしはいくら支払わなければなりませんか？" ぽーるがたずねます。 "watashi wa, Palatino no kagu dezain nitsuite no kono hon to, furasshu nitsuite no kono akai hon ga kai tai desu. watashi wa ikura shiharawa nakere ba

"I want to buy this book by Palatino about furniture design and this red book about Flash. How much must I pay for them?" Paul asks.

"あなたはこれらの 本 2 冊 で、95 どる支払う必 要 があります" 店 員 が 彼 に 言います。 "anata ha korera no hon ni satsu de, kyuu juu go doru shiharau hitsuyou ga ari masu" ten'in ga kare ni ii masu.

"You need to pay 95 dollars for these two books," the shop assistant says to him.

ぽーるは支払いをします。そして 本 とCDを受け取ります。 po―ru wa shiharai wo shi masu. soshite hon to shi― di― wo uketori masu.

Paul pays. Then he takes the books and the CDs.

"さようなら" 店 員 が 彼 に 言います。 "sayounara" ten'in ga kare ni ii masu.

"Bye," the shop assistant says to him.

"さようなら" ぽーるは 彼 女 に 言い、出ます。 "sayounara" po―ru wa kanojo ni ii, de masu.

"Bye," Paul says to her and goes.

11

Audio

ロバートはお金を稼ぎたいです（パート１）
Robert wants to earn some money (Part 1)

A

単語
Words

1. いつもの、通常の [itsumo no, tsuujou no] - usual
2. いつもは、通常は、普段は [itsumo wa, tsuujou wa, fudan wa] - usually
3. エネルギー、元気 [enerugiー, genki] - energy
4. こたえる [kotaeru] - answer
5. トラック [torakku] - truck
6. メモ [memo] - note
7. もう一度 [mouichido] - one more
8. より良い [yori yoi] - better
9. リスト、リストする [risuto, risuto suru] - list

10. 一部、部品、部分 [ichibu, buhin, bubun] - part
11. 人事部 [jinji bu] - personnel department
12. 大丈夫、平気、わかる [daijoubu, heiki, wakaru] - OK, well
13. 大変な [taihen na] - hard
14. 後で [atode] - after
15. 搬入する、積む；搬入作業員 [hannyuu suru, tsumu ; hannyuu sagyou in] - load; loader
16. 数字 [suuji] - number
17. 日；毎日、日常的に [nichi ; mainichi, nichijou teki ni] - day; daily
18. 時；２時です [ji ; ni ji desu] - o'clock; It is two o'clock.
19. 時間；毎時 [jikan ; maiji] - hour; hourly
20. 理解する、わかる [rikai suru, wakaru] - understand
21. 稼ぐ；わたしは時給１０ドルを稼ぎます [kasegu ; watashi wa jikyuu juu doru wo kasegi masu] - earn; I earn 10 dollars per hour.
22. 箱、ダンボール [hako, danbo―ru] - box
23. 素早く [subayaku] - quick, quickly
24. 終わる、終える；終えるために [owaru, oeru ; oeru tame ni] - finish; to finish
25. 続く [tsuzuku] - be continued
26. 運送する、運ぶ [unsou suru, hakobu] - transport

B

ロバートはお金を稼ぎたいです
（パート１）

roba―to wa okane wo kasegi tai desu （pa―to ichi）

ろばーとは大学の後、毎日空き時間があります。彼はお金を稼ぎたいです。彼は職業紹介所へ向かいます。彼ら

Robert wants to earn some money (Part 1)

Robert has free time daily after college. He wants to earn some money. He heads to a job agency. They give

は、ある運送会社の住所を彼に渡します。運送会社らぴっどは搬入作業員を必要としています。この仕事は本当に大変です。しかし彼らは時給11どるを支払います。ろばーとはこの仕事につきたいです。なので、彼は運送会社のおふぃすへ行きます。

roba―to wa daigaku no nochi, mainichi aki jikan ga ari masu. kare wa okane wo kasegi tai desu. kare wa shokugyou shoukai jo e mukai masu. karera wa, aru unsou gaisha no juusho wo kare ni watashi masu. unsou gaisha rapiddo wa hannyuu sagyou in wo hitsuyou to shi te i masu. kono shigoto wa hontouni taihen desu. shikashi karera wa jikyuu juu ichi doru wo shiharai masu. roba―to wa kono shigoto ni tsuki tai desu. na node, kare wa unsou gaisha no ofisu e iki masu.

him the address of a transport firm. The transport firm Rapid needs a loader. This work is really hard. But they pay 11 dollars per hour. Robert wants to take this job. So he goes to the office of the transport firm.

"こんにちは。職業紹介所からあなたがたへ、めもがあります" ろばーとは会社の人事部の女性に言います。彼は彼女にめもを渡します。"こんにちは。" 女性が言います。"私の名前はまーがれっと・ばーどです。わたしが人事部長です。あなたのお名前は何ですか？" "わたしの名前はろばーと・げんしゃーです" ろばーとが言います

"konnichiwa. shokugyou shoukai jo kara anata gata e, memo ga ari masu" roba―to wa kaisha no jinji bu no josei ni ii masu. kare wa kanojo ni memo wo watashi masu. "konnichiwa." josei ga ii masu. "watashi no namae

"Hello. I have a note for you from a job agency," Robert says to a woman in the personnel department of the firm. He gives her the note.

"Hello," the woman says, "My name is Margaret Bird. I am the head of the personnel department. What is your name?"

wa ma―garetto. ba―do desu. watashi ga jinji buchou desu. anata no o namae wa nan desu ka?" "watashi no namae wa roba―to. gensha― desu" roba―to ga ii masu.

"あなたはあめりか人ですか？"まーがれっとがききます。"いいえ。わたしはどいつ人です"ろばーとがこたえます。"あなたは英語を上手に話したり、読んだりできますか？"彼女が質問します。"はい、できます。"彼が言います。"あなたは何歳ですか、ろばーと？彼女が聞きます。"わたしは２０歳です。"ろばーとがこたえます。"anata wa amerika jin desu ka?" ma―garetto ga kiki masu. "iie. watashi wa doitsu jin desu" roba―to ga kotae masu. "anata wa eigo wo jouzu ni hanashi tari, yon dari deki masu ka?" kanojo ga shitsumon shi masu. "hai, deki masu." kare ga ii masu. "anata wa nan sai desu ka, roba―to? kanojo ga kiki masu. "watashi wa ni ju ssai desu." roba―to ga kotae masu.

"あなたは運送会社で搬入作業員として働きたいですか？"人事部長が彼にききます。ろばーとは英語が上手に話せないために、より良い仕事につくことができないと言うのを恥ずかしく思います。なので、彼は言います："時給１１どるを稼ぎたいのです。" "anata wa unsou gaisha de hannyuu sagyou in toshite hataraki tai desu ka?" jinji buchou ga kare ni kiki masu. roba―to wa eigo ga jouzu ni hanase nai tame ni, yori yoi shigoto ni tsuku koto ga deki nai to

"My name is Robert Genscher" Robert says.

"Are you American?" Margaret asks.

"No. I am German," Robert answers.

"Can you speak and read English well?" she asks.

"Yes, I can," he says.

"How old are you, Robert?" she asks.

"I am twenty years old," Robert answers.

"Do you want to work at the transport firm as a loader?" the head of the personnel department asks him.

Robert is ashamed to say that he cannot have a better job because he cannot speak English well. So he says: "I want to earn 11 dollars per hour."

iu no wo hazukashiku omoi masu. na node, kare wa ii masu : "jikyuu juu ichi doru wo kasegi tai no desu."

"Well-well," Margaret says, "Our transport firm usually does not have much loading work. But now we really need one more loader. Can you load quickly boxes with 20 kilograms of load?"

"これはこれは"まーがれっとが言います。"私たちの運送会社は通常、搬入の仕事はたくさんありません。しかし、私たちは一人だけ搬入作業員が本当に必要です。あなたは20きろの箱を素早く積むことができますか？" "はい、できます。わたしはえねるぎーがたくさんあります。" ろばーとがこたえます。"kore wa kore wa" まーgaretto ga ii masu. "watashi tachi no unsou gaisha wa tsuujou, hannyuu no shigoto wa takusan ari mase n. shikashi, watashi tachi wa hitori dake hannyuu sagyou in ga hontouni hitsuyou desu. anata wa ni ju kkiro no hako wo subayaku tsumu koto ga deki masu ka?" "hai, deki masu. watashi wa enerugi— ga takusan ari masu." ろばーto ga kotae masu.

"Yes, I can. I have a lot of energy," Robert answers.

"わたしたちは、毎日3時間搬入作業員が必要です。4時から7時まで働くことができますか？" 彼女がききます。

"We need a loader daily for three hours. Can you work from four to seven o'clock?" she asks.

"はい、わたしの授業は1時に終わります" 学生が彼女にこたえます。"いつから始めることができますか？" 人事部長が彼に質問します。 "今から始められますよ。" ろばーとはこたえます。 "watashi tachi wa, mainichi san jikan hannyuu sagyou in ga hitsuyou desu. yo ji kara nana ji made hataraku koto ga deki masu ka?" kanojo ga kiki masu. "hai, watashi no jugyou wa ichi ji ni owari masu" gakusei ga kanojo ni kotae masu. "itsu kara hajimeru koto ga deki masu ka?" jinji buchou ga kare ni shitsumon shi masu. "ima kara hajime rare masu yo."

"Yes, my lessons finish at one o'clock," the student answers to her.

"When can you begin the work?" the head of the personnel department asks him.

"I can begin now," Robert answers.

roba一to wa kotae masu.

"ええと。この搬入りすとを見てください。いくつかの会社とお店の名前がりすとにのっています。"まーがれっとは説明します。"全ての会社とお店に、いくつかの数字があります。それらは箱の数です。そしてこれらの番号は、あなたがこれらの箱を搬入しなければいけないとらっくの数です。とらっくは1時間ごとに来て、去って行きます。ですから、あなたは素早く働く必要があります。大丈夫ですか？" "大丈夫です" ろばーとは、まーがれっとを上手く理解せずに、こたえます。 "eeto. kono hannyuu risuto wo mi te kudasai. ikutsu ka no kaisha to o mise no namae ga risuto ni no tte i masu." ma一garetto wa setsumei shi masu." subete no kaisha to o mise ni, ikutsu ka no suuji ga ari masu. sorera wa hako no kazu desu. soshite korera no bangou wa, anata ga korera no hako wo hannyuu shi nakere ba ike nai torakku no kazu desu. torakku wa ichi jikan goto ni ki te, sa tte iki masu. desu kara, anata wa subayaku hataraku hitsuyou ga ari masu. daijoubu desu ka?" "daijoubu desu" roba一to wa, ma一garetto wo umaku rikai se zu ni, kotae masu.

"では、この搬入りすとを持って、搬入どあ番号3まで行ってください。"人事部長はろばーとに言います。ろばーとは搬入りすとを持ち、仕事に行きます。

"Well. Look at this loading list. There are some names of firms and shops in the list," Margaret explains, "Every firm and shop has some numbers. They are numbers of the boxes. And these are numbers of the trucks where you must load these boxes. The trucks come and go hourly. So you need to work quickly. OK?"

"OK," Robert answers, not understanding Margaret well.

"Now take this loading list and go to the loading door number three," the head of the personnel department says to Robert. Robert takes

（続く）

"dewa, kono hannyuu risuto wo mo tte, hannyuu doa bangou san made i tte kudasai." jinji buchou wa roba—to ni ii masu. roba—to wa hannyuu risuto wo mochi, shigoto ni iki masu.

(tsuzuku)

the loading list and goes to work.

(to be continued)

12

Audio

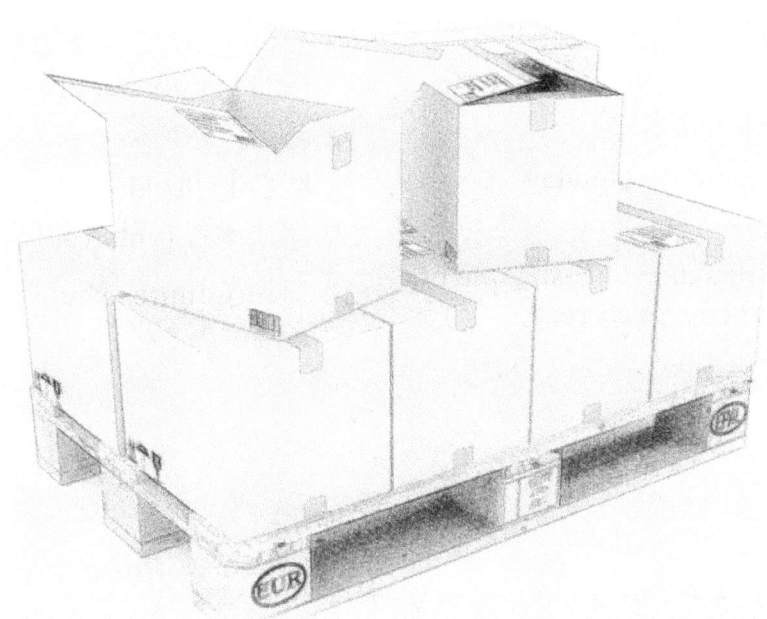

ロバートはお金を稼ぎたいです（パート２）
Robert wants to earn some money (Part 2)

A

単語
Words

1. あなたの [anata no] - your
2. あなたの代わりに [anata no kawari ni] - instead of you
3. いやがる、嫌う [iyagaru, kirau] - hate
4. お母さん、母親 [okaasan, hahaoya] - mom, mother
5. ここ [koko] - here (a place)
6. ここに、こちらに [koko ni, kochira ni] - here (a direction)
7. こちらは、これは [kochira wa, kore wa] - here is
8. さん、氏 [san, shi] - mister, Mr.
9. 代わりに [kawari ni] - instead of
10. 会う [au] - meet

11. 先生 [sensei] - teacher
12. 嬉しい [ureshii] - glad
13. 彼らの [karera no] - their
14. 息子 [musuko] - son
15. 悪い、良くない [warui, yoku nai] - bad
16. 戻る [modoru] - back
17. 月曜日 [getsuyoubi] - Monday
18. 正しく、正確に ; 直すために [tadashiku, seikaku ni ; naosu tame ni] - correct, correctly; to correct
19. 歩く [aruku] - walk
20. 理由 [riyuu] - reason
21. 申し訳ない、悪いと思う ; ごめんなさい [moushiwake nai, warui to omou ; gomennasai] - be sorry; I am sorry.
22. 誤って [ayama tte] - incorrectly
23. 起き上がる ; 起きて！ [okiagaru ; oki te!] - get up; Get up!
24. 運ぶ、持ってくる、 [hakobu, mo tte kuru,] - bring
25. 運転する [unten suru] - drive
26. 運転手 [unten shu] - driver

B

ロバートはお金を稼ぎたいです
（パート2）

roba—to wa okane wo kasegi tai desu (pa—to ni)

搬入どあ3番にはたくさんのとらっくがあります。彼らは積み荷を運んで戻ってきています。人事部長と社長がそこへ来ます。彼らはろばーとの方へ来ます。ろばーとは箱をとらっくに搬入しています。彼は素早く動いています。 hannyuu doa san ban ni wa takusan no torakku ga ari masu. karera wa tsumini wo hakon de modo tte ki te i masu. jinji buchou to shachou ga soko e ki masu. karera wa roba—to no hou e ki masu. roba—to wa hako wo torakku ni hannyuu

Robert wants to earn some money (Part 2)

There are many trucks at the loading door number three. They are coming back bringing back their loads. The head of the personnel department and the head of the firm come there. They come to Robert. Robert is loading boxes in a truck. He is working quickly.

shi te i masu. kare wa subayaku ugoi te i masu.

"やあ、ろばーと！こちらへ来てください。"まーがれっとが彼を呼びます。"こちらは社長のぷろふぃっとさんです。" "お会いできて嬉しいです。"ろばーとは彼らに向かいながら言います。"わたしもです。"ぷろふぃっとさんがこたえます。"あなたの搬入りすとはどこですか？" "ここです。"ろばーとは搬入りすとを彼に渡します。 "yaa, robaーto! kochira e ki te kudasai." maーgaretto ga kare wo yobi masu." kochira wa shachou no puro fitto san desu." "o ai deki te ureshii desu." robaーto wa karera ni mukai nagara ii masu. "watashi mo desu." puro fitto san ga kotae masu. "anata no hannyuu risuto wa doko desu ka?" "koko desu." robaーto wa hannyuu risuto wo kare ni watashi masu.

"これはこれは。" ぷろふぃっとさんはりすとを見ながら言います。"これらのとらっくを見てください。あなたが箱を誤って搬入するので、彼らは積み荷を運んで戻ってきています。本の箱が本屋の代わりに家具屋に行き、びでおかせっととDVDの箱がびでおしょっぷの代わりにかふぇに行き、さんどいっちの箱がかふぇではなくびでおしょっぷに行っています！よくない仕事ですね！ごめんなさい、しかしあなたはわたしたちの会社で働くことはできませ

"Hey, Robert! Please, come here," Margaret calls him, *"This is the head of the firm, Mr. Profit."*

"I am glad to meet you," Robert says coming to them.

"I too," Mr. Profit answers, *"Where is your loading list?"*

"It is here," Robert gives him the loading list.

"Well-well," Mr. Profit says looking in the list, *"Look at these trucks. They are coming back bringing back their loads because you load the boxes incorrectly. The boxes with books go to a furniture shop instead of the book shop, the boxes with videocassettes and DVDs go to a café instead of the video shop, and the boxes with sandwiches go to a video shop instead of the café! It is

ん。"ぷろふぃっとさんはそう言い、おふぃすにある 歩いて 戻 ります。 "kore wa kore wa." puro fitto san wa risuto wo mi nagara ii masu. "korera no torakku wo mi te kudasai. anata ga hako wo ayama tte hannyuu suru node, karera wa tsumini wo hakon de modo tte ki te i masu. hon no hako ga hon'ya no kawari ni kagu ya ni iki, bideokasetto to DVD no hako ga bideo shoppu no kawari ni kafe ni iki, sandoicchi no hako ga kafe de wa naku bideo shoppu ni i tte i masu! yoku nai shigoto desu ne! gomennasai, shikashi anata wa watashi tachi no kaisha de hataraku koto wa deki mase n." puro fitto san wa sou ii, ofisu ni arui te modori masu.

bad work! Sorry but you cannot work at our firm," Mr. Profit says and walks back to the office.

ろばーとは、とても 少 しの 英単語 しか読んで 理解 ができないため、箱を 正しく 搬入 することができません。まーがれっとはろばーとを 見ます。ろばーとは 恥ずかしく 思っています。 roba―to wa, totemo sukoshi no eitango shika yon de rikai ga deki nai tame, hako wo tadashiku hannyuu suru koto ga deki mase n. ma―garetto wa roba―to wo mi masu. roba―to wa hazukashiku omo tte i masu.

Robert cannot load boxes correctly because he can read and understand very few English words. Margaret looks at him. Robert is ashamed.

"ろばーと、あなたはもっと 英語を 学んで、その 後に、また 来てくださいね。 大丈夫 ですか?"まーがれっとが 言います。"わかりました"ろばーとがこたえます。"さようなら、まーがれっと。" "さようなら、ろばーと。"まーがれっとがこたえます。ろばーとは 家まで 歩きます。今の 彼は、もっと 英語を 勉強 して、そして 新しい 仕事につきたいです。 "roba―to, anata wa motto eigo wo manan de, sono ato

"Robert, you can learn English better and then come again. OK?" Margaret says.

"OK," Robert answers, "Bye Margaret."

"Bye Robert," Margaret answers.

Robert walks home. He wants to learn English better now

ni, mata ki te kudasai ne. daijoubu desu ka?" ma―garetto ga ii masu. "wakari mashi ta" roba―to ga kotae masu. "sayounara, ma―garetto." "sayounara, roba―to." ma―garetto ga kotae masu. roba―to wa ie made aruki masu. ima no kare wa, motto eigo wo benkyou shi te, soshite atarashii shigoto ni tsuki tai desu.

and then take a new job.

大学へ行く時間です

daigaku e iku jikan desu

月曜日の朝、母は部屋の中へ行き、息子を起こします。"起きなさい、7時よ。大学へ行く時間よ！" "でもなんで、お母さん？行きたくないよ。" getsuyoubi no asa, haha wa heya no naka e iki, musuko wo okoshi masu. "oki nasai, nana ji yo. daigaku e iku jikan yo!" "demo nande, okaasan? iki taku nai yo."

"行きたくない理由を2つ教えて" 母は息子に言います。"ひとつめは、生徒達がぼくを嫌っていて、先生達もぼくを嫌っている！" "まあ、大学へ行かない理由ではないわね。起きなさい！" "iki taku nai riyuu wo futatsu oshie te" haha wa musuko ni ii masu. "hitotsu me wa, seito tachi ga boku wo kira tte i te, sensei tachi mo boku wo kira tte iru!" "maa, daigaku e ika nai riyuu de wa nai wa ne. oki nasai!"

"わかった。大学へ行かなければ行けない理由を2つ教えてよ" 彼は母に言います。

It is time to go to college

Monday morning a mother comes into the room to wake up her son.

"Get up, it is seven o'clock. It is time to go to college!"

"But why, Mom? I don't want to go."

"Name me two reasons why you don't want to go," the mother says to the son.

"The students hate me for one and the teachers hate me too!"

"Oh, they are not reasons not to go to college. Get up!"

"OK. Name me two reasons why I must go to college," he says to his mother.

"ええと、ひとつめは、あなたは５５歳だから。そしてふたつめは、あなたが大学の学長だからよ！今すぐ起きなさい！" "waka tta. daigaku e ika nakere ba ike nai riyuu wo futatsu oshie te yo" kare wa haha ni ii masu. "eeto, hitotsu me wa, anata wa go juu go sai da kara. soshite futatsu me wa, anata ga daigaku no gakuchou da kara yo! ima sugu oki nasai!"

"Well, for one, you are 55 years old. And for two, you are the head of the college! Get up now!"

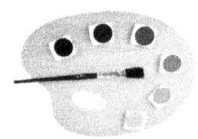

Elementary Course

13

Audio

<ruby>ホテル<rt></rt></ruby>の<ruby>名前<rt>なまえ</rt></ruby>

The name of the hotel

A

単語
Words

1. エレベーター [erebe―ta―] - lift
2. そして、その後 [soshite, sonogo] - then
3. タクシー [takushi―] - taxi
4. タクシードライバー [takushi― doraiba―] - taxi driver
5. とめる、とまる、終わりにする [tomeru, tomaru, owari ni suru] - stop
6. ばかげた、ばかな [bakage ta, baka na] - silly
7. ポーランド [po―rando] - Poland
8. また、再び、もう一度 [mata, futatabi, mouichido] - again
9. まわる [mawaru] - round
10. みる、わかる、理解する [miru, wakaru, rikai suru] - see
11. もうすでに [mou sudeni] - already
12. 下に [shita ni] - down
13. 中へ、抜けて、通して [naka e, nuke te, tooshi te] - through

14. 今、現在 [ima, genzai] - now
15. 別の、違う [betsu no, chigau] - another
16. 去って、離れて [sa tte, hanare te] - away
17. 向こうの、渡った [mukou no, watatta] - over, across
18. 夕方 [yuugata] - evening
19. 夜 [yoru] - night
20. 広告 [koukoku] - advert
21. 微笑みかけるために [hohoemikakeru tame ni] - to smile
22. 微笑む、笑いかける [hohoemu, waraikakeru] - smile
23. 怒っている [oko tte iru] - angry
24. 橋 [hashi] - bridge
25. 歩いて [arui te] - on foot
26. 歩く [aruku] - walk
27. 湖 [mizuumi] - lake
28. 疲れている [tsukare te iru] - tired
29. 眠る、寝る [nemuru, neru] - sleep
30. 立つ [tatsu] - stand
31. 見せる [miseru] - show
32. 見つける、探す [mitsukeru, sagasu] - find
33. 足 [ashi] - foot
34. 通り過ぎる [toorisugiru] - past
35. 道 [michi] - way
36. 開ける、開く [akeru, hiraku] - open
37. 驚いている [odoroi te iru] - surprised
38. 驚かせる [odoroka seru] - surprise
39. 驚かせるために [odoroka seru tame ni] - to surprise

ホテルの名前

hoteru no namae

こちらは学生です。彼の名前はかすぱーです。彼はぽーらんど出身です。彼は英語を話すことができません。彼はあめりかの大学で英語を学びたいです。かす

The name of the hotel

This is a student. His name is Kasper. Kasper is from Poland. He cannot speak English. He wants to learn English at a college in the USA. Kasper lives

ぱーはさんふらんしすこのほてるに、今住んでいます。kochira wa gakusei desu. kare no namae wa kasu pa― desu. kare wa pō―rando shusshin desu. kare wa eigo wo hanasu koto ga deki mase n. kare wa amerika no daigaku de eigo wo manabi tai desu. kasu pa― wa sanfuranshisuko no hoteru ni, ima sun de i masu.	in a hotel in San Francisco now.
彼は今自分の部屋にいます。彼は地図を見ています。この地図はとても良い地図です。かすぱーは、通り、広場そしてお店を地図で見ます。彼は部屋を出て長い廊下を抜けえれべーたに向かいます。えれべーたで下に行きます。かすぱーは大きなほーるを抜け、ほてるを出ます。彼はほてるの近くでとまり、ほてるの名前を自分ののーとに書きます。kare wa ima jibun no heya ni i masu. kare wa chizu wo mi te i masu. kono chizu wa totemo yoi chizu desu. kasu pa― wa, toori, hiroba soshite o mise wo chizu de mi masu. kare wa heya wo de te nagai rouka wo nuke erebē―ta ni mukai masu. erebē―ta de shita ni iki masu. kasu pa― wa ookina hō―ru wo nuke, hoteru wo de masu. kare wa hoteru no chikaku de tomari, hoteru no namae wo jibun no nō―to ni kaki masu.	He is in his room now. He is looking at the map. This map is very good. Kasper sees streets, squares and shops on the map. He goes out of the room and through the long corridor to the lift. The lift takes him down. Kasper goes through the big hall and out of the hotel. He stops near the hotel and writes the name of the hotel into his notebook.
ほてるには丸い広場と湖があります。かすぱーは広場から湖へ渡ります。彼は湖から橋へ一周歩きます。たくさんの車、とらっく、そして人々が橋を渡ります。かすぱーは橋の	There is a round square and a lake at the hotel. Kasper goes across the square to the lake. He walks round the lake to the bridge. Many cars, trucks and people go over the bridge.

下へ行きます。そして彼は中心街へ、道に沿って歩きます。彼はたくさんの素敵な建物を通り過ぎます。hoteru ni wa marui hiroba to mizuumi ga ari masu. kasu paー wa hiroba kara mizuumi e watari masu. kare wa mizuumi kara hashi e isshuu aruki masu. takusan no kuruma, torakku, soshite hitobito ga hashi wo watari masu. kasu paー wa hashi no shita e iki masu. soshite kare wa chuushin gai e, michi ni so tte aruki masu. kare wa takusan no suteki na tatemono wo toorisugi masu.

もうすでに夕方です。かすぱーは疲れていて、ほてるに戻りたいです。彼はたくしーをとめて、そしてのーとを開き、ほてるの名前をたくしーどらいばーにみせます。たくしーどらいばーはのーとをみて微笑み、走り去ります。かすぱーはそれが理解できません。彼は立って、自分のーとを覗きます。そして、彼は別のたくしーをとめ、たくしーどらいばーに再びのーとをみせます。たくしーどらいばーはのーとをみます。そしてかすぱーをみて、微笑み、また去って行きます。mou sudeni yuugata desu. kasu paー wa tsukare te i te, hoteru ni modori tai desu. kare wa takushiー wo tome te, soshite noーto wo hiraki, hoteru no namae wo takushiー doraibaー ni mise masu. takushiー doraibaー wa noーto wo mi te hohoemi, hashirisari masu. kasu paー wa sore ga rikai deki mase n. kare wa ta tte, jibun no noーto wo nozoki masu. soshite, kare

Kasper goes under the bridge. Then he walks along a street to the city centre. He goes past many nice buildings.

It is evening already. Kasper is tired and he wants to go back to the hotel. He stops a taxi, then opens his notebook and shows the name of the hotel to the taxi driver. The taxi driver looks in the notebook, smiles and drives away. Kasper cannot understand it. He stands and looks in his notebook. Then he stops another taxi and shows the name of the hotel to the taxi driver again. The driver looks in the notebook. Then he looks at Kasper, smiles and drives away too.

wa betsu no takushī wo tome, takushī doraibā ni futatabi nōto wo mise masu. takushī doraibā wa nōto wo mi masu. soshite kasu pā wo mi te, hohoemi, mata sa tte iki masu.

かすぱーは驚いています。彼は別のたくしーをとめます。しかしこのたくしーも去って行きます。かすぱーには理解ができません。彼は驚いて、怒っています。しかし彼はばかではありません。彼は自分の地図を開き、ほてるへの道をみつけます。彼は歩いてほてるまで戻ります。kasu pā wa odoroi te i masu. kare wa betsu no takushī wo tome masu. shikashi kono takushī mo sa tte iki masu. kasu pā ni wa rikai ga deki mase n. kare wa odoroi te, oko tte i masu. shikashi kare wa baka de wa ari mase n. kare wa jibun no chizu wo hiraki, hoteru e no michi wo mitsuke masu. kare wa arui te hoteru made modori masu.

Kasper is surprised. He stops another taxi. But this taxi drives away too. Kasper cannot understand it. He is surprised and angry. But he is not silly. He opens his map and finds the way to the hotel. He comes back to the hotel on foot.

夜です。かすぱーはべっどの中にいます。彼は眠っています。星は窓から部屋の中をのぞきこんでいます。のーとは机の上にあります。それは開いています。"ふぉーどは最高の車だ"これはほてるの名前ではありません。これはほてるの建物の広告です。yoru desu. kasu pā wa beddo no naka ni i masu. kare wa nemu tte i masu. hoshi wa mado kara heya no naka wo nozokikon de i masu. nōto wa tsukue no ue ni ari masu. sore wa hirai te i

It is night. Kasper is in his bed. He is sleeping. The stars are looking into the room through the window. The notebook is on the table. It is open. "Ford is the best car". This is not the name of the hotel. This is an advert on the building of the hotel.

masu. "fo―do wa saikou no kuruma da" kore wa hoteru no namae de ha ari mase n. kore wa hoteru no tatemono no koukoku desu.

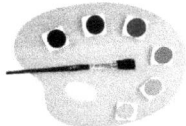

14

Audio

あすぴりん　ちんつうざい
アスピリン（鎮痛剤）

Aspirin

A

単語
Words

1. 10 [juu] - ten
2. １時に [ichi ji ni] - at one o'clock
3. ８時半に [hachi ji han ni] - at half past eight
4. アスピリン（鎮痛剤）[asupirin (chintsuu zai)] - aspirin
5. いくつかの、何人かの、いくらかの [ikutsu ka no, nan nin ka no, ikura ka no] - some
6. グレイ、灰色 [gurei, haiiro] - grey
7. こたえ、解決策 [kotae, kaiketsu saku] - solution, answer
8. 接続詞なので訳さない [setsuzokushi na node yakusa nai] - that *(conj)*
9. たどり着く [tadoritsuku] - get (somewhere)
10. ためす、してみる [tamesu, shi te miru] - try
11. テスト、試験 [tesuto, shiken] - test
12. テストをするために [tesuto wo suru tame ni] - to test
13. テストを通過するために [tesuto wo tsuuka suru tame ni] - to pass a test

14. とめる、停止する [tomeru, teishi suru] - break, pause
15. においのする [nioi no suru] - stinking
16. のために [no tame ni] - for
17. みる [miru] - watch
18. もちろん [mochiron] - of course
19. 何か [nani ka] - something
20. 化学 [kagaku] - chemistry
21. 化学の、化学的な [kagaku no, kagaku teki na] - chemical(adj)
22. 化学物質（複数）[kagaku busshitsu （fukusuu）] - chemicals
23. 半分 [hanbun] - half
24. 取る、手に入れる、得る [toru, te ni ireru, eru] - get (something)
25. 寮 [ryou] - dorms
26. 座る [suwaru] - sit down
27. 教室 [kyoushitsu] - classroom
28. 最後に [saigo ni] - at last
29. 机、デスク [tsukue, desuku] - desk
30. 用紙、シート [youshi, shi─to] - sheet (of paper)
31. 男の人、男性 [otoko no hito, dansei] - guy
32. 白い [shiroi] - white
33. 紙 [kami] - paper
34. 素晴らしい [subarashii] - wonderful
35. 考える [kangaeru] - think
36. 薬局 [yakkyoku] - pharmacy
37. 課題、タスク [kadai, tasuku] - task
38. 透明の、クリスタルの [toumei no, kurisutaru no] - crystal
39. 通り過ぎる、過ぎた [toorisugiru, sugi ta] - past
40. 錠剤、ピル [jouzai, piru] - pill
41. 頭の良い、賢い [atama no yoi, kashikoi] - smart
42. 頻繁に、よく [hinpan ni, yoku] - often

B

アスピリン（鎮痛剤）

asupirin （chintsuu zai）

Aspirin

こちらは、ろばーとの友達です。彼の名前はぽーるです。ぽーるはかなだ出身です。英語は彼の母国語です。彼はふらんす語もとても

This is Robert's friend. His name is Paul. Paul is from Canada. English is his native language. He can speak French very well too. Paul

　　　　じょうず　はな　　　　　　　りょう　す
　　上　手 に　話 せます。ぽーるは　寮　に住んでいま
　　　　　　　　　　　　いまかれ　へや
す。ぽーるは　今　彼 の部屋にいます。ぽーるは
きょうかがく　　　　　　　　　　　　かれ　とけい
今　日 化 学 のてすとがあります。　彼 は時 計 をみ
　　　　　　　じ　　い　じかん
ます。8時です。行く時 間 です。kochira wa, roba―
to no tomodachi desu. kare no namae wa po―ru desu.
po―ru wa kanada shusshin desu. eigo wa kare no
bokoku go desu. kare wa furansugo mo totemo jouzu ni
hanase masu. po―ru wa ryou ni sun de i masu. po―ru
wa ima kare no heya ni i masu. po―ru wa kyou kagaku
no tesuto ga ari masu. kare wa tokei wo mi masu. hachi
ji desu. iku jikan desu.

　　　　　　そと　で　　　かれ　だいがく　い
　ぽーるは　外 に出ます。　彼 は　大　学 へ行きます。
だいがく　　りょう　ちか　　　　　だいがく　い
　大　学 は　寮　の　近 くです。　大　学 へ行くのに
　　ふん　　　　　　　　　　　　　かがく
は10 分 ほどかかります。ぽーるは化 学 の
きょうしつ　い　　　　　かれ　あ
　教　室 に行きます。 彼 はどあを開けて、
きょうしつ　なか　のぞ　こ　　　　　　　　なん
　教　室 の 中 を 覗 き込みます。そこには 何
にん　　　　せいとたち　　せんせい
　人 かの生 徒 達 と 先　生 がいます。ぽーるは
きょうしつ　なか　はい
　教　室 の 中 へ 入 ります。po―ru wa soto ni de
masu. kare wa daigaku e iki masu. daigaku wa ryou no
chikaku desu. daigaku e iku no ni wa ju ppun hodo
kakari masu. po―ru wa kagaku no kyoushitsu ni iki
masu. kare wa doa wo ake te, kyoushitsu no naka wo
nozokikomi masu. soko ni wa nan nin ka no seito tachi
to sensei ga i masu. po―ru wa

kyoushitsu no naka e hairi masu.

　　　　　　　　　　かれ　い
　"こんにちは。" 彼 は言います。 "こんにち
　　　　　せんせい　せいとたち
は。" 先　生 と生 徒 達 がこたえます。ぽーる

lives in the dorms. Paul is in his room now. Paul has a chemistry test today. He looks at his watch. It is eight o'clock. It is time to go.

Paul goes outside. He goes to the college. The college is near the dorms. It takes him about ten minutes to go to the college. Paul comes to the chemical classroom. He opens the door and looks into the classroom. There are some students and the teacher there. Paul comes into the classroom.

"Hello," he says.

"Hello," the teacher and the students answer.

Paul comes to his desk and sits down. The chemistry test

は 机 に 座 ります。化学のてすとは8時半に
始 まります。 先 生 がぽーるの 机 へ来ます。
"konnichiwa." kare wa ii masu. "konnichiwa." sensei to
seito tachi ga kotae masu. po―ru wa tsukue ni suwari
masu. kagaku no tesuto wa hachi jihan ni hajimari masu.
sensei ga po―ru no tsukue e ki masu.

"これがあなたの 課 題 です。" 先 生 が言いま
す。そして 彼 はぽーるに 課 題 の書かれた 用 紙 を
渡 します。"あなたはあすぴりんを 作 らなけ
ればなりません。あなたは8時 半 から12時まで
作 業 をできます。 始 めてください。" 先 生
が言います。 "kore ga anata no kadai desu." sensei ga ii
masu. soshite kare wa po―ru ni kadai no kaka re ta
youshi wo watashi masu. "anata wa asupirin wo tsukura
nakere ba nari mase n. anata wa hachi jihan kara ichi ni
ji made sagyou wo deki masu. hajime te kudasai." sensei
ga ii masu.

ぽーるはこの 課 題 を知っています。 彼 はいくつか
の 薬 品 を取り、 始 めます。 彼 は10 分
作 業 をします。 最 後 には、ぐれーで 匂 いのす
る 何 かができます。これは良いあすぴり
ません。ぽーるは 大 きな 白 い 透 明 のあすぴり
んを 作 らなければならないことを知っています。そ
の後、彼 は 何 度 も 何 度 もためします。ぽーるは
一 時 間 作 業 をしますが、 何 度 もぐれーで

begins at half past eight. The teacher comes to Paul's desk.

"Here is your task," the teacher says. Then he gives Paul a sheet of paper with the task, "You must make aspirin. You can work from half past eight to twelve o'clock. Begin, please," the teacher says.

Paul knows this task. He takes some chemicals and begins. He works for ten minutes. At last he gets something grey and stinking. This is not good aspirin. Paul knows that he must get big white crystals of aspirin. Then he tries again and again. Paul works for an hour but he gets something

匂いのするものができます。po—ru wa kono kadai wo shi tte i masu. kare wa ikutsu ka no yakuhin wo tori, hajime masu. kare wa ju ppun sagyou wo shi masu. saigo ni wa, gure— de nioi no suru nani ka ga deki masu. kore wa yoi asupirin de wa ari mase n. po—ru wa ookina shiroi toumei no asupirin wo tsukura nakere ba nara nai koto wo shi tte i masu. sonogo, kare wa nan do mo nan do mo tameshi masu. po—ru wa ichi jikan sagyou wo shi masu ga, nan do mo gure— de nioi no suru mono ga deki masu.

grey and stinking again.

ぽーるは怒り、疲れています。彼には理解ができません。彼は、作業をやめて少し考えました。ぽーるは頭の良い男の人です。彼は1分考え、そして解決策をみつけます！彼は立ち上がります。"10分休憩してもいいですか？"ぽーるは先生に質問します。"もちろん、いいですよ。" 先生がこたえます。po—ru wa ikari, tsukare te i masu. kare ni wa rikai ga deki mase n. kare wa, sagyou wo yame te sukoshi kangae mashi ta. po—ru wa atama no yoi otoko no hito desu. kare wa i ppun kangae, soshite kaiketsu saku wo mitsuke masu! kare wa tachiagari masu. "ju puun kyuukei shi te mo ii desu ka?" po—ru wa sensei ni shitsumon shi masu. "mochiron, ii desu yo." sensei ga kotae masu.

Paul is angry and tired. He cannot understand it. He stops and thinks a little. Paul is a smart guy. He thinks for a minute and then finds the answer! He stands up.

"May I have a break for ten minutes?" Paul asks the teacher.

"Of course, you may," the teacher answers.

ぽーるは外へ出ます。彼は大学の近くの薬局をみつけます。彼は中へ入り、何錠かのあすぴりんを買います。10分で、彼は教室へ戻ります。生徒達は座って

Paul goes outside. He finds a pharmacy near the college. He comes in and buys some pills of aspirin. In ten minutes he comes back to the

作業をしています。ぽーるは座ります。po─ru wa soto e de masu. kare wa daigaku no

chikaku no yakkyoku wo mitsuke masu. kare wa naka e hairi, nan jou ka no asupirin wo kai masu. ju ppun de, kare wa kyoushitsu e modori masu. seito tachi wa suwa tte sagyou wo shi te i masu. po─ru wa suwari masu.

"てすとを終えてもいいですか？"ぽーるは、5分してから先生に言います。先生がぽーるの机へ来ます。彼は大きな、白い透明なあすぴりんをみつけます。先生は驚いて、とまります。彼は立って、あすぴりんを1分間みつめます。"tesuto wo oe te mo ii desu ka?" po─ru wa, go fun shi te kara sensei ni ii masu. sensei ga po─ru no tsukue e ki masu. kare wa ookina, shiroi toumei na asupirin wo mitsuke masu. sensei wa odoroi te, tomari masu. kare wa ta tte, asupirin wo i ppunkan mitsume masu.

"これは素晴らしい！あなたのあすぴりんはとても良いあすぴりんです。でもわたしにはわかりません！いつもあすぴりんを作るのですが、わたしにはぐれーで匂いのあるものしかできません" 先生が言います。"あなたはてすとを通過しました。" 彼が言います。 "kore wa subarashii! anata no asupirin wa totemo yoi asupirin desu. demo watashi ni wa wakari mase n! itsumo asupirin wo tsukuru no desu ga, watashi ni wa gure─ de nioi no aru mono shika deki mase n" sensei ga ii masu. " anata wa tesuto wo tsuuka shi mashi ta." kare ga ii masu.

ぽーるはてすとの後、外に出ました。先生は

classroom. The students sit and work. Paul sits down.

"May I finish the test?" Paul says to the teacher in five minutes.

The teacher comes to Paul's desk. He sees big white crystals of aspirin. The teacher stops in surprise. He stands and looks at aspirin for a minute.

"It is wonderful! Your aspirin is so nice! But I cannot understand it! I often try to get aspirin and I get only something grey and stinking," the teacher says, "You passed the test," he says.

Paul goes away after the test. The teacher sees something white at Paul's desk. He

ぽーるの 机 の 上に、何か 白いものを 見つけます。彼は 机 へ行き、あすぴりん 錠 の 包みをみつけます。"賢い 男 だ。おっけー、ぽーる。君 には 今 問題 があるよ。" 先生 が 言います。 po―ru wa tesuto no nochi, soto ni de mashi ta. sensei wa po―ru no tsukue no ue ni, nani ka shiroi mono wo mitsuke masu. kare wa tsukue e iki, asupirin jou no tsutsumi wo mitsuke masu. "kashikoi otoko da. okke―, po―ru. kimi ni wa ima mondai ga aru yo." sensei ga ii masu.

comes to the desk and finds the paper from the aspirin pills.

"Smart guy. Ok, Paul. Now you have a problem," the teacher says.

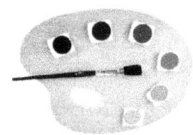

15

Audio

<ruby>ナンシー<rt>なんし</rt></ruby>と<ruby>カンガルー<rt>かんがる</rt></ruby>

Nancy and the kangaroo

A

単語
Words

1. アイスクリーム [aisukurī mu] - ice-cream
2. いじめる、邪魔をする、困らせる [ijimeru, jama wo suru, komaraseru] - bother
3. いつ [itsu] - when
4. おい！やあ！ [oi! yaa!] - Hey!
5. おもちゃ [omocha] - toy
6. カンガルー [kangarū] - kangaroo
7. これは何ですか？ [kore wa nan desu ka?] - What is this?
8. しっぽ [shippo] - tail
9. シマウマ [shimauma] - zebra
10. その [sono] - its *(for neuter)*
11. たたく、あてる [tataku, ateru] - hit, beat
12. なに [nani] - what
13. バケツ [baketsu] - pail
14. ライオン [raion] - lion
15. わあ！ああ！ [waa! aa!] - Oh!

16. わかった、ええと [waka tta, eeto] - okay, well
17. わたしたちに [watashi tachi ni] - us
18. わたしたちにさせる、しよう [watashi tachi ni sa seru, shiyo u] - let us
19. わたしに [watashi ni] - me
20. 一緒に [issho ni] - together
21. 予定、計画 [yotei, keikaku] - plan
22. 人形 [ningyou] - doll
23. 何のテーブルですか？ [nan no te—buru desu ka?] - What table?
24. 勉強する [benkyou suru] - study
25. 動物園 [doubutsu en] - zoo
26. 喜んでいる、幸せ [yorokon de iru, shiawase] - happy
27. 年 [toshi] - year
28. 広く [hiroku] - wide, widely
29. 引っ張る、引く [hipparu, hiku] - pull
30. 強く [tsuyoku] - strong, strongly
31. 本棚 [hondana] - bookcase
32. 水 [mizu] - water
33. 泣く、叫ぶ [naku, sakebu] - cry
34. 満ちている、いっぱいの [michi te iru, ippai no] - full
35. 濡れている [nure te iru] - wet
36. 猿 [saru] - monkey
37. 耳 [mimi] - ear
38. 落ちる [ochiru] - fall
39. 落ちるために [ochiru tame ni] - to fall
40. 虎 [tora] - tiger
41. 計画するために [keikaku suru tame ni] - to plan
42. 貧しい [mazushii] - poor
43. 静かに [shizuka ni] - quietly
44. 髪の毛 [kaminoke] - hair

B

ナンシーとカンガルー
なんし かんがる

nanshi— to kangaru—

ろばーとは 今、学生です。彼は大学で 勉強をしています。彼は英語を 勉強します。ろばーとは 寮に住んでいま

Nancy and the kangaroo

Robert is a student now. He studies at a college. He studies English. Robert lives at the dorms. He lives next

かれ はぽーるの 隣 に住んでいます。ろばーと は 今 、部屋にいます。 彼 は 電 話をとり、 友 達 のでいびっどに 電 話 をします。 robaーto wa ima, gakusei desu. kare wa daigaku de benkyou wo shi te i masu. kare wa eigo wo benkyou shi masu. robaーto wa ryou ni sun de i masu. kare wa poーru no tonari ni sun de i masu. robaーto wa ima, heya ni i masu. kare wa denwa wo tori, tomodachi no deibiddo ni denwa wo shi masu.

"もしもし。"でいびっどが 電 話 をとります。
"やあ、でいびっど。ろばーとだよ。元 気 ?"ろばーとが言います。 "やあ、ろばーと。元 気 だよ。ありがとう。君 は 元 気 ?"でいびっどがこたえます。 "ぼくも 元 気 だよ。ありがとう。ぼくは散 歩 に行くんだ。君 の今 日 の予 定 は?"ろばーとが 言 います。 "moshimoshi." deibiddo ga denwa wo tori masu. "yaa, deibiddo. robaーto da yo. genki?" robaーto ga ii masu. "yaa, robaーto. genki da yo. arigatou. kimi wa genki?" deibiddo ga kotae masu. "boku mo genki da yo. arigatou. boku wa sanpo ni iku n da. kimi no kyou no yotei wa?" robaーto ga ii masu.

" 妹 のなんしーに、彼 女 を動 物 園 につれていくよう 頼 まれたんだ。今 から、そこへ連 れて行くんだ。君 も一 緒 に行こうよ。"でいびっどが言います。 "imouto no nanshiー ni, kanojo wo doubutsu en ni tsure te iku you tanoma re ta n da. ima kara, soko e tsure te iku n da. kimi mo issho ni iko u yo."

door to Paul's. Robert is in his room now. He takes the telephone and calls his friend David.

"Hello," David answers the call.

"Hello David. It is Robert here. How are you?" Robert says.

"Hello Robert. I am fine. Thanks. And how are you?" David answers.

"I am fine too. Thanks. I will go for a walk. What are your plans for today?" Robert says.

"My sister Nancy asks me to take her to the zoo. I will take her there now. Let us go together," David says

deibiddo ga ii masu.

"いいよ。君たちと一緒に行くよ。どこで会う？"ろばーとが聞きます。 "ii yo. kimitachi to issho ni iku yo. doko de au?" roba―to ga kiki masu.

"おりんぴっくのばす停で会おうよ。そしてぽーるにも、ぼくらと一緒にこないか聞いてみてよ。"でいびっどが言います。 "orinpikku no basutei de ao u yo. soshite po―ru ni mo, boku ra to issho ni ko nai ka kii te mi te yo." deibiddo ga ii masu.

"いいよ。じゃあね。"ろばーとがこたえます。

"またね。じゃあ。"でいびっどが言います。 "ii yo. jaa ne." roba―to ga kotae masu. "mata ne. jaa." deibiddo ga ii masu.

その後、ろばーとはぽーるの部屋へ行きます。ぽーるは彼の部屋にいます。 sonogo, roba―to wa po―ru no heya e iki masu. po―ru wa kare no heya ni i masu.

"やあ"ろばーとがいいます。 "やあ、こんにちはろばーと。入っておいで"ぽーるが言います。 "yaa" roba―to ga ii masu. "yaa, konnichiha roba―to. hai tte oide" po―ru ga ii masu.

"でいびっどと彼の妹とぼくで動物園に行くんだ。ぼくたちと一緒に行かない？"ろばーとが質問します。 "もちろん、ぼくも行くよ！"ぽーるが言います。 ろばーととぽーるはおりんぴっくのばす停まで運転します。そこで、で

"Okay. I will go with you. Where will we meet?" Robert asks.

"Let us meet at the bus stop Olympic. And ask Paul to come with us too," David says.

"Okay. Bye," Robert answers.

"See you. Bye," David says.

Then Robert goes to Paul's room. Paul is in his room.

"Hello," Robert says.

"Oh, hello Robert. Come in, please," Paul says. Robert comes in.

"David, his sister and I will go to the zoo. Will you go together with us?" Robert asks.

"Of course, I will go too!" Paul says.

いびっどと 彼の 妹 を見つけます。"deibiddo to kare no imouto to boku de doubutsu en ni iku n da. boku tachi to issho ni ika nai?" roba―to ga shitsumon shi masu. "mochiron, boku mo iku yo!" po―ru ga ii masu. roba―to to po―ru wa orinpikku no basutei made unten shi masu. sokode, deibiddo to kare no imouto wo mitsuke masu.

でいびっどの 妹 はまだ5歳です。彼女は小さな 女 の子で、えねるぎーに満ちています。彼女は動物が大好きです。でもなんしーは動物をおもちゃだと思っています。動物は彼女から逃げ出します。なぜなら、彼女は動物達をたくさんいじめるからです。彼女はしっぽや鼻を引っ張ったり、手やおもちゃで、たたいたりします。なんしーは犬と猫を家で飼っています。なんしーが家にいるときは、犬はべっどの下にいて、猫は本棚に座ります。そうすれば、彼女が触れないからです。なんしー、でいびっど、ろばーと、ぽーるは動物園に来ました。deibiddo no imouto wa mada go sai desu. kanojo wa chiisana onnanoko de, enerugi― ni michi te i masu. kanojo wa doubutsu ga daisuki desu. demo nanshi― ha doubutsu wo omocha da to omo tte i masu. doubutsu ha kanojo kara nigedashi masu. nazenara, kanojo wa doubutsu tachi wo takusan ijimeru kara desu. kanojo wa shippo ya hana wo hippa ttari, te ya omocha de, tatai tari shi masu. nanshi― wa inu to neko wo ie de ka tte i masu. nanshi― ga ie ni iru toki ha, inu wa beddo

Robert and Paul drive to the bus stop Olympic. They see David and his sister Nancy there.

David's sister is only five years old. She is a little girl and she is full of energy. She likes animals very much. But Nancy thinks that animals are toys. The animals run away from her because she bothers them very much. She can pull tail or ear, hit with a hand or with a toy. Nancy has a dog and a cat at home. When Nancy is at home the dog is under a bed and the cat sits on the bookcase. So she cannot get them.

Nancy, David, Robert and Paul come into the zoo.

no shita ni i te, neko ha hondana ni suwari masu. sou sure ba, kanojo ga fure nai kara desu. nanshī, deibiddo, robāto, pōru ha doubutsu en ni ki mashi ta.

動物園にはたくさんの動物達がいます。なんしーはとても喜んでいます。彼女はらいおんと虎へ向かって走って行きます。彼女は、自分の人形でしまうまをたたきます。彼女が猿のしっぽをとても強く引っ張るので、猿は皆泣きながら逃げて行きます。そして、なんしーはかんがるーを見つけます。かんがるーはばけつから水を飲みます。なんしーは微笑み、かんがるーのほうへとても静かにやってきます。そして…

There are many animals in the zoo. Nancy is very happy. She runs to the lion and to the tiger. She hits the zebra with her doll. She pulls the tail of a monkey so strong that all the monkeys run away crying. Then Nancy sees a kangaroo. The kangaroo drinks water from a pail. Nancy smiles and comes to the kangaroo very quietly. And then…

doubutsu en ni wa takusan no doubutsu tachi ga i masu. nanshī wa totemo yorokon de i masu. kanojo wa raion to tora e muka tte hashi tte iki masu. kanojo wa, jibun no ningyou de shimauma wo tataki masu. kanojo ga saru no shippo wo totemo tsuyoku hipparu node, saru wa mina naki nagara nige te iki masu. soshite, nanshī wa kangarū wo mitsuke masu. kangarū wa baketsu kara mizu wo nomi masu. nanshī wa hohoemi, kangarū no hou e totemo sizukani yatteki masu. soshite …

"やあ！！かんがるーーー！！"なんしーは叫んで、しっぽを引っ張ります。かんがるーはなんしーを、大きな目で見ます。驚いてじゃんぷをしたので、水の入ったばけつが飛び上がり、なんしーに落ちます。水は、彼女の髪、顔、そして

"Hey!! Kangaroo-oo-oo!!" Nancy cries and pulls its tail. The kangaroo looks at Nancy with wide open eyes. It jumps in surprise so that the pail with water flies up and falls

106

服を流れ落ちます。なんしーはびしょ濡れです。"とても悪いかんがるーね！ひどい！"彼女は泣きます "yaa!! kangaru—–!!" nanshi— wa saken de, shippo wo hippari masu. kangaru— wa nanshi— wo, ookina me de mi masu. odoroi te janpu wo shi ta node, mizu no hai tta baketsu ga tobiagari, nanshi— ni ochi masu. mizu wa, kanojo no kami, kao, soshite fuku wo nagareochi masu. nanshi— wa bishonure desu. "totemo warui kangaru— ne! hidoi!" kanojo wa naki masu.

何人かの人たちは微笑み、他の人たちは言います："かわいそうな女の子だね。"でいびっとはなんしーをつれて家へ帰ります。 nan nin ka no hito tachi wa hohoemi, hoka no hito tachi wa ii masu : "kawaisou na onnanoko da ne." deibitto ha nanshi— wo tsure te ie e kaeri masu.

"動物をいじめちゃだめだよ。"でいびっどは言い、それからあいすくりーむを彼女にあげます。なんしーはあいすくりーむを食べます。"わかったよ。とても大きくて、怒っている動物とは遊ばない"なんしーは考えます。"わたしは小さい動物とだけ遊ぶのよ"彼女はまた嬉しそうです。 "doubutsu wo ijime cha dame da yo." deibiddo wa ii, sorekara aisukuri—mu wo kanojo ni age masu. nanshi— wa aisukuri—mu wo tabe masu. "waka tta yo. totemo ookiku te, oko tte iru doubutsu to wa asoba nai" nanshi— wa kangae masu. "watashi wa chiisai doubutsu to dake asobu no yo" kanojo wa mata ureshi sou desu.

on Nancy. Water runs down her hair, her face and her dress. Nancy is all wet.

"You are a bad kangaroo! Bad!" she cries.

Some people smile and some people say: "Poor girl." David takes Nancy home.

"You must not bother the animals," David says and gives an ice-cream to her. Nancy eats the ice-cream.

"Okay. I will not play with very big and angry animals," Nancy thinks, "I will play with little animals only." She is happy again.

16

Audio

<ruby>パ<rt>ぱ</rt></ruby><ruby>ラ<rt>ら</rt></ruby><ruby>シュ<rt>しゅ</rt></ruby><ruby>ー<rt></rt></ruby><ruby>ト<rt>と</rt></ruby>

Parachutists

 A

単語

Words

1. あとで、あとに [atode, ato ni] - after
2. エアーショー [eaー shoー] - airshow
3. クラブ [kurabu] - club
4. ゴム [gomu] - rubber
5. ズボン（複数）[zubon（fukusuu）] - trousers
6. する、やる、行う [suru, yaru, okonau] - do
7. だけ [dake] - just
8. チーム [chiーmu] - team

9. ところで [tokorode] - by the way
10. トリック、技 [torikku, waza] - trick
11. なる [naru] - be
12. パパ、お父さん [papa, otousan] - daddy
13. パラシュート [parashuーto] - parachute
14. パラシュートをする人 [parashuーto wo suru hito] - parachutist
15. メンバー [menbaー] - member
16. もし [moshi] - if
17. 9 [kyuu] - nine
18. 一部 [ichibu] - part
19. 上の、以上の、こえた [ue no, ijou no, koe ta] - over
20. 上着 [uwagi] - jacket
21. 中に、中へ [naka ni, naka e] - inside
22. 人命救助のトリック [jinmei kyuujo no torikku] - life-saving trick
23. 他の、別の [ta no, betsu no] - other
24. 信じる；の目を信じない [shinjiru ; no me wo shinji nai] - believe; to not believe one's eyes
25. 命 [inochi] - life
26. 屋根 [yane] - roof
27. 座る；席に座る [suwaru ; seki ni suwaru] - seat; take a seat
28. 怒って [oko tte] - angrily
29. 押す [osu] - push
30. 捕まえる、掴む、引っかかる [tsukamaeru, tsukamu, hikkakaru] - catch
31. 操縦席、パイロット [soujuu seki, pairotto] - pilot
32. 救う、助ける [sukuu, tasukeru] - save
33. 服 [fuku] - clothes
34. 服を着ている [fuku wo ki te iru] - dressed
35. 本当の、実際の [hontou no, jissai no] - real
36. 用意する、準備する [youi suru, junbi suru] - prepare
37. 人形（パラシュートをする人） [ningyou(parashuーto wo suru hito)] - stuffed parachutist
38. 着る、身に着ける [kiru, mi ni tsukeru] - put on
39. 空中、空気、エアー [kuuchuu, kuuki, eaー] - air
40. 素晴らしい、偉大な [subarashii, idai na] - great
41. 自身の [jishin no] - own
42. 落ちた [ochi ta] - fallen
43. 落ちる [ochiru] - falling
44. 観客 [kankyaku] - audience
45. 訓練する、鍛える；訓練されている、鍛えられている [kunren suru, kitaeru ; kunren sa re te iru, kitae rare te iru] - train; trained
46. 赤い [akai] - red
47. 金属 [kinzoku] - metal

48. 閉じる、閉める、近い [tojiru, shimeru, chikai] - close
49. 降りる [oriru] - get off
50. 陸上、着陸する [rikujou, chakuriku suru] - land
51. 静かに、黙って [shizuka ni, damatte] - silent, silently
52. 飛行機 [hikouki] - airplane
53. 黄色い [kiiroi] - yellow

B

ぱらしゅーと
パラシュート

parashu―to wo suru hito

朝のことです。ろばーとはぽーるの部屋へ行きます。ぽーるは机に座り、何かを書いています。ぽーるの猫、ふぇいばりっとはぽーるのべっどの上にいます。静かに眠っています。 asa no koto desu. roba―to wa po―ru no heya e iki masu. po―ru wa tsukue ni suwari, nani ka wo kai te i masu. po―ru no neko, feibaritto wa po―ru no beddo no ue ni i masu. shizuka ni nemu tte i masu.

"入(はい)っていいかい?" ろばーとが聞(き)きます。"元気だよ。ありがとう。座って。" ぽーるはこたえます。ろばーとはいすに座ります。 "hai tte i ikai?" roba―to ga kiki masu. "yaa, roba―to. hai tte oide. genki?" po―ru ga kotae masu. "genki da yo. arigatou. kimi wa genki?" po―ru ga ii masu. "genki da yo. arigatou. suwa tte." po―ru wa kotae masu. roba―to wa isu ni suwari masu.

"ぼくがぱらしゅーとくらぶのめんばーなのは知

Parachutists

It is morning. Robert comes to Paul's room. Paul is sitting at the table and writing something. Paul's cat Favorite is on Paul's bed. It is sleeping quietly.

"May I come in?" Robert asks.

"Oh, Robert. Come in please. How are you?" Paul answers.

"Fine. Thanks. How are you?" Robert says.

"I am fine. Thanks. Sit down, please," Paul answers.

Robert sits on a chair.

"You know I am a member of a parachute club. We are having

っているよね。今日、えあーしょーをやるんだ。"ろばーとが言います。"ぼくもしょーで、じゃんぷするんだ" "boku ga parashu—to kurabu no menba— na no wa shi tte iru yo ne. kyou, ea—sho— wo yaru n da." roba—to ga ii masu." boku mo sho— de, janpu suru n da"

"とても面白そうだね。"ぽーるがこたえます。"ぼくもえあーしょーみにいくかも。" "もし君がよければ、ぼくが君をそこまで連れていくよ、そして君も飛行機にのれるよ。"ろばーとが言います。 "totemo omoshiro sou da ne." po—ru ga kotae masu. "boku mo ea— sho— mi ni iku kamo." "moshi kimi ga yokere ba, boku ga kimi wo soko made tsure te iku yo, soshite kimi mo hikouki ni noreru yo." roba—to ga ii masu.

"本当に？それは素晴らしい！"ぽーるが叫びます。"えあーしょーは何時からかな？" "hontouni? sore wa subarashii!" po—ru ga sakebi masu. "ea— sho— wa nan ji kara ka na?"

"しょーは午前10時に始まるよ。"ろばーとがこたえます。"でいびっどもくるよ。ところで、ぼくたち、飛行機から人形（ぱらしゅーとする人）を押す助けが必要なんだ。手伝ってくれる？" "sho— ha gozen juu ji ni hajimaru yo." roba—to ga kotae masu. "deibiddo mo kuru yo. tokorode, boku tachi, hikouki kara ningyou (parashu—to suru hito) wo osu tasuke ga hitsuyou na n da. tetsuda tte kureru?"

an airshow today," Robert says, "I am going to make some jumps there."

"It is very interesting," Paul answers, "I may come to see the airshow."

"If you want I can take you there and you can fly in an airplane," Robert says.

"Really? That will be great!" Paul cries, "What time is the airshow?"

"It begins at ten o'clock in the morning," Robert answers, "David will come too. By the way we need help to push a stuffed parachutist out of the airplane. Will you help?"

"人形？どうして？"ぽーるは驚いてたずねます。"ほら、しょーの一部だよ。"ろばーとは言います。"これは人命救助のとりっくなんだ。人形が落ちる。ここで、本物のぱらしゅーと士が飛んできて彼を掴み、彼自身のぱらしゅーとを開く。"人"が救助されるんだ！"
"ningyou? doushite?" poーru wa odoroi te tazune masu. "hora, shoー no ichibu da yo." robaーto wa iimasu. "kore wa jinmei kyuujo no torikku na n da. ningyouga ochiru. koko de, honmono no parashuーto shi ga ton de ki te kare wo tsukami, kare jishin no parashuーto wo hiraku. "hito" ga kyuujo sa reru n da!"

"すごいね！"ぽーるはこたえます。"手伝うよ。さあ、行こう！"ぽーるとろばーとは外へ出ます。彼らはおりんぴっくのばす停へ行きばすに乗ります。えあーしょーへ行くには、たった５分でつきます。彼らがばすを降りるときにでいびっどがみえます。"sugoi ne!" poーru wa kotae masu. "tetsudau yo. saa, ikou!" poーru to robaーto wa soto e de masu. karera wa orinpikku no basutei e iki basu ni nori masu. eaー shoー e iku ni wa, tatta go fun de tsuki masu. karera ga basu wo oriru toki ni deibiddo ga mie masu.

"こんにちは、でいびっど。"ろばーとが言います"飛行機へ行こう" "konnichiwa,

"A stuffed parachutist? Why?" Paul says in surprise.

"You see, it is a part of the show," Robert says, "This is a life-saving trick. The stuffed parachutist falls down. At this time a real parachutist flies to it, catches it and opens his own parachute. The "man" is saved!"

"Great!" Paul answers, "I will help. Let's go!"

Paul and Robert go outside. They come to the bus stop Olympic and take a bus. It takes only ten minutes to go to the airshow. When they get off the bus, they see David.

"Hello David," Robert says, "Let's go to the airplane."

deibiddo." roba―to ga ii masu   "hikouki e iko u"
　　彼らは、飛行機でぱらしゅーとのちーむをみ
つけます。彼らはちーむのりーだーのところへ
行きます。ちーむのりーだーは赤いずぼんと
赤い上着を着ています。karera wa, hikouki de
parashu―to no chi―mu wo mitsuke masu. karera
wa chi―mu no ri―da― no tokoro e iki masu. chi―
mu no ri―da― wa akai zubon to akai uwagi wo ki te
i masu.

　　"こんにちは、まーてぃん。"ろばーとは言い
ます。"ぽーるとでいびっどが人命
救助のとりっくの手伝いをしてくれる
よ。"konnichiwa, ma―tin." roba―to wa ii masu. "po
―ru to deibiddo ga jinmei kyuujo no torikku no
tetsudai wo shi te kureru yo."

　　"わかった。人形はここだよ。"まーて
ぃんが言います。彼は、ninngyouを彼らに
渡します。着ぐるみでぱらしゅーとをする
人は赤いずぼんと赤い上着を着ていま
す。"waka tta. wa koko da yo."   ma―tin ga ii
masu. kare wa, ningyou wo karera ni watashi masu.
ningyou wa akai zubon to akai uwagi wo ki te i masu.

　　"君みたいな服装だね"でいびっどがまー
てぃんに笑いながら言います。"それについて
は話している時間はないんだ"まーてぃんが言
います。"飛行機の中にそれを持って行っ

They see a parachute team at the airplane. They come to the head of the team. The head of the team is dressed in red trousers and a red jacket.

"Hello Martin," Robert says, "Paul and David will help with the life-saving trick."

"Okay. The stuffed parachutist is here," Martin says. He gives them the stuffed parachutist. The stuffed parachutist is dressed in red trousers and a red jacket.

"It is dressed like you," David says smiling to Martin.

"We have no time to talk about it," Martin says, "Take it into this

113

て。" "kimi mitai na fukusou da ne" deibiddo ga ma―tin ni warai nagara ii masu. "sore nitsuite hanashite iru jikan ha nai n da" ma―tin ga ii masu. "hikouki no naka ni sore wo motte i tte."

ぽーるとでいびっどは、人形を飛行機の中に持って行きます。彼らはぱいろっとの席に座ります。ぱらしゅーとちーむのへっど以外の全員は飛行機へ乗り込みます。彼らはどあを閉じます。5分すると、飛行機は空中にいます。さんふらんしすこの上を飛ぶとき、でいびっどは自分の家をみつけます。po―ru to deibiddo wa, ningyou wo hikouki no naka ni motte iki masu. karera wa pairotto no seki ni suwari masu. parashu―to chi―mu no heddo igai no zen'in wa hikouki e norikomi masu. karera wa doa wo toji masu. go fun suru to, hikouki wa kuuchuu ni i masu. sanfuranshisuko no ue wo tobu toki, deibiddo wa jibun no ie wo mitsuke masu.

"みて！あれ、ぼくの家！" でいびっどが叫びます。ぽーるは、通り、広場そして街の公園を窓越しにのぞきます。飛行機で飛ぶのは素晴らしい！ "じゃんぷする準備をして！" ぱいろっとが叫びます。ぱらしゅーとする人達は立ち上がります。彼らはどあを開けます。"10、9、8、7、6、5、4、3、2、1。行くんだ！" ぱいろっとが叫びます。

airplane."

Paul and David take the stuffed parachutist into the airplane. They take seats at the pilot. All the parachute team but its head gets into the airplane. They close the door. In five minutes the airplane is in the air. When it flies over San Francisco David sees his own house.

"Look! My house is there!" David cries.

Paul looks through the window at streets, squares, and parks of the city. It is wonderful to fly in an airplane.

"Prepare to jump!" the pilot cries. The parachutists stand up. They open the door.

"mi te! are, boku no ie!" deibiddo ga sakebi masu. po―ru wa, toori, hiroba soshite machi no kouen wo mado goshi ni nozoki masu. hikouki de tobu no wa subarashii! "janpu suru junbi wo shi te!" pairotto ga sakebi masu. parashu―to suru hitotachi wa tachiagari masu. karera wa doa wo ake masu. "juu, kyuu, hachi, nana, roku, go, yon, san, ni, ichi. iku n da!" pairotto ga sakebi masu.

ぱらしゅーとをする人達は飛行機から飛び降り始めます。陸上の観客は、赤、緑、白、青、黄色のぱらしゅーとを見つけます。とても綺麗です。まーてぃん、ぱらしゅーとちーむのりーだーも見上げています。ぱらしゅーとをしょった人達は降下をしていて、何人かはすでに着陸しています。parashu―to wo suru hitotachi wa hikouki kara tobiori hajime masu. rikujou no kankyaku wa, aka, midori, shiro, ao, oushoku no parashu―to wo mitsuke masu. totemo kirei desu. ma―tin, parashu―to chi―mu no ri―da― mo miage te i masu. parashu―to wo sho tta hitotachi wa kouka wo shi te i te, nan nin ka wa sudeni chakuriku shi te i masu.

"おっけー。よくやったね。"まーてぃんは言い、近くのかふぇへこーひーをのみにいきます。えあーしょーは続きます。"人命救助のとりっくの準備をして!"ぱいろっとが叫びます。でいびっどとぽーるは、人形をどあまで持って行きます。"10、

"Ten, nine, eight, seven, six, five, four, three, two, one. Go!" the pilot cries.

The parachutists begin to jump out of the airplane. The audience down on the land sees red, green, white, blue, yellow parachutes.

It looks very nice. Martin, the head of the parachute team is looking up too. The parachutists are flying down and some are landing already.

"Okay. Good work guys," Martin says and goes to the nearby café to drink some coffee.

The airshow goes on.

"Prepare for the life-saving trick!" the pilot cries.

David and Paul take the stuffed

9、8、7、6、5、4、3、2、1。行くんだ！" ぱいろっとが叫びます。"okkeー. yoku yatta ne." maーtin wa ii, chikaku no kafe e koーhiー wo nomi ni iki masu. eaー shoー wa tsuzuki masu. "jinmei kyuujo no torikku no junbi wo shi te!" pairotto ga sakebi masu. deibiddo to poーru wa, ningyou wo doa made motte iki masu. "juu, kyuu, hachi, nana, roku, go, yon, san, ni, ichi. iku n da!" pairotto ga sakebi masu.

ぽーるとでいびっどは、人形をどあから押します。出て行ったのですが、止まっています。飛行機の金属部品に、ごむの"手"が引っかかっています。poーru to deibiddo wa, ningyouwo doa kara oshi masu. de te i tta no desu ga, toma tte i masu. hikouki no kinzoku buhin ni, gomu no "te" ga hikkaka tte i masu.

"行って、行って！"ぱいろっとが叫びます。男の子達は、着ぐるみでぱらしゅーとをする人をとても強く押しますが、離すことができません。"itte, itte!" pairotto ga sakebi masu. otokonoko tachi wa, ningyou wo totemo tsuyoku oshi masu ga, hanasu koto ga deki mase n.

陸上の観客は赤い服を着た人が飛行機のどあにいるのを見つけます。別の2人の男性が、その男を押しだそうとしています。彼らは自分たちが見ているもの

parachutist to the door.

"Ten, nine, eight, seven, six, four, three, two, one. Go!" the pilot cries.

Paul and David push the stuffed parachutist through the door. It goes out but then stops. Its rubber "hand" catches on some metal part of the airplane.

"Go-go boys!" the pilot cries.

The boys push the stuffed parachutist very strongly but cannot get it out.

The audience down on the land sees a man dressed in red in the airplane door. Two other men are trying to push him out. People cannot believe their eyes. It goes on about a minute. Then

を信じることができません。それは1分ほど続きます。そして、赤い服を着た人が落ちてきます。ぱらしゅーとをしょった別の人が飛んできて、彼を掴もうとします。しかし彼は掴むことができません。赤い服の人は落ちて行きます。かふぇの中の屋根を抜けて落ちます。観客は静かにみつめます。そして人々はかふぇの外を赤い服の男が走っているのをみつけます。この赤い男はまーてぃん、ぱらしゅーとちーむの部長です。しかし、観客は、彼は落ちてきたぱらしゅーとの人だと考えています。彼は見上げて、怒ったように叫びます。"もし、人を掴むことができないのなら、試さないでよ！" rikujou no kankyaku wa akai fuku wo ki ta hito ga hikouki no doa ni iru no wo mitsuke masu. betsu no futari no dansei ga, sono otoko wo oshidaso u to shi te i masu. karera wa jibun tachi ga mi te iru mono wo shinjiru koto ga deki mase n. sore wa i ppun hodo tsuzuki masu. soshite, akai fuku wo kita hito ga ochi te ki masu. parashu―to wo sho tta betsu no hito ga ton de ki te, kare wo tsukamo u to shi masu. shikashi kare wa tsukamu koto ga deki mase n. akai fuku no hito wa ochi te iki masu. kafe no naka no yane wo nuke te ochi masu. kankyaku wa shizuka ni mitsume masu. soshite hitobito wa kafe no soto wo akai fuku no otoko ga hashi tte iru no wo mitsuke masu. kono akai fuku no

the parachutist in red falls down. Another parachutist jumps out of the airplane and tries to catch it. But he cannot do it. The parachutist in red falls down. It falls through the roof inside of the café. The audience looks silently. Then the people see a man dressed in red run outside of the café. This man in red is Martin, the head of the parachutist team. But the audience thinks that he is that falling parachutist. He looks up and cries angrily, "If you cannot catch a man then do not try it!"

otoko wa ma―tin, parashu―to chi―mu no buchou desu. shikashi, kankyaku wa, kare wa ochi te ki ta parashu―to no hito da to kangae te i masu. kare wa miage te, oko tta you ni sakebi masu. "moshi, hito wo tsukamu koto ga deki nai no nara, tamesa nai de yo!"

観客は黙っています。"ぱぱ、この人はとても強いんだよ"小さな女の子がお父さんに言います。"彼はとても鍛えられているね"お父さんはこたえます。えあーしょーのあと、ぽーるとでいびっどはろばーとのところへ行きます。"ぼくたちの仕事、どうだった？"でいびっどがききます。"ええと...ああ、とてもよかったよ。ありがとう。"ろばーとがこたえます。"もし助けが必要だったら、言ってね！"ぽーるが言います。kankyaku wa dama tte i masu. "papa, kono hito wa totemo tsuyoi n da yo" chiisana onnanoko ga otousan ni ii masu. "kare wa totemo kitae rare te iru ne" otousan wa kotae masu. ea― sho― no ato, po―ru to deibiddo wa roba―to no tokoro e iki masu. "boku tachi no shigoto, dou da tta?" deibiddo ga kiki masu. "eeto... aa, totemo yoka tta yo. arigatou." roba―to ga kotae masu. "moshi tasuke ga hitsuyou da ttara, i tte ne!" po―ru ga ii masu.

The audience is silent.

*"Daddy, this man is very strong,"
a little girl says to her dad.*

*"He is well trained," the dad
answers.*

*After the airshow Paul and David
go to Robert.*

"How is our work?" David asks.

*"Ah... Oh, it is very good. Thank
you," Robert answers.*

*"If you need some help just say,"
Paul says.*

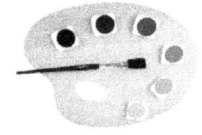

17

Audio

<ruby>ガス<rt>がす</rt></ruby>を<ruby>消<rt>け</rt></ruby>して！

Turn the gas off!

A

単語

Words

1. （これから）する [（korekara） suru] - will
2. １１ [juu ichi] - eleven
3. ２０ [ni juu] - twenty
4. ４４ [yon juu yon] - forty-four
5. おかしな、変な [okashina, hen na] - strange
6. ガス [gasu] - gas
7. キロメートル(km) [kirome—toru (km)] - kilometer
8. サンドイッチ [sandoicchi] - sandwich
9. ずるい、いたずらに [zurui, itazurani] - sly, slyly

10. だから、では [dakara, dewa] - so
11. チケット、券 [chiketto, ken] - ticket
12. つける [tsukeru] - turn on
13. やかん [yakan] - kettle
14. 一方で、その間に [ippou de, sonokan ni] - meanwhile
15. 一瞬、その時、その瞬間 [isshun, sono toki, sono shunkan] - moment
16. 今すぐに [ima suguni] - immediately
17. 住んでいる [sun de iru] - living
18. 全て、全部 [subete, zenbu] - everything
19. 受話器 [juwaki] - phone handset
20. 命令する、言いつける [meirei suru, ii tsukeru] - order
21. 固まる、凍える、凍る [katamaru, kogoeru, kooru] - freeze
22. 声 [koe] - voice
23. 幼稚園 [youchien] - kindergarten
24. 広める、広げる [hiromeru, hirogeru] - spread
25. 忘れる [wasureru] - forget
26. 暖かい [atatakai] - warm
27. 暖める [atatameru] - warm up
28. 曲がる、曲げる、向ける、向く [magaru, mageru, mukeru, muku] - turn
29. 気をつける、注意深い [ki wo tsukeru, chuuibukai] - careful
30. 気持ち、感じる、思う [kimochi, kanjiru, omou] - feeling
31. 消す [kesu] - turn off
32. 満たす、いっぱいにする [mitasu, ippai ni suru] - fill up
33. 火 [hi] - fire
34. 猫 [neko] - pussycat
35. 秘書 [hisho] - secretary
36. 突然 [totsuzen] - suddenly
37. 素早く、速く、急いで [subayaku, hayaku, isoi de] - quick, quickly
38. 蛇口 [jaguchi] - tap
39. 言う、伝える [iu, tsutaeru] - tell, say
40. 誰 [dare] - who
41. 電話をする、鳴らす；電話をするために [denwa wo suru, narasu ; denwa wo suru tame ni] - ring; to ring
42. 電車 [densha] - train
43. 電車の駅 [densha no eki] - railway station
44. 青白い [aojiroi] - pale

B

ガスを消して！
gasu wo keshi te!!

朝7時です。でいびっどとなんしーは眠っています。彼らの母はきっちんにいます。母の名前はりんだです。りんだは４４歳です。彼女は注意深い女性です。りんだは仕事に行く前にきっちんを掃除します。彼女は秘書です。彼女はさんふらんしすこから２０きろめーとる離れたところで働いています。りんだはいつも電車で仕事に行きます。 asa nana ji desu. deibiddo to nanshi― wa nemutte i masu. karera no haha wa kicchin ni i masu. haha no namae wa rinda desu. rinda wa yon juu yon sai desu. kanojo wa chuuibukai josei desu. rinda wa shigoto ni iku mae ni kicchin wo souji shi masu. kanojo wa hisho desu. kanojo wa sanfuranshisuko kara niju kkiro me―toru hanare ta tokoro de hatarai te i masu. rinda wa itsumo densha de shigoto ni iki masu.

彼女は外に出ます。電車の駅は近くなので、りんだはそこへ歩いて行きます。彼。りんだは電車に座り、窓の外をみつめます。 kanojo wa soto ni de masu. densha no eki wa chikaku na node, rinda wa soko e arui te iki masu. kanojo wa chiketto wo ka tte, densha ni nori masu. shigoto e iku no ni ni ju ppun hodo kakari masu. rinda

Turn the gas off!

It is seven o'clock in the morning. David and Nancy are sleeping. Their mother is in the kitchen. The mother's name is Linda. Linda is forty-four years old. She is a careful woman. Linda cleans the kitchen before she goes to work. She is a secretary. She works twenty kilometers away from San Francisco. Linda usually goes to work by train.

She goes outside. The railway station is nearby, so Linda goes there on foot. She buys a ticket and gets on a train. It takes about twenty minutes to go to work. Linda sits in the train and looks out of the window.

wa densha ni suwari, mado no soto wo mitsume masu.
女はちけっとを買って、電車に乗ります。仕事へ行くのに２０分ほどかかります。突然彼女は凍り付きます。やかん！こんろにおいたままで、彼女はがすを消し忘れたのです！でいびっどとなんしーは眠っている。火は家具へ広がって、そして...りんだは青白くなります。しかし、彼女は頭の良い女性で、１分でどうすべきかわかります。彼女は近くに座る女性と男性に、彼女の家へ電話をしてでいびっとにやかんのことを伝えるよう頼みます。totsuzen kanojo wa kooritsuki masu. yakan! konro ni oi ta mama de, kanojo wa gasu wo keshi wasure ta no desu! deibiddo to nanshī wa nemu tte iru. hi wa kagu e hiroga tte, soshite... rinda wa aojiroku nari masu. shikashi, kanojo wa atama no yoi josei de, i ppun de dou su beki ka wakari masu. kanojo wa chikaku ni suwaru josei to dansei ni, kanojo no ie e denwa wo shi te deibitto ni yakan no koto wo tsutaeru you tanomi masu.

一方、でいびっどは起き上がり、（顔を）洗い、きっちんへ行きます。彼はでーぶるからやかんを取り、水で満たし、こんろに置きます。そして彼はぱんとばたーを取りさんどいっちを作ります。なんしーがきっちんへ入ってきま

Suddenly she freezes. The kettle! It is standing on the cooker and she forgot to turn the gas off! David and Nancy are sleeping. The fire can spread on the furniture and then... Linda turns pale. But she is a smart woman and in a minute she knows what to do. She asks a woman and a man, who sit nearby, to telephone her home and tell David about the kettle.

Meanwhile David gets up, washes and goes to the kitchen. He takes the kettle off the table, fills it up with water and puts it on the cooker. Then he takes bread and butter and makes sandwiches. Nancy

す。ippou, deibiddo wa okiagari, (kao wo) arai, kicchin e iki masu. kare wa de―buru kara yakan wo tori, mizu de mitashi, konro ni oki masu. soshite kare wa pan to bata― wo tori sandoicchi wo tsukuri masu. nanshi― ga kicchin e hai tte ki masu.

comes into the kitchen.

"わたしの猫はどこ？" 彼女はききます。
"知らないよ。" でいびっどがこたえます。"お手洗いに行って、顔を洗っておいで。今からお茶をのんで、さんどいっちをたべるよ。それからぼくが幼稚園に連れて行くよ。" なんしーは洗いたくありません。"わたし、蛇口を開けられないの。" 彼女は意地悪そうに言います。"ぼくが手伝うよ" 彼女の兄が言います。その時、電話が鳴ります。なんしーは素早く電話へ走り、受話器を取ります。
"watashi no neko wa doko?" kanojo wa kiki masu. "shira nai yo." deibiddo ga kotae masu. "o tearai ni i tte, kao wo ara tte oide. ima kara ocha wo non de, sandoicchi wo taberu yo. sorekara boku ga youchien ni tsure te iku yo." nanshi― wa arai taku ari mase n. "watashi, jaguchi wo ake rare nai no." kanojo wa ijiwaru sou ni ii masu. "boku ga tetsudau yo" kanojo no ani ga ii masu.

sono toki, denwa ga nari masu. nanshi― wa subayaku denwa e hashiri, juwaki wo tori masu.

"Where is my little pussycat?" she asks.

"I do not know," David answers, "Go to the bathroom and wash your face. We will drink some tea and eat some sandwiches now. Then I will take you to the kindergarten."

Nancy does not want to wash. "I cannot turn on the water tap," she says slyly.

"I will help you," her brother says. At this moment the telephone rings. Nancy runs quickly to the telephone and takes the handset.

"もしもし、こちら動物園です。誰ですか？" 彼女はいいます。でいびっどは受話器を彼女から取って、言います。"もしもし、で

"Hello, this is the zoo. And who are you?" she says. David takes the handset from her and says,

びっどです。" "くいーん通り１１番地に住んでいるでいびっど・ついーたーさんですか？" 知らない女性の声がたずねます。"はい。" でいびっどはこたえます。 "moshimoshi, kochira doubutsu en desu. dare desu ka?" kanojo wa ii masu. deibiddo wa juwaki wo kanojo kara to tte, ii masu. "moshimoshi, debiddo desu." "kui―n doori juu ichi banchi ni sun de iru deibiddo.tsui―ta― san desu ka?" shira nai josei no koe ga tazune masu. "hai." deibiddo wa kotae masu.

"今すぐきっちんへ行って、がすを消してください！" 女性の声が叫びます。"あなたはどなたですか？なぜぼくががすを消さなければならないのですか？" でいびっどが驚いて言います。 "今すぐ消してください！" その声がいいつけます。 "ima sugu kicchin e i tte, gasu wo keshi te kudasai!" josei no koe ga sakebi masu. "anata wa donata desu ka? naze boku ga gasu wo kesa nakere ba nara nai no desu ka?" deibiddo ga odoroi te ii masu. "ima sugu keshi te kudasai!" sono koe ga iitsuke masu.

でいびっどはがすを消します。なんしーとでいびっどは驚いてやかんを見ます。"わからないよ。" でいびっどが言います。"どうして、この女性はぼくたちがお茶を飲もうとしていたのを知ることができたんだ？" "わたし、お腹すいた。" 彼の妹は言います。"わたしたち、いつたべるの？" "ぼくもお腹すいたよ。"

"Hello. This is David."

"Are you David Tweeter living at eleven Queen street?" the voice of a strange woman asks.

"Yes," David answers.

"Go to the kitchen immediately and turn the gas off!" the woman's voice cries.

"Who are you? Why must I turn the gas off?" David says in surprise.

"Do it now!" the voice orders.

David turns the gas off. Nancy and David look at the kettle in surprise.

"I do not understand," David says, "How can this woman know that we will drink tea?"

"I am hungry," his sister says,

でいびっどはそう言い、がすを再びつけます。このとき また電話が鳴ります。deibiddo wa gasu wo keshi masu. nanshー to deibiddo wa odoroi te yakan wo mi masu. "wakara nai yo." deibiddo ga ii masu. "doushite, kono josei wa boku tachi ga ocha wo nomo u to shi te i ta no wo shiru koto ga deki ta n da?" "watashi, onaka sui ta." kare no imouto wa ii masu. "watashi tachi, itsu taberu no? "boku mo onaka sui ta yo." deibiddo wa sou ii, gasu wo futatabi tsuke masu. kono toki mata denwa ga nari masu.

"もしもし。"でいびっどが言います。"くいーん通り１１番地に住んでいるでいびっど・ついーたーさんですか？"知らない男性の声がたずねます。"はい。"でいびっどがこたえます。"moshimoshi." deibiddo ga ii masu. "kuiーn doori juu ichi banchi ni sun de iru deibiddo.tsuiーtaー san desu ka?" shira nai dansei no koe ga tazune masu. "hai." deibiddo ga kotae masu.

"今すぐきっちんへ行って、こんろのがすを消してください！気をつけて！"その声は命令します。"わかりました。"でいびっどはそう言い、再びがすを消します。"さあ、幼稚園へ行こう。"でいびっどは、今日はお茶は飲まないなと感じながら、なんしーに言います。"やだ。お茶とばたーのぱんが欲しいの。"なんしーは怒って言います。"ima sugu kicchin e i tte, konro no gasu wo keshi te kudasai! ki wo tsuke te!" sono koe wa meirei shi masu. "wakari mashi ta." deibiddo wa sou ii, futatabi gasu wo keshi

"When will we eat?"

"I am hungry too," David says and turns the gas on again. At this minute the telephone rings again.

"Hello," David says.

"Are you David Tweeter who lives at eleven Queen street?" the voice of a strange man asks.

"Yes," David answers.

"Turn off the cooker gas immediately! Be careful!" the voice orders.

"Okay," David says and turns the gas off again.

"Let's go to the kindergarten," David says to Nancy feeling that they will not drink tea today.

"No. I want some tea and bread with butter," Nancy says angrily.

masu. "saa, youchien e iko u." deibiddo wa, kyou wa ocha wa noma nai na to kanji nagara, nanshī ni ii masu. "ya da. ocha to batā no pan ga hoshii no." nanshī wa oko tte ii masu.

"ええと、じゃあやかんをもう一度暖めよう。"彼女の兄はそう言い、またがすをつけます。電話がまた鳴り、今回は彼らの母親ががすを消すように言いつけます。そして彼女は全てを説明します。最後には、なんしーとでいびっどはお茶を飲み幼稚園へ行きます。 "eeto, jaa yakan wo mouichido atatameyo u." kanojo no ani wa sou ii, mata gasu wo tsuke masu. denwa ga mata nari, konkai wa karera no hahaoya ga gasu wo kesu you ni iitsuke masu. soshite kanojo wa subete wo setsumei shi masu. saigo ni wa, nanshī to deibiddo wa ocha wo nomi youchien e iki masu.

"Well, let's try to warm up the kettle again," her brother says and turns the gas on.

The telephone rings and this time their mother orders to turn the gas off. Then she explains everything. At last Nancy and David drink tea and go to the kindergarten.

18

Audio

しょくぎょうしょうかいじょ
職 業 紹 介 所

A job agency

A

単語

Words

1. 15 [juu go] - fifteen
2. 60 [roku juu] - sixty
3. お互いを知る [otagai wo shiru] - know each other
4. ケーブル、電線 [keーburu, densen] - cable
5. コンサルタント [konsarutanto] - consultant

6. させる [sa seru] - let
7. だった [da tta] - was
8. ひどい、命とりの [hidoi, inochitori no] - deadly
9. ポジション、場所 [pojishon, basho] - position
10. また、同じく [mata, onajiku] - also
11. マットレス [mattoresu] - mattress
12. 個別に、別々に [kobetsu ni, betsubetsu ni] - individually
13. 全ての、全部 [subete no, zenbu] - all
14. 出版 [shuppan] - publishing
15. 助手 [joshu] - helper
16. 半分の [hanbun no] - half
17. 同じ [onaji] - the same
18. 同時に [douji ni] - at the same time
19. 同じように、同じ程度 [onaji you ni, onaji teido] - as
20. 同意する [doui suru] - agree
21. 床 [yuka] - floor
22. 強い、強く [tsuyoi, tsuyoku] - strong, strongly
23. 心配しないで！ [shinpai shi nai de!] - Do not worry!
24. 心配する [shinpai suru] - worry
25. 手作業 [tesagyou] - manual work
26. 振る、揺れる [furu, yureru] - shake
27. 推薦する [suisen suru] - recommend
28. 数字 [suuji] - number
29. 毎時、1時間ごと [maiji, ichi jikan goto] - per hour
30. 注意してきく、注意深くきく [chuui shi te kiku, chuuibukaku kiku] - listen carefully
31. 注意深く [chuuibukaku] - carefully
32. 混乱する [konran suru] - confused
33. 物語、ストーリー [monogatari, sutoーriー] - story
34. 町 [machi] - town
35. 白髪の [hakuhatsu no] - grey-headed
36. 相談する [soudan suru] - consult
37. 真剣に [shinken ni] - seriously
38. 確信している [kakushin shi te iru] - sure
39. 精神作業 [seishin sagyou] - mental work
40. 経験 [keiken] - experience
41. 腕相撲する、腕 [udezumou suru, ude] - arm
42. 走る、動かす [hashiru, ugokasu] - running
43. 電気の [denki no] - electric
44. 電流 [denryuu] - current

B

しょくぎょうしょうかいじょ
職業紹介所

shokugyou shoukai jo

ある日、ぽーるはろばーとの部屋へ行き、彼の友達がべっどの上で震えているのをみつけます。ぽーるは、ろばーとから電気のやかんまで電線が続いているのをみつけます。ぽーるはろばーとがひどい電流を受けていると考えます。彼は急いでべっどへ行き、まっとれすを掴み、強く引きます。ろばーとは床へ落ちます。そして彼は立ち上がって、ぽーるを驚きの目でみます。aru hi, po—ru wa roba—to no heya e iki, kare no tomodachi ga beddo no ue de furue te iru no wo mitsuke masu. po—ru wa, roba—to kara denki no yakan made densen ga tsuzui te iru no wo mitsuke masu. po—ru wa roba—to ga hidoi denryuu wo uke te iru to kangae masu. kare wa isoi de beddo he iki, mattoresu wo tsukami, tsuyoku hiki masu. roba—to wa yuka e ochi masu. soshite kare wa tachiaga tte, po—ru wo odoroki no me de mi masu.

"何だったの？"ろばーとがききます。"君は電流をうけていたんだ。"ぽーるが言います。"ちがうよ、音楽をきいていたんだよ。"ろばーとがそう言い、彼のCDぷれーやー

A job agency

One day Paul goes to Robert's room and sees that his friend is lying on the bed shaking. Paul sees some electrical cables running from Robert to the electric kettle. Paul believes that Robert is under a deadly electric current. He quickly goes to the bed, takes the mattress and pulls it strongly. Robert falls to the floor. Then he stands up and looks at Paul in surprise.

"What was it?" Robert asks.

"You were on electrical current," Paul says.

"No, I was listening to the

をみせます。"わぁ、ごめん。"ぽーるは言います。彼は混乱しています。"大丈夫だよ。心配しないで！"ろばーとは静かにこたえ、ずぼんを綺麗にしています。"でいびっどとぼくは職業紹介所へいくんだ。ぼくたちと一緒にいく？"ぽーるが聞きます。"もちろん。さあ、一緒にいこう。"ろばーとが言います。 "nan da tta no?" roba一to ga kiki masu. "kimi wa denryuu wo uke te i ta n da." po一ru ga ii masu. "chigau yo, ongaku wo kii te i ta n da yo." roba一to ga sou ii, kare no shi一di一pure一ya一 wo mise masu. "waa, gomen." po一ru wa ii masu. kare wa konran shi te i masu. "daijoubu da yo. shinpai shi nai de!" roba一to wa shizuka ni kotae, zubon wo kirei ni shi te i masu. "deibiddo to boku wa shokugyou shoukai jo e iku n da. boku tachi to issho ni iku?" po一ru ga kiki masu. "mochiron. saa, issho ni iko u." roba一to ga ii masu.

彼らは外に出て、７番のばすに乗ります。職業紹介所へ行くのには、１５分ほどかかります。でいびっどはすでにそこにいます。彼らは建物の中へ入ります。職業紹介所の前には長い列ができています。彼らも列に並びます。３０分で建物の中に入ります。部屋の中には机と本棚がいくつかあります。白髪

music," Robert says and shows his CD player.

"Oh, I am sorry," Paul says. He is confused.

"It's okay. Do not worry," Robert answers quietly cleaning his trousers.

"David and I go to a job agency. Do you want to go with us?" Paul asks.

"Sure. Let's go together," Robert says.

They go outside and take the bus number seven. It takes them about fifteen minutes to go to the job agency. David is already there. They come into the building. There is a long queue to the office of the job agency. They stand in the queue. In half an hour they come into the office. There is a

…の男性がてーぶるに座っています。彼は60歳くらいです。karera wa soto ni de te, nana ban no basu ni nori masu. shokugyou shoukai jo e iku no ni wa, juu go fun hodo kakari masu. deibiddo wa sudeni soko ni i masu. karera wa tatemono no naka e hairi masu. shokugyou shoukai jo no mae ni wa nagai retsu ga deki te i masu. karera mo retsu ni narabi masu. san ju ppun de tatemono no naka ni hairi masu. heya no naka ni wa tsukue to hondana ga ikutsu ka ari masu. hakuhatsu no dansei ga te―buru ni suwa tte i masu. kare wa roku ju ssai kurai desu.

"入ってください！"彼はふれんどりーに言います。"座ってください。"でいびっど、ろばーと、ぽーるは座ります。"私の名前はじょーじ・えすてぃめーたーです。わたしがじょぶこんさるたんとです。通常、訪問者とは個別にお話をします。しかし、あなたたちは皆学生で、お互いを知っているようなので、全員一緒に相談にのります。同意しますか？""はい。"でいびっどが言います。"ぼくたちは毎日3時間か4時間空き時間があります。その時間にできる仕事をみつける必要があるのです。" "hai tte kudasai!" kare wa furendori― ni ii masu. "suwa tte kudasai." deibiddo, roba―to, po―ru wa suwari masu. "watashi no namae ha jo―ji.esutime―ta― desu. watashi ga jobukonsarutanto desu. tsuujou, houmon sha to wa kobetsu ni ohanashi wo shi masu. shikashi, anata tachi wa mina gakusei de, otagai wo shi tte iru you na node,

table and some bookcases in the room. A gray-headed man is sitting at the table. He is about sixty years old.

"Come in guys!" he says friendly, "Take seats, please."
David, Robert and Paul sit down.

"My name is George Estimator. I am a job consultant. Usually I speak with visitors individually. But as you are all students and know each other I can consult you all together. Do you agree?"

"Yes, sir," David says, "We have three or four hours of free time every day. We need to find jobs for that time, sir."

zen'in issho ni soudan ni nori masu. doui shi masu ka?"
"hai." deibiddo ga ii masu. "boku tachi wa mainichi san jikan ka yon jikan aki jikan ga ari masu. sono jikan ni dekiru shigoto wo mitsukeru hitsuyou ga aru no desu."

"ええと。学生のための仕事がいくつかありますよ。それから、CDぷれーやーを外してくださいね。"えすてぃめーたー氏がろばーとに言います。"あなたと音楽、同時にきけます。"ろばーとが言います。"もし本気で仕事を見つけたいのであれば、CDぷれーやーを外してわたしが言うことを注意してきいてください。"えすてぃめーたー氏が言います。"では、どのような種類の仕事が必要ですか？精神作業ですか、それとも手作業ですか？"
"ぼくはどんな仕事もできます。"ぽーるが言います。"ぼくは強いんです。腕相撲しますか？"彼はそう言い、えすてぃめーたー氏の机の上に自分の腕を置きます。"eeto. gakusei no tame no shigoto ga ikutsu ka ari masu yo. sorekara, shi─di─pure─ya─ wo hazushi te kudasai ne." esutime─ta─ shi ga roba─to ni ii masu. "anata to ongaku, doujini kike masu." roba─to ga ii masu. "moshi honki de shigoto wo mitsuke tai no de are ba, shi─di─pure─ya─ wo hazushi te watashi ga iu koto wo chuui shi te kii te kudasai." esutime─ta─ shi ga ii masu. "deha, dono you na shurui no shigoto ga hitsuyou desu ka? seishin sagyou desu ka, soretomo tesagyou desu ka?" "boku wa donna shigoto mo deki

"Well. I have some jobs for students. And you take off your player," Mr. Estimator says to Robert.

"I can listen to you and to music at the same time," Robert says.

"If you seriously want to get a job take the player off and listen carefully to what I say;" Mr. Estimator says, "Now guys say what kind of job do you need? Do you need mental or manual work?"

"I can do any work," Paul says, "I am strong. Want to arm?" he says and puts his arm on Mr. Estimator's table.

masu." poーru ga ii masu. "boku wa tsuyoi n desu. udezumou shi masu ka?" kare wa sou ii, esutimeーtaーshi no tsukue no ue ni jibun no ude wo oki masu.

"ここはすぽーつくらぶではないんですけれど、でももしあなたがやりたいのであれば…" えすていめーたー氏が言います。彼は机の上に自分の腕を置き、素早くぽーるの腕を押し倒します。"みてわかるように、強いだけではなく、賢くもなければいけないんですよ。" "koko wa supoーtsu kurabu de wa nai n desu keredo, demo moshi anata ga yari tai no de are ba…" esutimeーtaー shi ga ii masu. kare wa tsukue no ue ni jibun no ude wo oki, subayaku poーru no ude wo oshitaoshi masu. "mi te wakaru you ni, tsuyoi dake de wa naku, kashikoku mo nakere ba ike nai n desu yo."

"It is not a sport club here but if you want…" Mr. Estimator says. He puts his arm on the table and quickly pushes down Paul's arm, "As you see son, you must be not only strong but also smart."

"ぼくは精神作業もできます。" ぽーるは再び言います。彼は仕事がとても欲しいのです。"ぼくは物語が書けます。自分の生まれた街についての物語をいくつか持っています。" "boku wa seishin sagyou mo deki masu." poーru wa futatabi ii masu. kare wa shigoto ga totemo hoshii no desu. "boku wa monogatari ga kake masu. jibun no umare ta machi nitsuite no monogatari wo ikutsu ka mo tte i masu."

"I can work mentally too, sir," Paul says again. He wants to get a job very much.
"I can write stories. I have some stories about my native town."

"それはとても興味深い" えすてぃめーたー氏が言います。彼は用紙を一枚取ります。"出版社 "おーるらうんど" はらいてぃんぐのぽじしょんで、若い助手をひとり

"This is very interesting," Mr. Estimator says. He takes a sheet of paper, "The publishing house "All-round" needs a

133

必要としています。彼らは時給9どる支払いますよ。" "sore wa totemo kyoumibukai" esutimeーtaー shi ga ii masu. kare wa youshi wo ichi mai tori masu. "shuppan sha "oーruraundo" wa raitingu no pojishon de, wakai joshu wo hitori hitsuyou to shi te i masu. karera wa jikyuu kyuu doru shiharai masu yo."

young helper for a writing position. They pay nine dollar per hour."

"いいですね！" ぽーるが言います。" 試すことができますか？" "もちろん。これが彼らのでんわばんごうと住所です。" えすてぃめーたー氏はそう言い、一枚の紙をぽーるに渡します。 "ii desu ne!" poーru ga ii masu. "tamesu koto ga deki masu ka?" "mochiron. kore ga karera no denwa bangou to juusho desu." esutimeーtaー shi wa sou ii, ichi mai no kami wo poーru ni watashi masu.

"Cool!" Paul says, "Can I try?"

"Sure. Here are their telephone number and their address," Mr. Estimator says and gives a sheet of paper to Paul.

"それから、君たちは農場、こんぴゅーたー会社、新聞社もしくはすーぱーで仕事を選べますよ。君たちは経験がないので、農場で働き始めることをわたしは推薦します。彼らは従業員をふたり必要としています。" えすてぃめーたー氏がでいびっどとぽーるに言います。 "sorekara, kimitachi wa noujou, konpyuーtaー kaisha, shinbun sha moshikuha suーpaー de shigoto wo erabe masu yo. kimitachi wa keiken ga nai node, noujou de hataraki hajimeru koto wo watashi wa suisen shi masu. karera wa juugyou in wo fu tari hitsuyou to shi te i masu." esutimeーtaー shi ga deibiddo to poーru ni

"And you guys can choose a job on a farm, in a computer firm, on a newspaper or in a supermarket. As you do not have any experience I recommend you to begin to work in a farm. They need two workers," Mr. Estimator says to David and Robert.

134

ii masu.

"彼らはいくら支払いますか？"でいびっどが質問します。"ちょっとまってください…"えすてぃめーたー氏はこんぴゅーたーをのぞきこみます。"彼らは毎日3-4時間労働者が必要で、時給7どる支払います。土曜日と日曜日はお休みです。同意しますか？彼が聞きます。"はい、同意します。"でいびっどが言います。"ぼくも同意します。"ろばーとが言います。"ええと。農場の電話番号と住所を持って行ってください。"えすてぃめーたー氏はそう言い、一枚の用紙を彼らに渡します。"ありがとうございます。"男の子たちはそう言って、外にでていきます。"karera wa ikura shiharai masu ka?" deibiddo ga shitsumon shi masu. "chotto ma tte kudasai …" esutime—ta— shi wa konpyu—ta— wo nozokikomi masu. "karera wa mainichi san yo jikan roudou sha ga hitsuyou de, jikyuu nana doru shiharai masu. doyoubi to nichiyoubi wa o yasumi desu. doui shi masu ka? kare ga kiki masu. "hai, doui shi masu." deibiddo ga ii masu. "boku mo doui shi masu." roba—to ga ii masu. "eeto. noujou no denwa bangou to juusho wo mo tte i tte kudasai." esutime—ta— shi wa sou ii, ichi mai no youshi wo karera ni watashi masu. "arigatou gozai masu." otokonoko tachi wa sou i tte, soto ni de te iki masu.

"How much do they pay?" David asks.

"Let me see…" Mr. Estimator looks into the computer, "They need workers for three or four hours a day and they pay seven dollars per hour. Saturdays and Sundays are days off. Do you agree?" he asks.

"I agree," David says.

"I agree too," Robert says.

"Well. Take the telephone number and the address of the farm," Mr. Estimator says and gives a sheet of paper to them.

"Thank you, sir," the boys say and go outside.

19

Audio

<ruby>デイビッド<rt>でいびっど</rt></ruby>と<ruby>ロバート<rt>ろばと</rt></ruby>は<ruby>トラック<rt>とらっく</rt></ruby>を<ruby>洗<rt>あら</rt></ruby>います
(<ruby>パート<rt>ぱと</rt></ruby>１)

David and Robert wash the truck (Part 1)

A

単語
Words

1. １０番目の [juu banme no] - tenth
2. ２番目の [ni banme no] - second
3. ３番目の [san banme no] - third
4. ４番目の [yon banme no] - fourth
5. ５番目の [go banme no] - fifth
6. ６番目の [roku banme no] - sixth
7. ８番目の [hachi banme no] - eighth
8. ９番目の [kyuu banme no] - ninth
9. エンジン [enjin] - engine

10. オーナー、持ち主 [oーnaー, mochinushi] - owner
11. タイヤ [taiya] - wheel
12. はじめに、最初に [hajime ni, saisho ni] - at first
13. ブレーキ [bureーki] - brake
14. ブレーキをかけるために [bureーki wo kakeru tame ni] - to brake
15. フロント、受付、前、玄関 [furonto, uketsuke, mae, genkan] - front
16. メートル [meーtoru] - meter
17. ゆっくりと [yukkuri to] - slowly
18. より近い [yori chikai] - closer
19. より遠く [yori tooku] - further
20. ロット [rotto] - lot
21. に沿って [ni sotte] - along
22. 使う [tsukau] - use
23. より大きな [yori ookina] - bigger
24. 到着する [touchaku suru] - arrive
25. 前輪 [zenrin] - front wheels
26. 力、強さ [chikara, tsuyo sa] - strength
27. 合っている、ぴったりの、ふさわしい [a tte iru, pittari no, fusawashii] - suitable
28. 始める、始まる [hajimeru, hajimaru] - start
29. 庭、場 [niwa, ba] - yard
30. 待つ [matsu] - wait
31. 揺れる [yureru] - pitch
32. 搬入する、積む [hannyuu suru, tsumu] - load
33. 機械 [kikai] - machine
34. 波 [nami] - wave
35. 洗う [arau] - wash
36. 浮く [uku] - float
37. 海 [umi] - sea
38. 海岸 [kaigan] - seashore
39. 畑、フィールド [hatake, fiーrudo] - field
40. 確認する [kakunin suru] - check
41. 種 [tane] - seed
42. 箱、ダンボール [hako, danboーru] - box
43. 綺麗、清潔 [kirei, seiketsu] - clean
44. 自動車免許証 [jidousha menkyo shou] - driving license
45. 船 [fune] - ship
46. 踏む [fumu] - step
47. 辞める、とめる [yameru, tomeru] - quite
48. 近い [chikai] - close
49. 7番目の [nana banme no] - seventh
50. 道路 [douro] - road
51. 遠い、離れた [tooi, hanare ta] - far
52. 降ろす、荷おろしをする [orosu, ni oroshi wo suru] - unload
53. 雇い主 [yatoinushi] – employer

B

デイビッドとロバートはトラックを洗います（パート１）

deibiddo to roba—to wa torakku wo arai masu (pa—to ichi)

でいびっどとろばーとは今、農場で働いています。彼らは毎日 3-4 時間働いています。仕事はとても大変です。彼らは毎日たくさん働かなければなりません。彼らは農場の庭を毎週2日目に掃除をします。彼らは毎週3日目に、機械を洗います。毎週4日目には、彼らは農場の畑で働きます。deibiddo to roba—to wa ima, noujou de hatarai te i masu. karera wa mainichi san yo jikan hatarai te i masu. shigoto wa totemo taihen desu. karera wa mainichi takusan hataraka nakere ba nari mase n. karera wa noujou no niwa wo maishuu futsuka me ni souji wo shi masu. karera wa maishuu mikka me ni, kikai wo arai masu. maishuu yokka me ni wa, karera wa noujou no hatake de hataraki masu.

彼らの雇い主の名前はだにえる・たふです。たふさんは農場のおーなーで、彼がほとんどの仕事をします。たふさんはとてもよく働きます。彼は、でいびっどとろばーとにも

David and Robert are working on a farm now. They work three or four hours every day. The work is quite hard. They must do a lot of work every day. They clean the farm yard every second day. They wash the farm machines every third day. Every fourth day they work in the farm fields.

Their employer's name is Daniel Tough. Mr. Tough is the owner of the farm and he does most of the work. Mr. Tough works very hard. He also gives

たくさんの仕事を与えます。karera no yatoinushi no namae wa danieru. tafu desu. tafu san wa noujou no o―na― de, kare ga hotondo no shigoto wo shi masu. tafu san wa totemo yoku hataraki masu. kare wa, deibiddo to roba―to ni mo takusan no shigoto wo atae masu.

a lot of work to David and Robert.

"やあ、君たち。機械を洗うのを終わらせて、とらっくで運送会社らぴっどまで行ってきて。"たふさんが言います。"彼らには、わたしの荷物があるんだよ。種の箱をとらっくに積んで農場へ運び、それから農場の庭に荷おろしをして。今日、種を使う必要があるから素早くやるんだよ。そして、とらっくを洗うのを忘れないでね。" "yaa, kimitachi. kikai wo arau no wo owara se te, torakku de unsou kaisha rapiddo made i tte ki te." tafu san ga ii masu. "karera ni wa, watashi no nimotsu ga aru n da yo. tane no hako wo torakku ni tsun de noujou e hakobi, sorekara noujou no niwa ni ni oroshi wo shi te. kyou, tane wo tsukau hitsuyou ga aru kara subayaku yaru n da yo. soshite, torakku wo arau no wo wasure nai de ne."

"Hey boys, finish cleaning the machines, take the truck and go to the transport firm Rapid," Mr. Tough says, "They have a load for me. Load boxes with the seed in the truck, bring them to the farm, and unload in the farm yard. Do it quickly because I need to use the seed today. And do not forget to wash the truck".

"わかりました。"でいびっどが言います。彼らは掃除を終え、とらっくに乗ります。でいびっどは運転免許証をもっているので、彼がとらっくを運転します。彼はえんじんをつけて、始めはゆっくり農場の庭を抜け、

"Okay," David says. They finish cleaning and get into the truck. David has a driving license so he drives the truck. He starts the engine and drives at first slowly through the farm yard,

そして道路沿いを素早く運転します。運送会社らぴっどは農場から離れていません。彼らは15分でそこに到着します。彼らはそこで搬入どあ10番をさがします。"wakari mashi ta." deibiddo ga ii masu. karera wa souji wo oe, torakku ni nori masu. deibiddo wa unten menkyo shou wo mo tte iru node, kare ga torakku wo unten shi masu. kare wa enjin wo tsuke te, hajime wa yukkuri noujou no niwa wo nuke, soshite douro zoi wo subayaku unten shi masu. unsou kaisha rapiddo wa noujou kara hanare te i mase n. karera wa juu go fun de soko ni touchaku shi masu. karera wa soko de hannyuu doa juu ban wo sagashi masu.

でいびっどは搬入場を注意深く運転して抜けます。彼らは最初の搬入どあを通り過ぎ、2番目の搬入どあを通り過ぎ、3番目の搬入どあを通り過ぎ、4番目の搬入どあを通り過ぎ、5番目の搬入どあを通り過ぎ、6番目の搬入どあを通り過ぎ、7番目の搬入どあを通り過ぎ、8番目の搬入どあを通り過ぎ、9番目の搬入どあを通り過ぎます。でいびっどは搬入どあ10番まで運転して止まります。deibiddo wa hannyuu jou wo chuuibukaku unten shi te nuke masu. karera wa saisho no hannyuu doa wo

then quickly along the road. The transport firm Rapid is not far from the farm. They arrive there in fifteen minutes. They look for the loading door number ten there.

David drives the truck carefully through the loading yard. They go past the first loading door, past the second loading door, past the third, past the fourth, past the fifth, past the sixth, past the seventh, past the eighth, then past the ninth loading door. David drives to the tenth loading door and stops.

toorisugi, ni banme no hannyuu doa wo toorisugi, san banme no hannyuu doa wo toorisugi, yon banme no hannyuu doa wo toorisugi, go banme no hannyuu doa wo toorisugi, roku banme no hannyuu doa wo toorisugi, nana banme no hannyuu doa wo toorisugi, hachi banme no hannyuu doa wo toorisugi, kyuu banme no hannyuu doa wo toorisugi masu. deibiddo wa hannyuu doa juu ban made unten shi te tomari masu.

"はじめに搬入りすとを確認しないといけないね。"この運送会社ですでに搬入りすとの経験があるろばーとが言います。彼はどあで働いている搬入作業員まで行き、搬入りすとを渡します。搬入作業員は素早く5つの箱をとらっくへ搬入します。ろばーとは箱を注意深く確認します。箱の全ての数字は、搬入りすとの数字です。"数字は合っていますね。さあ行こう。"ろばーとが言います。 "hajime ni hannyuu risuto wo kakunin shi nai to ike nai ne." kono unsou kaisha de sudeni hannyuu risuto no keiken ga aru roba—to ga ii masu. kare wa doa de hatarai te iru hannyuu sagyou in made iki, hannyuu risuto wo watashi masu. hannyuu sagyou in wa subayaku itsutsu no hako wo torakku e hannyuu shi masu. roba—to wa hako wo chuuibukaku kakunin shi masu. hako no subete no suuji wa, hannyuu risuto no suuji desu. "suuji wa a tte i masu ne. saa iko u." roba—to ga ii masu.

"わかった。"でいびっどはそう言い、えんじんを

"We must check the loading list first," Robert says who already has some experience with loading lists at this transport firm. He goes to the loader who works at the door and gives him the loading list. The loader loads quickly five boxes into their truck. Robert checks the boxes carefully. All numbers on the boxes have numbers from the loading list.

"Numbers are correct. We can go now," Robert says.

"Okay," David says and starts

すたーとします。"今、とらっくを洗えると思うんだ。ここから遠くないところに、ぴったりの場所があるんだ。"彼らは、5分で海岸へ到着しました。"waka tta." deibiddo wa sou ii, enjin wo suta―to shi masu. "ima, torakku wo araeru to omou n da. koko kara tooku nai tokoro ni, pittari no basho ga aru n da." karera wa, go fun de kaigan e touchaku shi mashi ta.

"君はここでとらっくを洗いたいの?"ろばーとが驚いてききます。"そうだよ！いい場所じゃない?"でいびっどが言います。"kimi wa koko de torakku wo arai tai no?" roba―to ga odoroi te kiki masu. "sou da yo! ii basho ja nai?" deibiddo ga ii masu.

"それでどこでばけつをとるの?"ろばーとがききます。"ばけつはいらないんだよ。ぼくが海のとても近くを運転するんだ。海からの水をつかうんだ。"でいびっどはそう言い、水のとても近くを運転します。前輪は水に入り、波が彼らのほうへ溢れます。"sorede doko de baketsu wo toru no?" roba―to ga kiki masu. "baketsu wa ira nai n da yo. boku ga umi no totemo chikaku wo unten suru n da. umi kara no mizu wo tsukau n da." deibiddo wa sou ii, mizu no totemo chikaku wo unten shi masu. zenrin wa mizu ni hairi, nami ga karera no hou e afure masu.

"さあ、外へ出て洗い始めよう。"ろばーと

the engine, "I think we can wash the truck now. There is a suitable place not far from here".

In five minutes they arrive to the seashore.

"Do you want to wash the truck here?" Robert asks in surprise.

"Yeah! It is a nice place, isn't it?" David says.

"And where will we take a pail?" Robert asks.

"We do not need any pail. I will drive very close to the sea. We will take the water from the sea," David says and drives very close to the water. The front wheels go in the water and the waves run over them.

"Let's get out and begin

が言います。"ちょっと待って。もう少し近くを運転するよ。"でいびっどはそう言い、1－2めーとるさらに遠くへ運転します。"このほうがいいね。"そして大きな波がきて、水がとらっくを少し持ち上げ、ゆっくりと海の方へむかって運びます。"saa, soto e de te arai hajimeyo u." roba─to ga ii masu. "chotto ma tte. mousukoshi chikaku wo unten suru yo." deibiddo wa sou ii, ichi ni me─toru sarani tooku e unten shi masu. "kono hou ga iine." soshite ookina nami ga ki te, mizu ga torakku wo sukoshi mochiage, yukkuri to umi no hou e muka tte hakobi masu.

"止めて！でいびっど、とらっくを止めて！"ろばーとが叫びます。"もうぼくらは水の中にいるんだよ！お願い、止めて！" "止まらないんだよ！！"でいびっどは、ぶれーきを力一杯踏みながら叫びます。"止められないんだ！！"とらっくは、小さな船のように波の上を揺られ、海の中へゆっくりとさらに流れていきます。"tome te! deibiddo, torakku wo tome te!" roba─to ga sakebi masu. "mou boku ra wa mizu no naka ni iru n da yo! onegai, tome te!" "tomara nai n da yo!!" deibiddo wa, bure─ki wo chikaraippai fumi nagara sakebi masu. "tome rare nai n da!!" torakku wa, chiisana fune no you ni nami no ue wo yura re, umi no naka e yukkuri to sarani nagare te iki masu.

(続く) (tsuzuku)

washing," Robert says.

"Wait a minute. I will drive a bit closer," David says and drives one or two meters further, "It is better now."

Then a bigger wave comes and the water lifts the truck a little and carries it slowly further into the sea.

"Stop! David, stop the truck!" Robert cries, "We are in the water already! Please, stop!"

"It will not stop!!" David cries stepping on the brake with all his strength, "I cannot stop it!!"

The truck is slowly floating further in the sea pitching on the waves like a little ship.

(to be continued)

20

Audio

<ruby>デイビッド<rt>でいびっど</rt></ruby>と<ruby>ロバート<rt>ろばーと</rt></ruby>は<ruby>トラック<rt>とらっく</rt></ruby>を<ruby>洗<rt>あら</rt></ruby>います
(<ruby>パート<rt>ぱーと</rt></ruby>2)

David and Robert wash the truck (Part 2)

A

単語
Words

1. １年前 [ichi nen mae] - a year ago
2. ２５ [ni juu go] - twenty-five
3. お金 [okane] - money
4. くじら, シャチ [kujira, shachi] - whale; killer whale
5. コントロールする [kontoroーru suru] - control
6. ジャーナリスト [jaーnarisuto] - journalist

7. すごい、大きな [sugoi, ookina] - killer
8. スピーチ [supi—chi] - speech
9. タンカー [tanka—] - tanker
10. であった [de a tta] - were
11. ハンドルをきる [handoru wo kiru] - steer
12. リハビリ [rihabiri] - rehabilitation
13. リハビリする [rihabiri suru] - rehabilitate
14. 一定に、定期的に [ittei ni, teiki teki ni] - constant
15. 事故 [jiko] - accident
16. 例 [rei] - example
17. 例えば [tatoeba] - for example
18. 写真; カメラマン [shashin ; kameraman] - photograph; photographer
19. 前 [mae] - ago
20. 助ける、救助する [tasukeru, kyuujo suru] - rescue
21. 右 [migi] - right
22. 岸 [kishi] - shore
23. 左 [hidari] - left
24. 式典 [shikiten] - ceremony
25. 放す、自由にする [hanasu, jiyuu ni suru] - set free
26. 救助サービス [kyuujo sa—bisu] - rescue service
27. 明日 [ashita] - tomorrow
28. 楽しむ [tanoshimu] - enjoy
29. 欲しがられる [hoshi gara reru] - wanted
30. 決してない、二度とない [kesshite nai, nidoto nai] - never
31. 泳ぐ [oyogu] - swim
32. 流れる [nagareru] - flow
33. 浅い [asai] - swallow
34. 浮いている [ui te iru] - floating
35. 状況、シチュエーション [joukyou, shichue—shon] - situation
36. 知らせる [shiraseru] - inform
37. 石油 [sekiyu] - oil
38. 笑う [warau] - laugh
39. 素晴らしい [subarashii] - wonderful
40. 綺麗な [kirei na] - cleaned
41. 親愛なる [shinai naru] - dear
42. 解雇する [kaiko suru] - fire
43. 起きた、起こった [oki ta, oko tta] - happened
44. 起きる、起こる [okiru, okoru] - happen
45. 風 [kaze] - wind
46. 餌付けする [ezuke suru] - feed
47. 鳥 [tori] - bird

B

デイビッドとロバートはトラックを洗います（パート2）

deibiddo to roba—to wa torakku wo arai masu (pa—to ni)

トラックは、小さな船のように波の上を揺られ、海の中へゆっくりとさらに流れていきます。でいびっどは、左、右とはんどるをきり、ぶれーきとがすを踏みます。しかし彼はとらっくをこんとろーるできません。強い風がとらっくを海岸沿いへ押しています。

torakku wa, chiisana fune no you ni nami no ue wo yura re, umi no naka e yukkuri to sarani nagare te iki masu. deibiddo wa, hidari, migi to handoru wo kiri, bure—ki to gasu wo fumi masu. shikashi kare wa torakku wo kontoro—ru deki mase n. tsuyoi kaze ga torakku wo kaigan zoi he oshi te i masu.

でいびっどとろばーとはどうしていいかわかりません。彼らはただ座って、窓の外を見ています。海水が中に流れ始めます。

deibiddo to roba—to wa doushite ii ka wakari mase n. karera wa tada suwa tte, mado no soto wo mi te i masu. kaisui ga naka ni nagare hajime masu.

"外へでて屋根に座ろう。"ろばーとが言います。彼らは屋根に座ります。"たふ氏は

David and Robert wash the truck (Part 2)

The truck is floating slowly further in the sea pitching on the waves like a little ship. David is steering to the left and to the right stepping on the brake and gas. But he cannot control the truck.
A strong wind is pushing it along the seashore.

David and Robert do not know what to do. They are just sitting, looking out of the windows. The sea water begins to run inside.

"Let's go out and sit on the roof," Robert says.

なんて言うかな？" ろばーとが言います。 とらっくは海岸から２０めーとるほどのところでゆっくりと浮いています。海岸の人達の何人かが、とまって驚きの目で見ています。"たふ氏はぼくたちを解雇するかもしれないね。"でいびっどがこたえます。 "soto e de te yane ni suwaro u." roba―to ga ii masu. karera wa yane ni suwari masu. "tafu shi wa nante iu ka na?" roba―to ga ii masu. torakku wa kaigan kara ni juu me―toru hodo no tokoro de yukkuri to ui te i masu. kaigan no hitotachi no nan nin ka ga, toma tte odoroki no me de mi te i masu. "tafu shi wa boku tachi wo kaiko suru kamo shire nai ne." deibiddo ga kotae masu.

一方で、大学の学長、かいと氏は彼のおふぃすに入ってきます。本日は式典がありますよ、と秘書は彼に言います。彼らはりはびり後の２羽の海鳥を放すのです。たんかー、ぐらんぽりゅーしょんの事故後に、りはびりせんたーの従業員は、石油の汚れを掃除しました。事故は１ヶ月前に起こりました。かいと氏はそこですぴーちをします。式典はあと２５分で始まります。かいと氏と彼の秘書はたくしーに乗り、１０分後には式典の場所に到着します。鳥たちも、すでにそこにい

They sit on the roof.

"What will Mr. Tough say, I wonder?" Robert says.

The truck is floating slowly about twenty meters away from the shore. Some people on the shore stop and look at it in surprise.

"Mr. Tough may fire us," David answers.

Meanwhile the head of the college Mr. Kite comes to his office. The secretary says to him that there will be a ceremony today. They will set free two sea birds after rehabilitation. Workers of the rehabilitation centre cleaned oil off them after the accident with the tanker Gran Pollución. The accident happened one month ago. Mr. Kite must make a speech there. The ceremony begins in twenty-five minutes.

ます。今、彼らは普段ほどは、白くはありません。しかし彼らは、泳いだり、飛んだりすることが再びできます。そこには今、たくさんの人々、じゃーなりすと、かめらまんがいます。あと2分で、式典が始まります。かいと氏はすぴーちを始めます。ippou de, daigaku no gakuchou, kaito shi wa kare no ofisu ni hai tte ki masu. honjitsu wa shikiten ga ari masu yo, to hisho wa kare ni ii masu. karera wa rihabiri go no ni wa no umidori wo hanasu no desu. tanka―, guranporyu―shon no jiko go ni, rihabiri senta― no juugyou in wa, sekiyu no yogore wo souji shi mashi ta. jiko wa i kkagetsu mae ni okori mashi ta. kaito shi wa soko de supi―chi wo shi masu. shikiten wa ato ni juu go fun de hajimari masu. kaito shi to kare no hisho wa takushi― ni nori, ju ppun go ni wa shikiten no basho ni touchaku shi masu. tori tachi mo, sudeni soko ni i masu. ima, karera wa fudan hodo wa, shiroku wa ari mase n. shikashi karera wa, oyoi dari, ton dari suru koto ga futatabi deki masu. soko ni wa ima, takusan no hitobito, ja―narisuto, kameraman ga i masu. ato ni fun de, shikiten ga hajimari masu. kaito shi wa supi―chi wo hajime masu.

"親愛なる諸君へ！" 彼は言います。"ぐらんぽりゅーしょんのたんかーの事故は、一ヶ月前にここで起きました。今、わたしたちは、多くの鳥と動物たちをりはびりしなければなりません。たくさんのお金がかかります。例えば、この鳥たちのりはびりには、それぞれ5000どるがかかります！

Mr. Kite and his secretary take a taxi and in ten minutes arrive to the place of the ceremony. These two birds are already there. Now they are not so white as usually. But they can swim and fly again now. There are many people, journalists, photographers there now. In two minutes the ceremony begins. Mr. Kite begins his speech.

"Dear friends!" he says, "The accident with the tanker Gran Pollución happened at this place a month ago. We must rehabilitate many birds and animals now. It costs a lot of money. For example the rehabilitation of each of these

そして、1ヶ月のりはびりを終えた、素晴らしい2羽の鳥たちが自由になることを、みなさんに今お伝えすることを、わたしは嬉しく思います。"

二人の男性が、鳥の箱を持って水まで運び、箱を開けます。鳥たちは箱から外に出て、それから水の中にじゃんぷをし、泳ぎます。かめらまん達は写真をとります。じゃーなりすとたちはりはびりせんたーの従業員たちに動物たちについて質問をします。 "shinai naru shokun e!" kare wa ii masu. "guranporyu―shon no tanka― no jiko wa, i kkagetsu mae ni koko de oki mashi ta. ima, watashi tachi wa, ooku no tori to doubutsu tachi wo rihabiri shi nakere ba nari mase n. takusan no okane ga kakari masu. tatoeba, kono tori tachi no rihabiri ni wa, sorezore go sen doru ga kakari masu! soshite, i kkagetsu no rihabiri wo oe ta, subarashii ni wa no tori tachi ga jiyuu ni naru koto wo, minasan ni ima otsutae suru koto wo, watashi wa ureshiku omoi masu." futari no dansei ga, tori no hako wo mo tte mizu made hakobi, hako wo ake masu. tori tachi wa hako kara soto ni de te, sorekara mizu no naka ni janpu wo shi, oyogi masu. kameraman tachi wa shashin wo tori masu. ja―narisuto tachi hw rihabiri senta― no juugyou in tachi ni doubutsu tachi nitsuite shitsumon wo shi masu.

突然大きなしゃちが現れ、2羽の鳥たちを素早く飲み込み、また沈みます。

birds costs 5,000 dollars! And I am glad to inform you now that after one month of rehabilitation these two wonderful birds will be set free."

Two men take a box with the birds, bring it to the water and open it. The birds go out of the box and then jump in the water and swim. The photographers take pictures. The journalists ask workers of the rehabilitation centre about the animals.

Suddenly a big killer whale comes up, quickly swallows those two birds and goes down again.

鳥たちがいた場所を、全員が見つめています。大学の学長は自分の目が信じられません。しゃちは再び現れ、さらに鳥を探しています。そこには鳥はいないため、また沈みます。かいと氏は今、すぴーちを終えなければなりません。"ええと…。"彼はふさわしい言葉を選びます。totsuzen ookina shachi ga araware, ni wa no tori tachi wo subayaku nomikomi, mata shizumi masu. tori tachi ga i ta basho wo, zen'in ga mitsume te i masu. daigaku no gakuchou wa jibun no me ga shinji rare mase n. shachi wa futatabi araware, sarani tori wo sagashi te i masu. soko ni wa tori wa i nai tame, mata shizumi masu. kaito shi wa ima, supi―chi wo oe nakere ba nari mase n. "eeto …." kare wa fusawashii kotoba wo erabi masu.

"人生の、素晴らしい、一定の流れは決して止まりません。大きな動物は、より小さな動物を食べたりします。そして…ええと…あれは何ですか?"彼は水を見ながら言います。全員がそこを見て、そして船のように波の上を揺られる大きなとっくが、海岸沿いに浮いているのをみつけます。二人の男の人がそこには座っていて、式典会場を見ています。"jinsei no, subarashii, ittei no nagare wa kesshite tomari mase n. ookina doubutsu wa, yori chiisana doubutsu wo

All the people look at the place where the birds were before. The head of the college does not believe his eyes. The killer whale comes up again looking for more birds. As there are no other birds there, it goes down again. Mr. Kite must finish his speech now.

"Ah…," he chooses suitable words,

"The wonderful constant flow of life never stops. Bigger animals eat smaller animals and so on… ah… what is that?" he says looking at the water. All the people look there and see a big truck floating along the shore pitching on the waves like a ship. Two guys sit on it looking at the place of the ceremony.

tabe tari shi masu. soshite... eeto... are wa nan desu ka?" kare wa mizu wo mi nagara ii masu. zen'in ga soko wo mi te, soshite fune no you ni nami no ue wo yura reru ookina torakku ga, kaigan zoi ni ui te iru no wo mitsuke masu. futari no otoko no hito ga soko ni wa suwa tte i te, shikiten kaijou wo mi te i masu.

"こんにちは、かいとさん。"ろばーとが言います。"なんでしゃちに鳥を餌付けしているんですか？""こんにちは、ろばーと。"かいと氏はこたえます。"そこで君たちは何をしているんだい？""ぼくたちはとらっくを洗いたかったんです。"でいびっどはこたえます。

"konnichiha, kaito san." robāto ga ii masu. "nande shachi ni tori wo ezuke shi te iru n desu ka?" "konnichiwa, robāto." kaito shi wa kotae masu. "sokode kimitachi wa nani wo shi te iru n dai?" "boku tachi wa torakku wo arai taka tta n desu." deibiddo wa kotae masu.

"Hello Mr. Kite," Robert says, "Why are you feeding killer whales with birds?"

"Hello Robert," Mr. Kite answers, "What are you doing there boys?"

"We wanted to wash the truck," David answers.

"なるほどね。"かいと氏は言います。何人かの人達は、この状況を楽しみ始めます。彼らは笑い始めます。"ええと、わたしは今から救助さーびすを呼びます。彼らが君たちを水から助けだします。そして明日、わたしのおふぃすに来てくださいね。"大学の学長はそう言い、救助さーびすを呼びます。"naruhodo ne." kaito shi wa ii masu. nan nin ka no hitotachi wa, kono joukyou wo tanoshimi hajime masu. karera wa warai hajime masu. "eeto, watashi wa ima kara kyuujo sā-

"I see," Mr. Kite says. Some of the people begin to enjoy this situation. They begin to laugh.

"Well, I will call the rescue service now. They will get you out of the water. And I want to see you in my office tomorrow," the head of the college says and calls the rescue service.

bisu wo yobi masu. karera ga kimitachi wo mizu kara tasuke dashi masu. soshite ashita, watashi no ofisu ni ki te kudasai ne." daigaku no gakuchou wa sou ii, kyuujo sa―bisu wo yobi masu.

21

Audio

じゅぎょう
授　業

A lesson

A

単語
Words

1. いつも [itsumo] - always
2. 彼女、女の子の友達 [kanojo, onnanoko no tomodachi] - girlfriend
3. クラス、授業 [kurasu, jugyou] - class
4. これ [kore] - this stuff
5. テレビ [terebi] - television
6. どの [dono] - which
7. なしで、せずに [nashi de, se zu ni] - without
8. に注意を払う [ni chuui wo harau] - pay attention to
9. の代わりに [no kawari ni] - instead
10. の間 [no aida] - between

11. 彼氏、男の子の友達 [kareshi, otokonoko no tomodachi] - boyfriend

12. まだ、それでも [mada, soredemo] - still

13. もの、こと [mono, koto] - thing

14. より少ない [yori sukunai] - less

15. わずかに [wazuka ni] - slightly

16. 両親 [ryoushin] - parent

17. 他の、別の [taj no, betsu no] - else

18. 何も言わずに [nani mo iwa zu ni] - without a word

19. 健康 [kenkou] - health

20. 医療の [iryou no] - medical

21. 大事な [daiji na] - important

22. 失う、なくす [ushinau, nakusu] - loose

23. 子供たち [kodomo tachi] - children

24. 小さい、少ない [chiisai, sukunai] - small

25. 幸せ [shiawase] - happiness

26. 本当に [hontouni] - really

27. 残る、とどまる [nokoru, todomaru] - remain

28. 気にする [ki ni suru] - care

29. 注ぐ [sosogu] - pour

30. 注意 [chuui] - attention

31. 瓶 [bin] - jar

32. 石 [ishi] - stone

33. 砂 [suna] - sand

34. 空の、空いている [kara no, ai te iru] - empty

35. 費やす、かける、過ごす [tsuiyasu, kakeru, sugosu] - spend

B

授業
じゅぎょう
Jugyou

A lesson

大学の学長はくらすの前に立っています。彼の前の机の上には、いくつかの箱とその他のものがあります。くらすが始

The head of the college is standing before the class. There are some boxes and other things on the table before him. When

まると、彼は大きな空の瓶を、何も言わずに大きな石で満たします。"あなたは、瓶がすでにいっぱいだと思いますか？" かいと氏は生徒たちに聞きます。daigaku no gakuchou wa kurasu no mae ni ta tte i masu. kare no mae no tsukue no ue ni wa, ikutsu ka no hako to sonota no mono ga ari masu. kurasu ga hajimaru to, kare wa ookina kara no bin wo, nani mo iwa zu ni ookina ishi de mitashi masu. "anata wa, bin ga sudeni ippai da to omoi masu ka?" kaito shi wa seito tachi ni kiki masu.

"はい、いっぱいです。" 生徒たちは同意します。そして、彼は小さな石の入ったひとつの箱を取り、それを瓶の中へ注ぎます。彼は瓶をわずかに振ります。小さな石は、もちろん、大きな石の間を埋めます。"どう思いますか？ 瓶はすでにいっぱいでしょう？" かいと氏は生徒たちに再び聞きます。"hai, ippai desu." seito tachi wa doui shi masu. soshite, kare wa chiisana ishi no hai tta hitotsu no hako wo tori, sore wo bin no naka e sosogi masu. kare wa bin wo wazuka ni furi masu. chiisana ishi wa, mochiron, ookina ishi no aida wo ume masu. "dou omoi masu ka? bin wa sudeni ippai desho u?" kaito shi wa seito tachi ni futatabi kiki masu.

"はい、そうです。今はいっぱいです。" 生徒たちは再び同意します。彼らはこの授業を楽しみ始めています。彼ら

the lesson begins he takes a big empty jar and without a word fills it up with big stones.

"Do you think the jar is already full?" Mr. Kite asks students.

"Yes, it is," agree students.

Then he takes a box with very small stones and pours them into the jar. He shakes the jar slightly. The little stones, of course, fill up the room between the big stones.

"What do you think now? The jar is already full, isn't it?" Mr. Kite asks them again.

"Yes, it is. It is full now," the students agree again. They begin to enjoy this lesson. They begin to laugh.

は、笑い始めます。その後、かいと氏は砂の入った箱を取り、瓶の中に注ぎます。もちろん、砂は隙間を埋めます。"hai, sou desu. ima wa ippai desu." seito tachi wa futatabi doui shi masu. karera wa kono jugyou wo tanoshimi hajime te i masu. karera wa, warai hajime mashi ta. sonogo, kaito shi wa suna no hai tta hako wo tori, bin no naka ni sosogi masu. mochiron, suna wa sukima wo ume masu.

"では、この瓶を、人の人生のように思ってください。大きな石は大事なものたちです。-あなたたちの家族、彼女・彼氏、健康、子供、両親-もしあなたが全てを失っても、それらが残っていれば、あなたの人生はそれでも満たされたものになります。小さな石は、その他のもう少し大事ではないものたちです。あなたの家、仕事、車などです。砂はその他全てです。- 小さなものたちです。もしあなたが砂を最初に瓶に入れてしまえば、小さな石や、大きな石の入る余地はなくなります。

同じことが、人生でも言えます。もしあなたが全ての時間とえねるぎーを小さなこと

Then Mr. Kite takes a box of sand and pours it into the jar. Of course, the sand fills up all the other room.

"Now I want that you to think about this jar like a man's life. The big stones are important things - your family, your girlfriend and boyfriend, your health, your children, your parents - things that if you loose everything and only they remain, your life still will be full. Little stones are other things which are less important. They are things like your house, your job, your car. Sand is everything else - small stuff. If you put sand in the jar at first, there will be no room for little or big stones. The same goes for life. If you spend all of your time and energy on the small stuff, you will never

に使えば、自分にとって大事なことへの機会を、あなたは決して持つことができないでしょう。自分の幸せにとって、最も大事なことに、注意してください。子供や両親と遊びましょう。健康診断に時間を使いましょう。ぼーいふれんどやがーるふれんどをかふぇに連れて行きましょう。仕事にいったり、家の掃除をしたり、そしててれびを見たりする時間はいつでもあります。"かいと氏は言います。"先に大きな石を大事にしましょう。

"deha, kono bin wo, hito no jinsei no you ni omo tte kudasai. ookina ishi wa daiji na mono tachi desu. - anata tachi no kazoku, kanojo. kareshi, kenkou, kodomo, ryoushin - moshi anata ga subete wo ushina tte mo, sorera ga noko tte ire ba, anata no jinsei wa soredemo mitasa re ta mono ni nari masu. chiisana ishi wa, sonota no mousukoshi daiji de wa nai mono tachi desu. anata no ie, shigoto, kuruma nado desu. suna wa sonota subete desu. - chiisana mono tachi desu. moshi anata ga suna wo saisho ni bin ni ire te shimae ba, chiisana ishi ya, ookina ishi no hairu yochi wa nakunari masu. onaji koto ga, jinsei de mo ie masu. moshi anata ga subete no jikan to enerugi—wo chiisana koto ni tsukae ba, jibun nitotte daiji na koto e no kikai wo, anata wa kesshite motsu koto ga deki nai desho u. jibun no shiawase nitotte, mottomo daiji na koto ni, chuui shi te kudasai. kodomo ya ryoushin to asobi masho u. kenkou shindan ni jikan wo tsukai masho u. bo—ifurendo ya ga—rufurendo wo kafe ni tsure te iki masho u. shigoto ni i ttari, ie

have room for things that are important to you. Pay attention to things that are most important to your happiness. Play with your children or parents. Take time to get medical tests. Take your girlfriend or boyfriend to a café. There will be always time to go to work, clean the house and watch television," Mr. Kite says, "Take care of the big stones first - things that are really important.

no souji wo shi tari, soshite terebi wo mi tari suru jikan wa itsu demo ari masu." kaito shi wa ii masu. " saki ni ookina ishi wo daiji ni shi masho u.

とても大事なことや、ものです。その他は全てただの砂です。" 彼は生徒たちを見ます。"じゃあ、ろばーととでいびっど、君たちにとっては、何がもっと大事ですかーとらっくを洗うこと、それとも君たちの命ですか？君たちはとらっくが洗いたくて、それでとらっくで船のように海に浮かぶ。君たちは、他には洗う方法がないと思いますか？" totemo daiji na koto ya, mono desu. sonota wa subete tada no suna desu." kare wa seito tachi wo mi masu. "jaa, roba―to to deibiddo, kimitachi nitotte wa, nani ga motto daiji desu ka - torakku wo arau koto, soretomo kimitachi no inochi desu ka? kimitachi wa torakku ga arai taku te, sorede torakku de fune no you ni umi ni ukabu. kimitachi wa, hoka ni wa arau houhou ga nai to omoi masu ka?"

"いいえ、そうは思いません。" でいびっどが言います。"洗車場で、とらっくを洗えますよね？" かいと氏は言います。"はい、そうですね。" 生徒たちが言います。"何かをする前に、考えなければいけません。大きな石をいつも大事にしなければなりません。そうですよね？ "はい、そうですね。" 生徒たちがこたえます。"iie, sou wa omoi mase

Everything else is just sand," he looks at the students, "Now Robert and David, what is more important to you - washing a truck or your lives? You float on a truck in the sea like on a ship just because you wanted to wash the truck. Do you think there is no other way to wash it?"

"No, we do not think so," David says.

"You can wash a truck in a washing station instead, can't you?" says Mr. Kite.

"Yes, we can," say the students.

"You must always think before you do something. You must always take care of the big stones, right?"

n." deibiddo ga ii masu. "sensha jou de, torakku wo arae masu yo ne?" kaito shi wa ii masu. "hai, sou desu ne." seito tachi ga ii masu. "nani ka wo suru mae ni, kangae nakere ba ike mase n. ookina ishi wo itsumo daiji ni shi nakere ba nari mase n. sou desu yo ne? "hai, sou desu ne." seito tachi ga kotae masu.

"Yes, we must," answer the students.

22

Audio

ポールは出版社で働きます
（ぽ　る　しゅっぱんしゃ　はたら）

Paul works at a publishing house

A

単語
Words

1. ３０ [san juu] - thirty
2. お客さん、カスタマー [okyaku san, kasutamaー] - customer
3. コーディネーション [koーdineーshon] - co-ordination
4. スキル、腕前 [sukiru, udemae] - skill
5. ストーリー、物語、話 [sutoーriー, monogatari, hanashi] - story
6. できるだけ頻繁に [dekirudake hinpan ni] - as often as possible
7. ない、何も [nai, nani mo] - nothing
8. なぜなら、から [nazenara, kara] - since, as
9. など、等 [nado, tou] - etc.
10. ピーという音 [piー toiu oto] - beep
11. やあ、こんにちは [yaa, konnichiwa] - hi

12. ルール、規則 [ru—ru, kisoku] - rule
13. 世界 [sekai] - world
14. 人間 [ningen] - human
15. 会社 [kaisha] - company
16. 作る、構成する、文章を作る [tsukuru, kousei suru, bunshou wo tsukuru] - compose
17. 冷たい [tsumetai] - cold *(adj)*
18. 冷たさ [tsumeta sa] - coldness
19. 創造的な [souzou teki na] - creative
20. 可能である [kanou de aru] - possible
21. 売る [uru] - sell
22. 外で [soto de] - outdoors
23. 将来 [shourai] - future
24. 少なくとも [sukunakutomo] - at least
25. 得る、着く、なる [eru, tsuku, naru] - get
26. 悲しい [kanashii] - sad
27. 文章、原稿、コンポジション（文章構成法）[bunshou, genkou, konpojishon（bunshou kousei hou）] - composition
28. 断る、拒否する [kotowaru, kyohi suru] - refuse
29. 新聞、新聞社 [shinbun, shinbun sha] - newspaper
30. 暗い、黒い [kurai, kuroi] - dark
31. 本文、文章、原稿、メッセージ [honbun, bunshou, genkou, messe—ji] - text

32. 歩いている [arui te iru] - walking
33. 特に [tokuni] - especially
34. 生産する、作る [seisan suru, tsukuru] - produce
35. 用意できている、準備できている [youi deki te iru, junbi deki te iru] - ready
36. 留守番電話 [rusuban denwa] - answering machine
37. 異なる、違う [kotonaru, chigau] - different
38. 眠っている [nemu tte iru] - sleeping
39. 職業 [shokugyou] - profession
40. 記録 [kiroku] - record
41. 話す、喋る [hanasu, shaberu] - talk
42. 誰も、一人も〜ない [dare mo, hitori mo 〜 nai] - nobody
43. 遊んでいる、プレイしている [ason de iru, purei shi te iru] - playing
44. 開発する、育てる [kaihatsu suru, sodateru] - develop
45. 階段（複数）[kaidan（fukusuu）] - stairs
46. 雑誌 [zasshi] - magazine
47. 難しい、困難な [muzukashii, konnan na] - difficult
48. 雨 [ame] - rain
49. 電話をかける、呼ぶ [denwa wo kakeru, yobu] - call
50. 面白い [omoshiroi] - funny
51. 鼻 [hana] - nose

B

ポールは出版社で働きます

po―ru wa shuppan sha de hataraki masu

Paul works at a publishing house

ぽーるは若い助手として、出版社おーるらうんどで働いています。彼はものを書く仕事をしています。po―ru wa wakai joshu toshite, shuppan sha o―ruraundo de hatarai te i masu. kare wa mono wo kaku shigoto wo shi te i masu.

Paul works as a young helper at the publishing house All-round. He does writing work.

"ぽーる、私たちの会社の名前はおーるらうんどです。"社長のふぉっくす氏が言います。"そして、これはどんな文章構成やでざいんわーくも、どんなお客さんにもできるという意味です。わたしたちは、新聞社、雑誌、そしてその他のお客さんから数多くの依頼を受けます。全ての依頼は異なるものですが、わたしたちはどれも断りません。" "po―ru, watashi tachi no kaisha no namae wa o―ruraundo desu." shachou no fokkusu shi ga ii masu. "soshite, kore wa donna bunshou kousei ya dezain wa―ku mo, donna okyaku san ni mo dekiru toiu imi desu. watashi tachi wa, shinbun sha, zasshi, soshite sonota no okyaku san kara kazu ooku no irai wo uke masu. subete no irai wa kotonaru mono desu ga, watashi tachi wa dore mo kotowari mase n."

"Paul, our firm's name is All-round," the head of the firm Mr. Fox says, "And this means we can do any text composition and design work for any customer. We get many orders from newspapers, magazines and from other customers. All of the orders are different but we never refuse any."

ぽーるは、創造的なすきるを育てることができるので、この仕事がとても好きです。彼は、文章

Paul likes this job a lot because he can develop creative skills. He enjoys

やでざいんを書いたりする創造的な仕事を楽しんでいます。彼は大学ででざいんを勉強しているので、これは彼の将来の職業に、とてもふさわしい仕事です。po—ru wa, souzou teki na sukiru wo sodateru koto ga dekiru node, kono shigoto ga totemo suki desu. kare wa, bunshou ya dezain wo kai tari suru souzou teki na shigoto wo tanoshin de i masu. kare wa daigaku de dezain wo benkyou shi te iru node, kore wa kare no shourai no shokugyou ni, totemo fusawashii shigoto desu.

creative works like writing compositions and design. Since he studies design at college it is a very suitable job for his future profession.

ふぉっくす氏は今日、彼に新しい課題があります。fokkusu shi wa kyou, kare ni atarashii kadai ga ari masu.

Mr. Fox has some new tasks for him today.

"わたしたちには、依頼がいくつかあります。あなたには、その内の2つができます。"ふぉっくす氏が言います。"最初の依頼は電話会社からです。彼らは留守番電話をつくっています。彼らは、留守番電話に使う、面白いめっせーじを必要としています。面白いもの以上によく売れるものはありません。4つか5つめっせーじをつくってください。お願いします。" "watashi tachi ni wa, irai ga ikutsu ka ari masu. anata ni wa, sono uchi no futatsu ga deki masu." fokkusu shi ga ii masu. "saisho no irai wa denwa gaisha kara desu. karera wa rusuban denwa wo tsuku tte i masu. karera wa, rusuban denwa ni tsukau, omoshiroi messe—ji wo hitsuyou to shi te i masu. omoshiroi mo no ijou ni yoku ureru mono wa ari mase n. yottsu ka itsutsu messe—ji wo tsuku tte kudasai. onegai shi masu."

"We have some orders. You can do two of them," Mr. Fox says, "The first order is from a telephone company. They produce telephones with answering machines. They need some funny texts for answering machines. Nothing sells better than funny things. Compose four or five texts, please."

"どれくらいの長さでないといけませんか?"ぽーるが

"How long must they

質問します。"5から30語です。"ふぉっくす氏がこたえます。"そして、2つ目の依頼は、雑誌の"ぐりーんわーるど"からです。この雑誌は動物、鳥、魚などについて書いています。彼らはどんなぺっとに関してでもいいので、原稿を必要としています。面白いものでも、悲しいものでも、又はあなたのぺっとに関しての話でもいいです。動物を飼っていますか？" "dore kurai no naga sa de nai to ike mase n ka?" po―ru ga shitsumon shi masu. "go kara san juu go desu." fokkusu shi ga kotae masu. "soshite, futatsu me no irai wa, zasshi no "guri―n wa―rudo" kara desu. kono zasshi wa doubutsu, tori, sakana nado nitsuite kai te i masu. karera wa donna petto nikanshite demo ii node, genkou wo hitsuyou to shi te i masu. omoshiroi mono de mo, kanashii mono de mo, matawa anata no petto nikanshite no hanashi de mo ii desu. doubutsu wo ka tte i masu ka?"

"はい。ねこを飼っています。名前はふぇいばりっとです。"ぽーるはこたえます。"それから、ぼくはふぇいばりっとのとりっくについての話がかけると思います。いつまでに用意しなければなりませんか？" "この2つの依頼は明日までに用意しなければなりません。"ふぉっくす氏がこたえます。"わかりました。今から始めていいですか？"ぽーるがたずねます。

"はい、ぽーる。"ふぉっくす氏が言います。"hai. neko wo ka tte i masu. namae wa feibaritto desu." po―ru wa kotae masu. "sorekara, boku wa feibaritto no torikku nitsuite no hanashi ga kakeru to omoi masu. itsu made ni youi shi

be?" Paul asks.

"They can be from five to thirty words," Mr. Fox answers, "And the second order is from the magazine "Green world". This magazine writes about animals, birds, fish etc. They need a text about any home animal. It can be funny or sad, or just a story about your own animal. Do you have an animal?"

"Yes, I do. I have a cat. Its name is Favorite," Paul answers, "And I think I can write a story about its tricks. When must it be ready?"

"These two orders must be ready by tomorrow," Mr. Fox answers.

"Okay. May I begin now?" Paul asks.

nakere ba nari mase n ka?" "kono futatsu no irai wa ashita made ni youi shi nakere ba nari mase n." fokkusu shi ga kotae masu. "wakari mashi ta. ima kara hajimete ii desu ka?" poーru ga tazune masu. "hai, poーru." fokkusu shi ga ii masu.

"Yes, Paul," Mr. Fox says.

ぽーるは次の日原稿を持ってきます。彼は、るすばんでんわよう留守番電話用に、5つのめっせーじがあります。ふぉっくす氏がそれらを読みます。：1."もしもし。じゃあ何かいってね。" 2."もしもし。留守番電話です。あなたは？" poーru wa tsugi no hi genkou wo mo tte ki masu. kare wa, rusuban denwa you ni, itsutsu no messeーji ga ari masu. fokkusu shi ga sorera wo yomi masu. : ichi. " moshimoshi. jaa nani ka i tte ne. " ni. " moshimoshi. rusuban denwa desu. anata wa?"

Paul brings those texts the next day. He has five texts for the answering machines. Mr. Fox reads them:

1. "Hi. Now you say something."

2. "Hello. I am an answering machine. And what are you?"

3."もしもし。今はわたしの留守電以外に誰も家にはいないの。だからわたしの代わりに、留守電と話してね。ぴーという音が鳴るのを待ってね。" 4."これは留守電ではありません。これは考え記録器です。ぴーという音の後に、あなたの名前と電話した理由、それからわたしがかけ直せる電話番号について考えてくださいね。それから、あなたにかけ直すことについてわたしは考えます。"
san." moshimoshi. ima wa watashi no rusuden igai ni dare mo ie ni wa i nai no. dakara watashi no kawari ni, rusuden to hanashi te ne. piー toiu oto ga naru no wo ma tte ne." yon." kore wa rusuden de wa ari mase n. kore wa kangae kiroku ki desu. piー toiu oto no ato ni, anata no namae to denwa shi ta riyuu, sorekara watashi ga kake naoseru denwa bangou nitsuite kangae te kudasai ne. sorekara, anata nikake naosu koto ni tsuite watashi wa kangae masu."

3. "Hi. Nobody is at home now but my answering machine is. So you can talk to it instead of me. Wait for the beep."

4. "This is not an answering machine. This is a thought-recording machine. After the beep, think about your name, your reason for calling and a number which I can call you back. And I will think about calling

5."ぴーという音の後に話してね！あなたには、黙る権利もあるよ。あなたが言うことの全てを記録して使わせてもらうのよ。" "悪くないね。動物については？" ふぉっくす氏が聞きます。ぽーるは彼に別の紙を渡します。ふぉっくす氏が読みます： go." pi─ toiu oto no ato ni hanashi te ne! anata ni wa, damaru kenri mo aru yo. anata ga iu koto no subete wo kiroku shi te tsukawa se te morau no yo." "waruku nai ne. doubutsu nitsuite wa?" fokkusu shi ga kiki masu. po─ru wa kare ni betsu no kami wo watashi masu. fokkusu shi ga yomi masu :

猫のルール

neko no ru─ru

歩くとき：できる限り頻繁に、素早く、そして人間の前では、特に：階段の上、彼らが手に何かを持っているとき、暗闇の中、そして彼らが朝起きるときには、できる限り彼らの近くを走りましょう。これで彼らのこーでぃねーしょんが鍛えられます。 aruku toki : dekiru kagiri hinpan ni, subayaku, soshite ningen no mae dewa, tokuni : kaidan no ue, karera ga te ni nani ka wo mo tte iru toki, kurayami no naka, soshite karera ga asa okiru toki ni wa, dekiru kagiri karera no chikaku wo hashirimashou. kore de karera no ko─dine─shon ga kitae rare masu.

べっどの中では：夜は必ず人間の上で寝ましょう。そうすれば、彼又は彼女はべっどの

you back."

5. "Speak after the beep! You have the right to be silent. I will record and use everything you say."

"It is not bad. And what about animals?" Mr. Fox asks. Paul gives him another sheet of paper. Mr. Fox reads:

Some rules for cats

Walking:

As often as possible, run quickly and as close as possible in front of a human, especially: on stairs, when they have something on their hands, in the dark, and when they get up in the morning. This will train their co-ordination.

In bed:

Always sleep on a human

中で寝返りをうてません。彼又は彼女の顔の上にねっころがるようにしてみましょう。あなたのしっぽが、彼又は彼女の鼻の上、ぴったりにあることを確認しましょう。beddo no naka de wa : yoru wa kanarazu ningen no ue de ne masho u. sou sure ba, kare matawa kanojo wa beddo no naka de negaeri wo ute mase n. kare matawa kanojo no kao no ue ni nekkorogaru you ni shi te mi masho u. anata no shippo ga, kare matawa kanojo no hana no ue, pittari ni aru koto wo kakunin shi masho u.

at night. So he or she cannot turn in the bed. Try to lie on his or her face. Make sure that your tail is right on their nose.

寝るとき： 遊ぶときにえねるぎーをたくさん持つためには、猫はたくさん（最低毎日１６時間）寝なければなりません。眠るのにふさわしい場所をみつけるのは大変ではありません。人間が座るのが好きな場所であればどこでも良いのです。外にも良い場所はあります。でも雨や、寒いときには使うことができません。その代わりに、開いた窓が使えます。neru toki : asobu toki ni enerugi— wo takusan motsu tame ni wa, neko wa takusan (saitei mainichi juu roku jikan) ne nakere ba nari mase n. nemuru noni fusawashii basho wo mitsukeru no wa taihen de wa ari mase n. ningen ga suwaru no ga suki na basho de are ba doko demo yoi no desu. soto ni mo yoi basho wa ari masu. demo ame ya, samui toki ni ha tsukau koto ga deki mase n. sono kawari ni, hirai ta mado ga tsukae masu.

Sleeping:

To have a lot of energy for playing, a cat must sleep a lot (at least 16 hours per day). It is not difficult to find a suitable place to sleep. Any place where a human likes to sit is good. There are good places outdoors too. But you cannot use them when it rains or when it is cold. You can use open windows instead.

ふぉっくす氏は笑います。"よくやった、ぽーる！雑誌"ぐりーんわーるど"は君の原稿を気に入ってくれると思いますよ。"彼は言います。fokkusu shi

Mr. Fox laughs.

"Good work, Paul! I think the magazine "Green world" will like your wa warai masu. "yoku ya tta, po—ru! zasshi "guri—n wa—rudo" wa kimi no genkou wo kinii tte kureru to omoi masu yo." kare wa ii masu.

composition," he says.

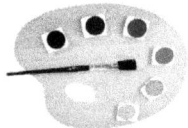

23

Audio

猫 のルール
Cat rules

A

単語
Words

1. おいしい [oishii] - tasty
2. お皿 [o sara] - plate
3. かくれんぼ [kakurenbo] - hide-and-seek
4. キーボード [kiーboーdo] - keyboard
5. キス [kisu] - kiss
6. ゲスト [gesuto] - guest
7. けれども、しかしながら [keredomo, shikashinagara] - although
8. こする [kosuru] - rub
9. こっそり手に入れる、取る、盗む [kossori te ni ireru, toru, nusumu] - steal
10. チャンス、確率 [chansu, kakuritsu] - chance
11. トイレ [toire] - toilet

12. ときどき、たまに [tokidoki, tamani] - sometimes
13. パニック；パニックするために [panikku ; panikku suru tame ni] - panic; to panic
14. ふりをする [furi wo suru] - pretend
15. 何でも [nani demo] - anything
16. 噛む [kamu] - bite
17. 天気 [tenki] - weather
18. 子供 [kodomo] - child
19. 季節 [kisetsu] - season
20. 学校 [gakkou] - school
21. 宿題 [shukudai] - homework
22. 少ない；いくつかの少ない [sukunai ; ikutsu ka no sukunai] - few; a few
23. 後ろ、あと [ushiro, ato] - behind
24. 得る、着く、なる [eru, tsuku, naru] - get
25. 忘れる [wasureru] - forget
26. 惑星 [wakusei] - planet
27. 愛 [ai] - love
28. 愛するために [aisuru tame ni] - to love
29. 料理をする [ryouri wo suru] - cooking
30. 楽しい [tanoshii] - fun
31. 秘密 [himitsu] - secret
32. 考えている [kangae te iru] - thinking
33. 蚊 [ka] - mosquito
34. 読んでいる [yon de iru] - reading
35. 謎、ミステリー [nazo, misuterī] - mystery
36. 走り去る、逃げる [hashirisaru, nigeru] - run away
37. 足 [ashi] - leg
38. 踏む；踏むために [fumu ; fumu tame ni] - step; to step
39. 隠れる [kakureru] - hide

B

猫のルール
neko no ru─ru

"雑誌 "ぐりーんわーるど" が 新しい依頼をしてきます。" 翌日、ふぉっくす氏はぽーるに言います。"そしてこれは 君への

Cat rules

"The magazine "Green world" places a new order," Mr. Fox says to Paul next day, "And this order is for you, Paul. They like

依頼ですよ、ぽーる。彼らは君の文章が気に入って、猫のるーるについてもっと大きな文章を欲しがっています。" この原稿を作るのに、ぽーるは２日間かかりました。これです。 "zasshi "guri—n wa—rudo" ga atarashii irai wo shi te ki masu." yokujitsu, fokkusu shi wa po—ru ni ii masu. "soshite kore wa kimi e no irai desu yo, po—ru. karera wa kimi no bunshou ga kinii tte, neko no ru—ru nitsuite motto ookina bunshou wo hoshi ga tte i masu." kono genkou wo tsukuru noni, po—ru wa futsuka kan kakari mashi ta. kore desu.

猫の秘密のルール

neko no himitsu no ru—ru

猫は一番であり、この惑星の中で最も素晴らしい動物ではありますが、彼らはとてもおかしなことをときどきやります。人間の内の一人が、何とかして猫の秘密をこっそり手に入れました。世界を支配するための人生のるーるです！しかし、これらのるーるがどう猫のためになるのかは、人間にとって全くの謎です。 neko wa ichiban de ari, kono wakusei no naka de mottomo subarashii doubutsu de wa ari masu ga, karera wa totemo okashina koto wo tokidoki yari masu. ningen no uchi no hitori ga, nan toka shi te neko no himitsu wo

your composition and they want a bigger text about "Cat rules".

It takes Paul two days to compose this text. Here it is.

Some secret rules for cats

Although cats are the best and the most wonderful animals on this planet, they sometimes do very strange things. One of the humans managed to steal some cat secrets. They are some rules of life in order to take over the world! But how these rules will help cats is still a total mystery to the humans.

kossori te ni ire mashi ta. sekai wo shihai suru tame no jinsei no ru―ru desu! shikashi, korera no ru―ru ga dou neko no tame ni naru no ka wa, ningen nitotte mattaku no nazo desu.

お手洗い：お手洗いとといれへは、いつもげすとと一緒に行きましょう。何もする必要はありません。ただ座って、見つめて、たまに彼らの足をこするのです。o tearai : o tearai to toire e wa, itsumo gesuto to issho ni iki masho u. nani mo suru hitsuyou wa ari mase n. tada suwa tte, mitsume te, tamani karera no ashi wo kosuru no desu.

どあ：全てのどあは開いていなければいけません。どあを開けるためには、たちあがり、悲しそうに人間をみつめましょう。彼らがどあを開けるときに通り抜ける必要はありません。この方法で外のどあを開けた後に、どあに立って何かについて考えましょう。特に、天気がとても寒い時、又は雨の時、そして蚊の季節の時に、これは大事です。doa : subete no doa wa hirai te i nakere ba ike mase n. doa wo akeru tame ni wa, tachiagari, kanashi sou ni ningen wo mitsume masho u. karera ga doa wo akeru toki ni toorinukeru hitsuyou wa ari mase n. kono houhou de soto no doa wo ake ta nochi ni, doa ni ta tte nani ka nitsuite kangae masho u. tokuni, tenki ga totemo samui toki, matawa ame no toki, soshite ka no kisetsu no toki ni, kore wa daiji desu.

料理をするとき：料理をしている人間

Bathrooms:

Always go with guests to the bathroom and to the toilet. You do not need to do anything. Just sit, look and sometimes rub their legs.

Doors:

All doors must be open. To get a door opened, stand looking sad at humans. When they open a door, you need not go through it. After you open in this way the outside door, stand in the door and think about something. This is especially important when the weather is very cold, or when it is a rainy day, or when it is the mosquito season.

Cooking:

Always sit just behind the right foot of cooking humans. So

の右足の後ろにだけ、いつも座りましょう。そうすれば、彼らはあなたのことをみることができず、彼らがあなたを踏むちゃんすが高まります。それが起きると、彼らはあなたを手にとり、何か美味しいものをくれるでしょう。ryouri wo suru toki : ryouri wo shi te iru ningen no migiashi no ushiro ni dake, itsumo suwari masho u. sou sure ba, karera wa anata no koto wo miru koto ga deki zu, karera ga anata wo fumu chansu ga takamari masu. sore ga okiru to, karera wa anata wo te nitori, nani ka oishii mono wo kureru desho u.

they cannot see you and you have a better chance that a human steps on you. When it happens, they take you in their hands and give something tasty to eat.

本を読むとき：読んでいる人間の顔に近づいてみてください。目と本の間です。本の上に寝そべるのが一番いい方法です。hon wo yomu toki : yon de iru ningen no kao ni chikazui te mi te kudasai. me to hon no aida desu. hon no ue ni nesoberu no ga ichiban ii houhou desu.

Reading books:

Try to get closer to the face of a reading human, between eyes and the book. The best is to lie on the book.

子供の宿題：本やのーとの上に寝そべって、眠っているふりをしましょう。時折ぺんの上に飛び乗りましょう。子供があなたを机からどかそうとしたら、噛みましょう。kodomo no shukudai : hon ya no—to no ue ni nesobe tte, nemu tte iru furi wo shi masho u. tokiori pen no ue ni tobi nori masho u. kodomo ga anata wo tsukue kara dokaso u to shi tara, kami masho u.

Children's school homework:

Lie on books and copy-books and pretend to sleep. But from time to time jump on the pen. Bite if a child tries to take you away from the table.

こんぴゅーたー：もし人間がこんぴゅーたーで働いていたら、机の上にじゃんぷして

Computer:

If a human works with a computer, jump up on the desk

きーぼーどの上を歩きましょう。konpyu—ta—: moshi ningen ga konpyu—ta— de hatarai te i tara, tsukue no ue ni janpu shi te ki—bo—do no ue wo aruki masho u.

食べ物：猫はたくさん食べる必要があります。しかし食べることは楽しみのうちの半分にすぎません。残りの半分は、食べ物を手に入れることです。人間が食べるときに、彼らが見てない間に、あなたのしっぽを彼らのお皿にのせましょう。これで、お皿の食べ物を全部手に入れるちゃんすが高まります。てーぶるから食べ物がとれるのであれば、自分のお皿からは決して食べないでください。人間のこっぷから飲めるのであれば、自分の水のお皿からは決して飲まないでください。tabemono : neko wa takusan taberu hitsuyou ga ari masu. shikashi taberu koto wa tanoshimi no uchi no hanbun ni sugi mase n. nokori no hanbun wa, tabemono wo te ni ireru koto desu. ningen ga taberu toki ni, karera ga mi te nai aida ni, anata no shippo wo karera no o sara ni nose masho u. kore de, o sara no tabemono wo zenbu te ni ireru chansu ga takamari masu. te—buru kara tabemono ga toreru no de are ba, jibun no o sara kara wa kesshite tabe nai de kudasai. ningen no koppu kara nomeru no de are ba, jibun no mizu no o sara kara wa kesshite noma nai de kudasai.

隠れるとき：人間が数日間あなたを

and walk over the keyboard.

Food:

Cats need to eat a lot. But eating is only half of the fun. The other half is getting the food. When humans eat, put your tail in their plate when they do not look. It will give you a better chance to get a full plate of food. Never eat from your own plate if you can take some food from the table. Never drink from your own water plate if you can drink from a human's cup.

Hiding:

Hide in places where humans

みつけられない場所に隠れましょう。これは、人間にあなたが逃げ出したと思わせ、ぱにっくにさせます（彼らはぱにっくが大好き）。隠れ場所から出てくるときには、人間はあなたにきすをして、彼らの愛をみせるでしょう。そして、何かおいしいものをもらえるかもしれません。kakureru toki : ningen ga suu jitsu kan anata wo mitsuke rare nai basho ni kakure masho u. kore wa, ningen ni anata ga nigedashi ta to omowa se, panikku ni sa se masu （karera ha panikku ga daisuki）. kakure basho kara de te kuru toki ni wa, ningen wa anata ni kisu wo shi te, karera no ai wo miseru desho u. soshite, nani ka oishii mono wo moraeru kamo shire mase n.

cannot find you for a few days. This will make humans panic (which they love) thinking that you ran away. When you come out of the hiding place, the humans will kiss you and show their love. And you may get something tasty.

人間：人間の仕事とは、わたしたちにえさをあたえること、わたしたちと遊ぶこと、そしてわたしたちの小屋を掃除することです。彼らが、家の主を誰だか忘れないでいるのは大事なことです。ningen : ningen no shigoto to wa, watashi tachi ni esa wo ataeru koto, watashi tachi to asobu koto, soshite watashi tachi no koya wo souji suru koto desu. karera ga, ie no aruji wo dare da ka wasure nai de iru no wa daiji na koto desu.

Humans:

Tasks of humans are to feed us, to play with us, and to clean our box. It is important that they do not forget who the head of the house is.

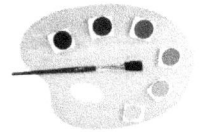

24

Audio

チームワーク
(ち　む わ　く)

Teamwork

A

単語

Words

1. 1000 [sen] - thousand
2. １０億 [juu oku] - billion
3. TV セット [tiー bui setto] - TV-set
4. あった [a tta] - had
5. あなたがたのどちらか [anata ga ta no dochira ka] - either of you
6. エイリアン [eirian] - alien
7. キャプテン [kyaputen] - captain
8. 連続ドラマ（読み方）[renzoku dorama（yomikata）] - serial
9. すぐに [suguni] - soon
10. ダンスした, 踊った [dansu shi ta, odo tta] - danced
11. ダンスしている [dansu shi te iru] - dancing
12. ダンスする、踊る [dansu suru, odoru] - dance

13. つけた [tsuke ta] - switched on
14. とめた、やめた、終えた [tome ta, yame ta, oe ta] - stopped
15. に対して [nitaishite] - against
16. はじめた [hajime ta] - began
17. まで [made] - until
18. みた [mi ta] - looked
19. ラジオ、無線 [rajio, musen] - radio
20. レーザー [re—za—] - laser
21. レーダー [re—da—] - radar
22. 中心の、真ん中の [chuushin no, mannaka no] - central
23. 動いた、動かした [ugoi ta, ugokashi ta] - moved
24. 動いている、働いている [ugoi te iru, hatarai te iru] - working
25. 去った、いなくなった [sa tta, i naku na tta] - went away
26. 同僚 [douryou] - colleague
27. 向ける [mukeru] - pointed
28. 地球 [chikyuu] - earth
29. 宇宙、スペース [uchuu, supe—su] - space
30. 宇宙船 [uchuusen] - spaceship
31. 庭 [niwa] - garden
32. 思い出した、覚えていた [omoidashi ta, oboe te i ta] - remembered
33. 愛した [aishi ta] - loved
34. 戦争 [sensou] - war
35. 振った [fu tta] - shook

36. 教える [oshieru] - teach
37. 来た、行った [ki ta, okona tta] - came
38. 死ぬ、亡くなる [shinu, nakunaru] - die
39. 死んだ、亡くなった [shin da, nakuna tta] - died
40. 殺した [koroshi ta] - killed
41. 知っていた、知った [shi tte i ta, shi tta] - knew
42. 知らせた [shirase ta] - informed
43. 短い [mijikai] - short
44. 破壊する、壊す [hakai suru, kowasu] - destroy
45. 積極的に参加する [sekkyoku teki ni sanka suru] - take part
46. 笑った、微笑んだ [wara tta, hohoen da] - smiled
47. 終わった、終えた [owa tta, oe ta] - finished
48. 続ける [tsuzukeru] - continue
49. 美しい、綺麗な [utsukushii, kirei na] - beautiful
50. 聞いた [kii ta] - heard
51. 花 [hana] - flower
52. 落ちた [ochi ta] - fell
53. 落ちる [ochiru] - fall
54. 見続ける [mi tsuzukeru] - continued to watch
55. 言った、発言した [i tta, hatsugen shi ta] - said
56. 飛び去った [tobi sa tta] - flew away

B

チームワーク
ちーむわーく

chi—muwa—ku

でいびっどはじゃーなりすとになりたいです。今日、彼は大学でこんぽじしょんの授業があります。かいと氏は生徒たちにこんぽじしょんの書き方を教えます。deibiddo wa ja—narisuto ni nari tai desu. kyou, kare wa daigaku de konpojishon no jugyou ga ari masu. kaito shi wa seito tachi ni konpojishon no kakikata wo oshie masu.

"親愛なる諸君"彼は言います。"君たちのうち何人かは、出版社、新聞社又は雑誌、らじお又はてれび局で働くでしょう。これは、ちーむで働くという意味です。ちーむで働くのは簡単ではありません。今から、君たちにじゃーなりすとこんぽじしょんを、ちーむで作ってみて欲しいのです。わたしは、男の子がひとりと女の子がひとり、必要です。" "shinai naru shokun" kare wa ii masu. "kimitachi no uchi nan nin ka wa, shuppan sha, shinbun sha matawa zasshi, rajio matawa terebikyoku de hataraku desho u. kore wa, chi—mu de hataraku toiu imi desu. chi—mu de hataraku no wa kantan de wa ari mase n. ima kara, kimitachi ni ja—narisuto konpojishon wo, chi—mu de tsuku tte mi te hoshii no desu. watashi wa, otokonoko

Teamwork

David wants to be a journalist. He studies at a college. He has a composition lesson today. Mr. Kite teaches students to write composition.

"Dear friends," he says, "some of you will work for publishing houses, newspapers or magazines, the radio or television. This means you will work in a team. Working in a team is not simple. Now I want that you try to make a journalistic composition in a team. I need a boy and a girl."

ga hitori to onnanoko ga hitori, hitsuyou desu."

たくさんの生徒たちがちーむわーくに積極的に参加したがります。かいと氏はでいびっどときゃろるを選びます。きゃろるはすぺいん出身ですが、彼女は英語をとても上手に話すことができます。takusan no seito tachi ga chi—muwa—ku ni sekkyoku teki ni sanka shi ta gari masu. kaito shi wa deibiddo to kyaroru wo erabi masu. kyaroru wa supein shusshin desu ga, kanojo wa eigo wo totemo jouzu ni hanasu koto ga deki masu.

Many students want to take part in the team work. Mr. Kite chooses David and Carol. Carol is from Spain but she can speak English very well.

"机に座ってください。それでは、君たちは同僚です。"かいと氏が彼らに言います。"tsukue ni suwa tte kudasai. soredewa, kimitachi wa douryou desu." kaito shi ga karera ni ii masu.

"Please, sit at this table. Now you are colleagues," Mr. Kite says to them,

"君たちは短いこんぽじしょんを書くのです。君たちのどちらかがこんぽじしょんを始め、そして同僚に渡しましょう。君の同僚は、こんぽじしょんを読んで続けるのです。その後同僚は、こんぽじしょんを君に返し、最初の人がそれを読んで続けるのです。そして、あなたの順番が終わるまで続けます。わたしは、君たちに２０分を与えます。"かいと氏は彼らに紙を渡し、きゃろるが始めます。彼女は少し考え、

"You will write a short composition. Either of you will begin the composition and then give it to your colleague. Your colleague will read the composition and continue it. Then your colleague will give it back and the first one will read and continue it. And so on until your time is over. I give you twenty minutes."

Mr. Kite gives them paper and Carol begins. She thinks a little

そして書(か)きます。 "kimitachi wa mijikai konpojishon wo kaku no desu. kimitachi no dochira ka ga konpojishon wo hajime, soshite douryou ni watashi masho u. kimi no douryou wa, konpojishon wo yon de tsuzukeru no desu. sonogo douryou wa, konpojishon wo kimi ni kaeshi, saisho no hito ga sore wo yon de tsuzukeru no desu. soshite, anata no junban ga owaru made tsuzuke masu. watashi wa, kimitachi ni ni ju ppun wo atae masu." kaito shi wa karera ni kami wo watashi, kyaroru ga hajime masu. kanojo wa sukoshi kangae, soshite kaki masu.

and then writes.

チーム(ち むこんぽじしょん)コンポジション

chi一mu konpojishon

Team composition

きゃろる：じゅりあは窓(まど)の外(そと)を覗(のぞ)いていました。彼女(かのじょ)の庭(にわ)のお花(はな)は、だんすをしているかのように風(かぜ)の中(なか)を揺(ゆ)れていました。彼女(かのじょ)はびりーとだんすをしたあの夜(よる)のことを思(おも)い出しました。あれは1年前(ねんまえ)のことですが、彼女(かのじょ)は全(すべ)てを覚(おぼ)えていました。-彼(かれ)の青(あお)い目(め)、彼(かれ)の微笑(ほほえ)み、そして彼(かれ)の声(こえ)。彼女(かのじょ)にとっては幸(しあわ)せな時間(じかん)でしたが、今(いま)ではもう終(お)わってしまいました。どうして彼(かれ)は彼女(かのじょ)とは一緒(いっしょ)ではなかったのでしょう？

kyaroru : juria wa mado no soto wo nozoi te i mashi ta. kanojo no niwa no ohana wa, dansu wo shi te iru ka no you ni kaze no naka wo yure te i mashi ta. kanojo wa biri一 to dansu wo shi ta ano yoru no koto wo omoidashi mashi ta. are wa ichi nen mae no koto desu ga, kanojo wea subete wo oboe te i mashi ta. - kare no

Carol: Julia was looking through the window. The flowers in her garden were moving in the wind as if dancing. She remembered that evening when she danced with Billy.

It was a year ago but she remembered everything - his blue eyes, his smile and his voice. It was a happy time for her but it was over now. Why was not he with her?

aoi me, kare no hohoemi, soshite kare no koe. kanojo nitotte wa shiawase na jikan deshi ta ga, ima de wa mou owa tte shimai mashi ta. doushite kare wa kanojo to wa issho de wa naka tta no desho u?

でいびっど:この時、宇宙船のきゃぷてん、びりー・ぶりすくは宇宙船、ほわいとすたーにいました。彼には大事な仕事があったので、1年前に一緒にだんすをした、おばかな女の子のことについて考えている時間はありませんでした。彼はほわいとすたーのれーざーを、えいりあんの宇宙船に素早く向けました。そして彼は、無線をつけ、えいりあんへ話しかけました。"ぎぶあっぷするのに1時間を、あなたに与えます。もし1時間でぎぶあっぷしないのであれば、わたしはあなた方を破壊します。"しかし、彼が終える前にえいりあんのれーざーはほわいとさーの左えんじんに当たりました。びりーのれーざーはえいりあんの宇宙船に当たり始め、同時に彼は中央と右のえんじんもつけました。えいりあんのれーざーは動いている右えんじんを破壊し、ほわいとさーをひどく揺らしました。びりーは床に落ち、落ちている間、どのえいりあん

David: At this moment space captain Billy Brisk was at the spaceship White Star. He had an important task and he did not have time to think about that silly girl who he danced with a year ago. He quickly pointed the lasers of White Star at alien spaceships. Then he switched on the radio and talked to the aliens: "I give you an hour to give up. If in one hour you do not give up I will destroy you." But before he finished an alien laser hit the left engine of the White Star. Billy's laser began to hit alien spaceships and at the same time he switched on the central and the right engines. The alien laser destroyed the working right engine and the White Star shook badly. Billy fell on the floor thinking

の宇宙船を先に破壊しなければいけないのだろうと考えました。deibiddo : kono toki, uchuusen no kyaputen, biri―. burisuku wa uchuusen, howaitosutā ni i mashi ta. kare ni wa daiji na shigoto ga a tta node, ichi nen mae ni issho ni dansu wo shi ta, o baka na onnanoko no koto nitsuite kangae te iru jikan wa ari mase n deshi ta. kare wa howaitosutā no rēzā wo, eirian no uchuusen ni subayaku muke mashi ta. soshite kare wa, musen wo tsuke, eirian e hanashikake mashi ta. "gibuappu suru no ni ichi jikan wo, anata ni atae masu. moshi ichi jikan de gibuappu shi nai no de are ba, watashi wa anata gata wo hakai shi masu." shikashi, kare ga oeru mae ni eirian no rēzā wa howaitosutā no hidari enjin ni atari mashi ta. biri― no rēzā wa eirian no uchuusen ni atari hajime, doujini kare wa chuuou to migi no enjin mo tsuke mashi ta. eirian no rēzā wa ugoi te iru migi enjin wo hakai shi, howaitosutā wo hidoku yurashi mashi ta. biri― wa yuka ni ochi, ochi te iru aida, dono eirian no uchuusen wo saki ni hakai shi nakere ba ike nai no daro u to kangae mashi ta.

during the fall which of the alien spaceships he must destroy first.

きゃろる：しかし彼は金属の床に自分の頭をぶつけ、それと同時に死んでしまいました。しかし亡くなる前に彼は、彼のことを愛した、かわいそうで美しい女の子を思い出し、彼女から去ったことを申し訳なく思いました。kyaroru : shikashi kare wa kinzoku no yuka ni jibun no atama wo butsuke, sore to doujini shin de shimai mashi ta. shikashi nakunaru mae ni kare wa, kare no koto wo aishi ta, kawaisou de utsukushii onnanoko wo omoidashi, kanojo kara sa tta koto wo moushiwake naku omoi mashi ta.

Carol: But he hit his head on the metal floor and died at the same moment. But before he died he remembered the poor beautiful girl who loved him and he was very sorry that he went away from her.

人々は、かわいそうなえいりあんとの、このばかげた戦争をすぐに止めました。彼らは自分たちの宇宙船とれーざーを全て破壊し、えいりあんに、人間は二度と彼らに対して戦争は始めないと知らせました。人々は、えいりあんと友達になりたかったのだ、と言いました。じゅりあはそれについて聞いたとき、とても喜びました。その後、彼女はTVせっとをつけ、素晴らしいどいつ語の連続どらまを見続けました。hitobito wa, kawaisou na eirian to no, kono bakage ta sensou wo suguni yame mashi ta. karera wa jibun tachi no uchuusen to re—za— wo subete hakai shi, eirian ni, ningen wa nidoto karera nitaishite sensou wa hajime nai to shirase mashi ta. hitobito wa, eirian to tomodachi ni nari taka tta no da, to ii mashi ta. juria wa sore nitsuite kii ta toki, totemo yorokobi mashi ta. sonogo, kanojo wa ti— bui setto wo tsuke, subarashii doitsugo no renzoku dorama wo mi tsuzuke mashi ta.

でいびっど：人々は、自分たちの宇宙船とれーざーを全て破壊したので、えいりあんの宇宙船が地球のとても近くに来たことを誰も知りませんでした。何千ものえいりあんのれーざーが地球にあたり、かわいそうでおばかなじゅりあと50億の人々を、たちまち殺しました。地球は破壊され

Soon people stopped this silly war on poor aliens. They destroyed all of their own spaceships and lasers and informed the aliens that people would never start a war against them again. People said that they wanted to be friends with the aliens. Julia was very glad when she heard about it. Then she switched on the TV-set and continued to watch a wonderful German serial.

David: Because people destroyed their own radars and lasers, nobody knew that spaceships of aliens came very close to the Earth. Thousands of aliens' lasers hit the Earth and killed poor silly Julia and five billion people in a second.

<ruby>回転<rt>かいてん</rt></ruby>する<ruby>部品<rt>ぶひん</rt></ruby>が<ruby>宇宙<rt>うちゅう</rt></ruby>へ<ruby>飛<rt>と</rt></ruby>んでい
てしまい、行きました。deibiddo : hitobito wa, jibun tachi no uchuusen to re―za― wo subete hakai shi ta node, eirian no uchuusen ga chikyuu no totemo chikaku ni ki ta koto wo dare mo shiri mase n deshi ta. nan zen mo no eirian no re―za― ga chikyuu niatari, kawaisou de o baka na juria to go juu oku no hitobito wo, tachimachi koroshi mashi ta. chikyuu wa hakai sa re te shimai, kaiten suru buhin ga uchuu e ton de iki mashi ta.

"あなたたちは<ruby>時間<rt>じかん</rt></ruby><ruby>切<rt>ぎ</rt></ruby>れになる<ruby>前<rt>まえ</rt></ruby>に<ruby>終<rt>お</rt></ruby>えたみたいですね。"かいと<ruby>氏<rt>し</rt></ruby>が<ruby>微笑<rt>ほほえ</rt></ruby>みます。"anata tachi wa jikangire ni naru mae ni oe ta mitai desu ne." kaito shi ga hohoemi masu.

"ええと、<ruby>授業<rt>じゅぎょう</rt></ruby>はこれで<ruby>終了<rt>しゅうりょう</rt></ruby>です。<ruby>次<rt>つぎ</rt></ruby>の<ruby>授業<rt>じゅぎょう</rt></ruby>の<ruby>時<rt>とき</rt></ruby>に、このちーむこんぽじしょんについて<ruby>読<rt>よ</rt></ruby>んだり<ruby>話<rt>はな</rt></ruby>したりしましょう。"
"eeto, jugyou wa kore de shuuryou desu. tsugi no jugyou no toki ni, kono chi―mu konpojishon nitsuite yon dari hanashi tari shi masho u."

The Earth was destroyed and its turning parts flew away in space.

"I see you came to the finish before your time is over," Mr. Kite smiled,

"Well, the lesson is over. Let us read and speak about this team composition during the next lesson."

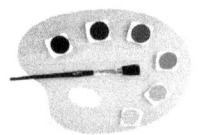

25

ろば と でいびっど あたら しごと さが
ロバートとデイビッドは 新しい仕事を探しています

Robert and David are looking for a new job

A

単語
Words

1. アーティスト、芸術家 [a―tisuto, geijutsu ka] - artist
2. アイディア、考え、案 [aidia, kangae, an] - idea
3. エンジニア [enjinia] - engineer
4. ギフト、贈り物、プレゼント [gifuto, okurimono, purezento] - gift
5. コンサルティング [konsarutingu] - consultancy
6. サービスする, 仕える [sa―bisu suru, tsukaeru] - serve

7. している間、その間 [shi te iru kan, sonokan] - while
8. スパニエル [supanieru] - spaniel
9. スペイン人、スペイン語 [supein jin, supein go] - Spanish
10. ずるい、ずる賢い [zurui, zuru kashikoi] - sly
11. ねずみ [nezumi] - rat
12. プログラマー [puroguramaー] - programmer
13. ペット [petto] - pet
14. リーダー [riーdaー] - leader
15. 予測する、予想する [yosoku suru, yosou suru] - estimate
16. 作家、ライター [sakka, raitaー] - writer
17. 個人的な、個人の、自分の [kojin teki na, kojin no, jibun no] - personal
18. 医者 [isha] - doctor
19. 単調な [tanchou na] - monotonous
20. 声に出して [koe ni dashi te] - aloud
21. 夢 [yume] - dream
22. 夢を見るために [yume wo miru tame ni] - to dream
23. 子犬 [koinu] - puppy
24. 子猫 [koneko] - kitten
25. 宣伝、広告 [senden, koukoku] - advert
26. 年、年齢 [toshi, nenrei] - age
27. 広告 [koukoku] - ad
28. 推薦、おすすめ [suisen, osusume] - recommendation
29. 推薦する、すすめる [suisen suru, susumeru] - recommend
30. 方法、やりかた [houhou, yari kata] - method
31. 旅行 [ryokou] - travel
32. 欄、題目 [ran, daimoku] - rubric
33. 汚い、汚れた [kitanai, yogore ta] - dirty
34. 獣医 [juui] - vet
35. 自然 [shizen] - nature
36. 芸術、アート [geijutsu, aーto] - art
37. 見つけた、見つかった、わかった [mitsuke ta, mitsuka tta, waka tta] - found
38. 質問表 [shitsumon hyou] - questionnaire
39. 農家 [nouka] - farmer
40. 近所の人 [kinjo no hito] - neighbour
41. 通訳、翻訳家 [tsuuyaku, hon'yaku ka] - translator
42. 食べ物 [tabemono] - food

B

ロバートとデイビッドは新しい仕事を探しています

roba─to to deibiddo wa atarashii shigoto wo sagashi te i masu

ろばーととでいびっどはでいびっどの家にいます。でいびっどは朝食の後、てーぶるを掃除していて、ろばーとは新聞の宣伝と広告を読んでいます。彼は動物というらんを読んでいます。でいびっどの妹のなんしーも部屋にいます。彼女はべっどの下に隠れている猫を捕まえようとしています。

roba─to to deibiddo wa deibiddo no ie ni i masu. deibiddo wa choushoku no nochi, te─buru wo souji shi te i te, roba─to wa shinbun no senden to koukoku wo yon de i masu. kare wa doubutsu toiu ran wo yon de i masu. deibiddo no imouto no nanshi─ mo heya ni i masu. kanojo wa beddo no shita ni kakure te iru neko wo tsukamaeyo u to shi te i masu.

"新聞にはたくさんのぺっとが無料でのっているよ。ぼくなら猫か犬を選ぶと思うな。でいびっど、どう思う？" ろばーとがでいびっどに聞きます。"なんしー、猫をいじめないで！" でいびっどが怒ったように言います。

"shinbun ni wa takusan no petto ga muryou de no tte

Robert and David are looking for a new job

Robert and David are at David's home. David is cleaning the table after breakfast and Robert is reading adverts and ads in a newspaper. He is reading the rubric "Animals". David's sister Nancy is in the room too. She is trying to catch the cat hiding under the bed.

"There are so many pets for free in the newspaper. I think I will choose a cat or a dog. David, what do you think?" Robert asks David.

"Nancy, do not bother the cat!"

iru yo. boku nara neko ka inu wo erabu to omou na. deibiddo, dou omou?" robāto ga deibiddo ni kiki masu. "nanshī, neko wo ijime nai de!" deibiddo ga oko tta you ni ii masu.

"ええと、ろばーと。そんなに悪くないあいでぃあだね。ぺっとはいつも君たちが帰ってくるのを家で待っていて、君たちが家に帰ってきて何か食べ物をあげるとき、とても喜ぶんだよ。そして、朝晩に散歩をして小屋を掃除するのを忘れてはいけないよ。たまには、床を掃除し、獣医につれて行かなくてはいけないよ。だから動物を飼う前に、よく考えるんだ。" "eeto, robāto. sonnani waruku nai aidia da ne. petto wa itsumo kimitachi ga kae tte kuru no wo ie de ma tte i te, kimitachi ga ie ni kae tte ki te nani ka tabemono wo ageru toki, totemo yorokobu n da yo. soshite, asaban ni sanpo wo shi te koya wo souji suru no wo wasure te wa ike nai yo. tama ni wa, yuka wo souji shi, juui nitsurete ika naku te wa ike nai yo. dakara doubutsu wo kau mae ni, yoku kangaeru n da."

"ええと、ここにいくつか広告があるよ。きいてね。" ろばーとはそう言い、声をだして読み始めます："ねずみのような、汚い白い犬を見つけました。外で長生きするかもしれません。お金を払ってくれる人に売ります。" こっちにもうひとつ："すぺいん犬、すぺ

David says angrily,

"Well Robert, it is not a bad idea. Your pet will always wait for you at home and will be so happy when you come back home and give some food. And do not forget that you will have to walk with your pet in mornings and evenings or clean its box. Sometimes you will have to clean the floor or take your pet to a vet. So think carefully before you get an animal."

"Well, there are some ads here. Listen," Robert says and begins to read aloud:

"Found dirty white dog, looks like a rat. It may live outside for a long time. I will give it away for money."

いん語を話します。無料です。それから、無料の子犬たちは、すぱにえると、近所のずる賢い犬のはーふです。" "eeto, koko ni ikutsu ka koukoku ga aru yo. kii te ne." roba─to wa sou ii, koe wo dashi te yomi hajime masu : "nezumi no you na, kitanai shiroi inu wo mitsukemashita. soto de nagaiki suru kamo shire mase n. okane wo hara tte kureru hito ni uri masu." kocchi ni mou hitotsu : "supein ken, supein go wo hanashi masu. muryou desu. sorekara, muryou no koinu tachi wa, supanieru to, kinjo no zuru kashikoi inu no ha─fu desu."

ろばーとはでいびっどを見ます。"どうやって犬がすぺいん語を話せるの？" "犬はすぺいん語を理解するのかもしれないね。すぺいん語、わかるの？" でいびっどが笑いながらききます。

"すぺいん語はわからないよ。きいて、もうひとつ広告があるよ：" 農場の子猫が無料です。食べ物も食べられます。彼らは何でも食べるでしょう。" roba─to wa deibiddo wo mi masu. "dou ya tte inu ga supein go wo hanaseru no?" "inu wa supein go wo rikai suru no kamo shire nai ne. supein go, wakaru no?" deibiddo ga warai nagara kiki masu. "supein go ha wakara nai yo. kii te, mou hitotsu koukoku ga aru yo : "noujou no koneko ga muryou desu. tabemono mo tabe rare masu. karera wa nan demo taberu desho u."

ろばーとは新聞をめくります。"ええと、ぺっとは急がなくてもいいと思うんだ。仕事のほ

Here is one more:

"Spanish dog, speaks Spanish. Give away for free. And free puppies half spaniel half sly neighbor's dog,"

Robert looks at David, "How can a dog speak Spanish?"

"A dog may understand Spanish. Can you understand Spanish?" David asks smiling.

"I cannot understand Spanish. Listen, here is one more ad:

"Give away free farm kittens. Ready to eat. They will eat anything,"

Robert turns the newspaper, "Well, I think pets can wait. I will better look for a job," he

うを 探さなきゃ。" 彼は仕事についての欄をみつけ、声を出して読みます。roba—to wa shinbun wo mekuri masu. "eeto, petto wa isoga naku te mo ii to omou n da. shigoto no hou wo sagasa nakya." kare wa shigoto nitsuite no ran wo mitsuke, koe wo dashi te yomi masu.

"自分に合った仕事を探していますか？職業こんさるてぃんぐの"すーたぶるぱーそねる（ふさわしい人材）"があなたをお手伝いします。わたしたちのこんさるたんとはあなた個人の才能を評価し、最もふさわしい職業について、あなたに推薦をします。" "jibun ni a tta shigoto wo sagashi te i masu ka? shokugyou konsarutingu no "su—taburupa—soneru（fusawashii jinzai）" ga anata wo otetsudai shi masu. watashi tachi no konsarutanto wa anata kojin no sainou wo hyouka shi, mottomo fusawashii shokugyou nitsuite, anata ni suisen wo shi masu."

ろばーとは見上げて言います。"でいびっど、どう思う？" "あなたにとって一番の仕事は、海の中でとらっくを洗って浮かべることよ。" なんしーはそう言い、部屋の外へ素早くはしっていきます。roba—to wa miage te ii masu. "deibiddo, dou omou?" "anata nitotte ichiban no shigoto wa, umi no naka de torakku wo ara tte ukaberu koto yo." nanshi— wa sou ii, heya no soto e subayaku hashi tte iki masu.

finds the rubric about jobs and reads aloud,

"Are you looking for a suitable job? The job consultancy "Suitable personnel" can help you. Our consultants will estimate your personal gifts and will give you a recommendation about the most suitable profession."

Robert looks up and says: "David what do you think?"
"The best job for you is washing a truck in the sea and let it float," Nancy says and quickly runs out of the room.

"悪くないあいでぃあだね。さあ、今いこうよ。" でいびっどはそうこたえ、なんしーが1分前にやかんに置いた猫を、気をつけてどかします。 "waruku nai aidia da ne. saa, ima iko u yo." deibiddo wa sou kotae, nanshi― ga i ppun mae ni yakan ni oi ta neko wo, ki wo tsuke te dokashi masu.

"It is not a bad idea. Let's go now," David answers and takes carefully the cat out of the kettle, where Nancy put the animal a minute ago.

ろばーととでいびっどは自転車で職業こんさるてぃんぐの "すーたぶるぱーそねる（ふさわしい人材）" に着きます。列はないので、中へ入ります。二人の女性がいます。そのうちの一人は電話で話をしています。別の女性は何かを書いています。彼女はろばーととでいびっどに、座るよう頼みます。彼女の名前はしゃーぷさんです。彼女は彼らの名前と年齢を聞きます。 roba―to to deibiddo wa jitensha de shokugyou konsarutingu no "su―taburupa―soneru（fusawashii jinzai）" ni tsuki masu. retsu wa nai node, naka e hairi masu. futari no josei ga i masu. sono uchi no hitori wa denwa de hanashi wo shi te i masu. betsu no josei wa nani ka wo kai te i masu. kanojo wa roba―to to deibiddo ni, suwaru you tanomi masu. kanojo no namae wa sha―pu san desu. kanojo wa karera no namae to nenrei wo kiki masu.

Robert and David arrive to the job consultancy "Suitable personnel" by their bikes. There is no queue, so they go inside. There are two women there. One of them is speaking on the telephone. Another woman is writing something. She asks Robert and David to take seats. Her name is Mrs. Sharp. She asks them their names and their age.

"ええと、わたしたちが使う方法を説明させてください。見てください、5種類の職業があります。 "eeto, watashi tachi ga

"Well, let me explain the method which we use. Look, there are five kinds of professions.

tsukau houhou wo setsumei sa se te kudasai. mi te kudasai, go shurui no shokugyou ga ari masu.

1種類目は人間と自然。職業：農家、動物園作業員など。

2種類目は人間と機械。職業：ぱいろっと、たくしー運転手、とらっく運転手など。

3種類目は人間と人間。職業：医者、先生、じゃーなりすとなど。

4種類目は人間とこんぴゅーたー。職業：翻訳家、えんじにあ、ぷろぐらまーなど。

5種類目は人間とあーと。職業：作家、あーてぃすと、歌手など。

i sshurui me wa ningen to shizen. shokugyou : nouka, doubutsu en sagyou in nado. ni shurui me wa ningen to kikai. shokugyou : pairotto, takushi— unten shu, torakku unten shu nado. san shurui me wa ningen to ningen. shokugyou : isha, sensei, ja—narisuto nado. yon shurui me wa ningen to konpyu—ta—. shokugyou : hon'yaku ka, enjinia, purogurama— nado. go shurui me wa ningen to a—to. shokugyou : sakka, a—tisuto, kashu nado.

わたしたちは、あなたたちについてもっと知ってから、ふさわしい職業についての推薦を

1. The first kind is man - nature. Professions: farmer, zoo worker etc.

2. The second kind is man - machine. Professions: pilot, taxi driver, truck driver etc.

3. The third kind is man - man. Professions: doctor, teacher, journalist etc.

4. The fourth kind is man - computer. Professions: translator, engineer, programmer etc.

5. The fifth kind is man - art. Professions: writer, artist, singer etc.

We give recommendations about a suitable profession

します。まず、あなたたちの才能(さいのう)を評価(ひょうか)させてください。あなたがたが、何(なに)が好きで何(なに)が好きでないかを知(し)らなくてはなりません。その後(ご)、どの種類(しゅるい)の職業(しょくぎょう)があなた方に最(もっと)もふさわしいかを知(し)ることができます。では、質問表(しつもんひょう)を埋(う)めてください。" watashi tachi wa, anata tachi nitsuite motto shi tte kara, fusawashii shokugyou nitsuite no suisen wo shi masu. mazu, anata tachi no sainou wo hyouka sa se te kudasai. anata ga ta ga, nani ga suki de nani ga suki de nai ka wo shira naku te ha nari mase n. sonogo, dono shurui no shokugyou ga anata gata ni mottomo fusawashii ka wo shiru koto ga deki masu. de wa, shitsumon hyou wo ume te kudasai."

しゃーぷさんはそう言(い)い、彼(かれ)らに質問表(しつもんひょう)を渡(わた)します。でいびっどとろばーとは質問表(しつもんひょう)を埋(う)めます。sha―pu san wa sou ii, karera ni shitsumon hyou wo watashi masu. deibiddo to roba―to wa shitsumon hyou wo ume masu.

質問表(しつもんおもて)

shitsumon hyou

名前(なまえ)：でいびっど ついーたー
namae : deibiddo tsuitta―

機械(きかい)を見(み)る－気(き)にしない
人(ひと)と話(はな)す－好(す)き

---

only when we learn about you more. First let me estimate your personal gifts. I must know what you like and what you dislike. Then we will know which kind of profession is the most suitable for you. Please, fill up the questionnaire now,"

Mrs. Sharp says and gives them the questionnaires. David and Robert fill up the questionnaires.

Questionnaire

Name: David Tweeter

Watch machines - I do not mind

Speak with people - I like

<ruby>接客<rt>せっきゃく</rt></ruby> - <ruby>気<rt>き</rt></ruby>にしない	Serve customers - I do not mind
<ruby>車<rt>くるま</rt></ruby>、とらっくの<ruby>運転<rt>うんてん</rt></ruby> - <ruby>好<rt>す</rt></ruby>き	Drive cars, trucks - I like
<ruby>中<rt>なか</rt></ruby>で<ruby>働<rt>はたら</rt></ruby>く - <ruby>好<rt>す</rt></ruby>き	Work inside - I like
<ruby>外<rt>そと</rt></ruby>で<ruby>働<rt>はたら</rt></ruby>く - <ruby>好<rt>す</rt></ruby>き	Work outside - I like
たくさん<ruby>記憶<rt>きおく</rt></ruby>する - <ruby>気<rt>き</rt></ruby>にしない	Remember a lot - I do not mind
<ruby>旅行<rt>りょこう</rt></ruby> - <ruby>好<rt>す</rt></ruby>き	Travel - I like
<ruby>予想<rt>よそう</rt></ruby>、<ruby>確認<rt>かくにん</rt></ruby> - <ruby>嫌<rt>ぎら</rt></ruby>い	Estimate, check - I hate
<ruby>汚<rt>よご</rt></ruby>れる<ruby>作業<rt>さぎょう</rt></ruby> - <ruby>気<rt>き</rt></ruby>にしない	Dirty work - I do not mind
<ruby>単調<rt>たんちょう</rt></ruby>な<ruby>作業<rt>さぎょう</rt></ruby> - <ruby>嫌<rt>ぎら</rt></ruby>い	Monotonous work - I hate
<ruby>厳<rt>きび</rt></ruby>しい<ruby>作業<rt>さぎょう</rt></ruby> - <ruby>気<rt>き</rt></ruby>にしない	Hard work - I do not mind
りーだーになる - <ruby>気<rt>き</rt></ruby>にしない	Be leader - I do not mind
ちーむで<ruby>働<rt>はたら</rt></ruby>く - <ruby>気<rt>き</rt></ruby>にしない	Work in team - I do not mind
<ruby>働<rt>はたら</rt></ruby>いている<ruby>間<rt>ま</rt></ruby>に<ruby>夢<rt>ゆめ</rt></ruby>を<ruby>見<rt>み</rt></ruby>る - <ruby>好<rt>す</rt></ruby>き	Dream while working - I like
<ruby>電車<rt>でんしゃ</rt></ruby> - <ruby>気<rt>き</rt></ruby>にしない	Train - I do not mind
<ruby>創造的<rt>そうぞうてき</rt></ruby>な<ruby>仕事<rt>しごと</rt></ruby>をする - <ruby>好<rt>す</rt></ruby>き	Do creative work - I like
<ruby>文章<rt>ぶんしょう</rt></ruby>の<ruby>作業<rt>さぎょう</rt></ruby> - <ruby>好<rt>す</rt></ruby>き	Work with texts - I like

kikai wo miru - ki ni shi nai
hito to hanasu - suki
sekkyaku - ki ni shi nai
kuruma, torakku no unten - suki

naka de hataraku - suki
soto de hataraku - suki
takusan kioku suru - ki ni shi nai
ryokou - suki
yosou, kakunin - kirai
yogoreru sagyou - ki ni shi nai
tanchou na sagyou - kirai
kibishii sagyou - ki ni shi nai
ri―da― ni naru - ki ni shi nai
chi―mu de hataraku - ki ni shi nai
hatarai te iru ma ni yume wo miru - suki
densha - ki ni shi nai
souzou teki na shigoto wo suru - suki
bunshou no sagyou - suki

質　問　表
しつもんおもて

shitsumon hyou

名前：ろばーと　げんしゃー
なまえ

namae : roba―to　gensha―

機械を見る-気にしない
きかい　み　　き

人と話す-好き
ひと　はな　す

接客-気にしない
せっきゃく　き

車、とらっくの運転-気にしない
くるま　　　　　　　うんてん　き

中で働く-好き
なか　はたら　す

外で働く-好き
そと　はたら　す

たくさん記憶する-気にしない
きおく　　　き

旅行-好き
りょこう　す

Questionnaire

Name: Robert Genscher

Watch machines - I do not mind

Speak with people - I like

Serve customers - I do not mind

Drive cars, trucks - I do not mind

Work inside - I like

Work outside - I like

Remember a lot - I do not mind

Travel - I like

Estimate, check - I do not mind

予想、確認 −気にしない

汚れる作業 −気にしない

単調な作業 −嫌い

厳しい作業 −気にしない

りーだーになる − 嫌い

ちーむで働く −好き

働いている間に夢を見る −好き

電車 −気にしない

創造的な仕事をする −好き

文章の作業 −好き

kikai wo miru - ki ni shi nai
hito to hanasu - suki
sekkyaku - ki ni shi nai
kuruma, torakku no unten - ki ni shi nai
naka de hataraku - suki
soto de hataraku - suki
takusan kioku suru - ki ni shi nai
ryokou - suki
yosou, kakunin - ki ni shi nai
yogoreru sagyou - ki ni shi nai
tanchou na sagyou - kirai
kibishii sagyou - ki ni shi nai
ri—da— ni naru - kirai
chi—mu de hataraku - suki
hatarai te iru ma ni yume wo miru - suki
densha - ki ni shi nai
souzou teki na shigoto wo suru - suki
bunshou no sagyou - suki

Dirty work - I do not mind

Monotonous work - I hate

Hard work - I do not mind

Be leader - I hate

Work in team - I like

Dream while working - I like

Train - I do not mind

Do creative work - I like

Work with texts - I like

26

Audio

<ruby>"サンフランシスコニュース"<rt>さんふらんしすこにゅーす</rt></ruby> へ <ruby>応募<rt>おうぼ</rt></ruby>

Applying to "San Francisco News"

A

単語
Words

1. １７ [juu nana] - seventeen
2. ２１ [ni juu ichi] - twenty-one
3. 情報 [jouhou] - information
4. かもしれない [kamo shire nai] - could
5. さようなら [sayounara] - goodbye
6. ステータス、事態 ; 家族ステータス [suteーtasu, jitai ; kazoku suteーtasu] - status; family status

7. について知った、について学んだ [nitsuite shi tta, nitsuite manan da] - learned about

8. パトロール、 [patoro—ru,] - patrol

9. ファイナンス、金融 [fainansu, kinyuu] - finance

10. フォーム [fo—mu] - form

11. ミス、さん [misu, san] - Miss

12. レポーター [repo—ta—] - reporter

13. レポート [repo—to] - report

14. 下線 [kasen] - underline

15. 与えた、渡した、あげた [atae ta, watashi ta, age ta] - gave

16. 乗った、取った、使った、食べた、飲んだ [no tta, to tta, tsuka tta, tabe ta, non da] - took

17. ミドルネーム [midoru ne—mu] - middle name

18. 働いた、 [hatarai ta,] - worked

19. 刑事上の、犯罪の [keiji jou no, hanzai no] - criminal

20. 到着した、ついた [touchaku shi ta, tsui ta] - arrived

21. 勧めた、推薦した [susume ta, suisen shi ta] - recommended

22. 去る、なくなる、出る [saru, nakunaru, deru] - leave

23. 同伴する [douhan suru] - accompany

24. 国籍 [kokuseki] - nationality

25. 女性 [josei] - female

26. 学歴、教育 [gakureki, kyouiku] - education

27. 応募する [oubo suru] - apply

28. 性別 [seibetsu] - sex

29. 流暢に、上手に [ryuuchou ni, jouzu ni] - fluently

30. 独身 [dokushin] - single

31. 男性 [dansei] - male

32. 空欄、空白 [kuuran, kuuhaku] - blank, empty

33. 星印（＊） [hoshi jirushi（＊）] - asterisk

34. 編集者 [henshuu sha] - editor

35. 評価した、予想した [hyouka shi ta, yosou shi ta] - estimated

36. 警察 [keisatsu] - police

37. 質問した、聞いた、頼んだ [shitsumon shi ta, kii ta, tanon da] - asked

38. 週 [shuu] - week

39. 項目 [koumoku] - field

B

さんふらんしすこにゅーす　　おうぼ
"サンフランシスコニュース"へ応募

"sanfuranshisuko nyu─su" e oubo

しゃーぷさんはでいびっどとろばーとの
しつもんひょう　かいとう　ひょうか
質問表の回答を評価しました。
かのじょ　かれ　さいのう　し
彼女は、彼らの才能について知ったとき
　　かれ　　　　　　しょくぎょう
に、彼らにふさわしい職業についての
すいせん
推薦をすることができました。sha─pu san wa deibiddo to roba─to no shitsumon hyou no kaitou wo hyouka shi mashi ta. kanojo wa, karera no sainou nitsuite shi tta toki ni, karera ni fusawashii shokugyou nitsuite no suisen wo suru koto ga deki mashi ta.

　　かのじょ　　　ばんめ　しょくしゅ　かれ
　彼女は、3番目の職種が彼らには
もっと あ　　　　い　　　　　いしゃ
最も合っていると言いました。それは、医者、
せんせい
先生、またはじゃーなりすとなどです。しゃーぷ
　　　　　かれ
さんは彼らに、"さんふらんしすこにゅーす"とい
　　しんぶんしゃ　　しごと　おうぼ　　　　　すす
う新聞社での仕事に応募するように勧め
　　　　　かれ　　けいじらんよう　けいさつ
ました。彼らは、刑事欄用に警察れぽー
　　　　　か　がくせい　　　　　　　しごと
とを書ける学生たちに、あるばいとの仕事を
わた　　　　　　　　　ご
渡しました。その後、ろばーととでいびっどは
しんぶんしゃ
新聞社、"さんふらんしすこにゅーす"に
とうちゃく　　　　　しごと　おうぼ
到着して、この仕事に応募しました。
kanojo wa, san banme no shokushu ga karera ni wa mottomo a tte iru to ii mashi ta. sore wa, isha, sensei,

Applying to "San Francisco News"

Mrs. Sharp estimated David's and Robert's answers in the questionnaires. When she learned about their personal gifts she could give them some recommendations about suitable professions. She said that the third profession kind is the most suitable for them. They could work as a doctor, a teacher or a journalist etc. Mrs. Sharp recommended them to apply for a job with the newspaper „San Francisco News". They gave a part time job to students who could compose police reports for the criminal rubric. So Robert and David arrived at the personnel department of the newspaper „San Francisco

matawa ja―narisuto nado desu. sha―pu san wa karera ni, "sanfuranshisuko nyu―su" toiu shinbun sha de no shigoto ni oubo suru you ni susume mashi ta. karera wa, keiji ran you ni keisatsu repo―to wo kakeru gakusei tachi ni, arubaito no shigoto wo watashi mashi ta. sonogo, roba―to to deibiddo wa shinbun sha, "sanfuranshisuko nyu―su" ni touchaku shi te, kono shigoto ni oubo shi mashi ta.

News "and applied for this job.

"わたしたちは職業こんさるてぃんぐの"すーたぶるぱーそねる"へ今日行きました。"でいびっどが、人事部長のすりむさんに言います。"彼らが、こちらの新聞社へ応募するよう、わたしたちに推薦しました。" "watashi tachi wa shokugyou konsarutingu no "su―taburupa―soneru" e kyou iki mashi ta." deibiddo ga, jinji buchou no surimu san ni ii masu. "karera ga, kochira no shinbun sha e oubo suru you, watashi tachi ni suisen shi mashi ta."

"We have been to the job consultancy "Suitable personnel" today," David said to Miss Slim, who was the head of the personnel department, "They have recommended us to apply to your newspaper."

"ええと、以前にれぽーたーとして働いたことはありますか?"すりむさんが質問しました。"eeto, izen ni repo―ta― toshite hatarai ta koto a ari masu ka?" surimu san ga shitsumon shi mashi ta.

"Well, have you worked as a reporter before?" Miss Slim asked.

"いいえ、ありません。"でいびっどがこたえました。"iie, ari mase n." deibiddo ga kotae mashi ta.

"No, we have not," David answered.

"これらの個人情報ふぉーむを埋めてください。"すりむさんはそう言って、彼らに2つのふぉーむを渡しました。ろばーととでいびっどは個人情報ふぉーむを埋めました。

"korera no kojin jouhou fo―mu wo umete kudasai."

"Please, fill up these personal information forms," Miss Slim said and gave them two forms. Robert and David filled up the personal

surimu san wa sou i tte, karera ni futatsu no fo―mu wo watashi mashita. roba―to to deibiddo wa kojin jouhou fo―mu wo ume mashita.

こじんじょうほうふぉ　む
個　人　情　報　フォーム

kojin jouhou fo―mu

　べいしるし　　こうもく　　かなら　う
　米　印＊の 項　目 は 必　ず 埋めてください。
　　　　た　こうもく　くうらん　　かま
　その他の 項　目 は 空　欄 でも 構　いません。

hoshi jirushi no koumoku wa kanarazu ume te kudasai.
sonota no koumoku wa kuuran demo kamai mase n.

なまえ
名 前 ＊-でいびっど

みどるねーむ

みょうじ
名 字 ＊-ついーたー

せいべつ　　かせん　おとこ
性　別 ＊(下　線)- 男　女

ねんれい
年　齢 ＊-20歳

こくせき
国　籍 ＊-あめりか

かぞく　　　　　　　かせん　　どくしん
家 族 すてーたす (下　線)- 独身　既婚

じゅうしょ　　　　　　　どおり　　ばん
住　所 ＊-くいーん 通　11 番 、さんふらんしす
こ、あめりか

がくれき だいがく　　ねんめ
学　歴 - 大　学 の 3 年目で、じゃーなりずむを
べんきょう
　勉　強 しています。

いぜん　　　はたら　　　　　　　　　　　のうか
以 前 どこで 働　いたことがありますか？-農家
さぎょういん　　　　　　　　かげつはたら
作　業　員 として 2ヶ月　働　きました。

---

information forms.

Personal information form

You must fill up fields with asterisk *. You can leave other fields blank

First name* - David

Middle name

Last name* - Tweeter

Sex* (underline) - <u>Male</u>
Female

Age* - Twenty years old

Nationality* - US

Family status (underline) - <u>single</u> married

Address* - 11 Queen street, San Francisco, USA

Education - I am studying Journalism in the third year at a college

Where have you worked before? -
I worked for two months as a farm worker

What experience and skills have you had?* - I can drive a

何の経験とすきるがありますか？*-車ととらっくが運転でき、こんぴゅーたーが使えます。

語学*0-なし, 10-流暢-すぺいん語-8, 英語-10

運転免許証*(下線)-いいえ はい
種類：BC, とらっくを運転できます。

必要な仕事*(下線)-正社員 あるばいと：毎週１５時間

稼ぎたい額-時給１５どる

car, a truck and I can use a computer

Languages* 0 - no, 10 - fluently - Spanish - 8, English - 10

Driving license* (underline) - No Yes Kind: BC, I can drive trucks

You need a job* (underline) - Full time Part time: 15 hours a week

You want to earn - 15 dollars per hour

namae - deibiddo
midorune─mu
myouji - tsui─ta─
seibetsu (kasen) - otoko onna
nenrei - ni ju ssai
kokuseki - amerika
kazoku sute─tasu (kasen) - dokushin kikon
juusho - kui─n doori juu ichi ban, sanfuranshisuko, amerika
gakureki - daigaku no san nen me de, ja─narizumu wo benkyou shi te i masu.
izen doko de hatarai ta koto ga ari masu ka? - nouka sagyou in toshite ni kagetsu hataraki mashi ta.
nan no keiken to sukiru ga ari masu ka? - kuruma to torakku ga unten deki, konpyu─ta─ ga tsukae masu.
gogaku zero - nashi, juu - ryuuchou - supein go - hachi, eigo - juu
unten menkyo shou (kasen) - iie hai shurui : BC, torakku wo unten deki masu.
hitsuyou na shigoto (kasen) - seishain arubaito : maishuu juu go jikan
kasegi tai gaku - jikyuu juu go doru

<ruby>個人情報<rt>こじんじょうほう</rt></ruby>フォーム

kojin jouhou fo—mu

<ruby>米印<rt>べいしるし</rt></ruby>*の<ruby>項目<rt>こうもく</rt></ruby>は<ruby>必<rt>かなら</rt></ruby>ず<ruby>埋<rt>う</rt></ruby>めてください。
その<ruby>他<rt>た</rt></ruby>の<ruby>項目<rt>こうもく</rt></ruby>は<ruby>空欄<rt>くうらん</rt></ruby>でも<ruby>構<rt>かま</rt></ruby>いません。

hoshi jirushi no koumoku wa kanarazu ume te kudasai.
sonota no koumoku wa kuuran demo kamai mase n.

<ruby>名前<rt>なまえ</rt></ruby>＊-ろばーと

みどるねーむ

<ruby>名字<rt>みょうじ</rt></ruby>＊-げんしゃー

<ruby>性別<rt>せいべつ</rt></ruby>＊(<ruby>下線<rt>かせん</rt></ruby>)-<ruby>男<rt>おとこ</rt></ruby> 女

<ruby>年齢<rt>ねんれい</rt></ruby>＊-21歳

<ruby>国籍<rt>こくせき</rt></ruby>＊-どいつ

<ruby>家族<rt>かぞく</rt></ruby>すてーたす(<ruby>下線<rt>かせん</rt></ruby>)-<ruby>独身<rt>どくしん</rt></ruby> 既婚

<ruby>住所<rt>じゅうしょ</rt></ruby>＊-<ruby>学生寮<rt>がくせいりょう</rt></ruby>218<ruby>号室<rt>ごうしつ</rt></ruby>、<ruby>大学通<rt>だいがくどおり</rt></ruby>36<ruby>番<rt>ばん</rt></ruby>、さんふらんしすこ,あめりか

<ruby>学歴<rt>がくれき</rt></ruby>-<ruby>大学<rt>だいがく</rt></ruby>の2<ruby>年目<rt>ねんめ</rt></ruby>で、こんぴゅーたーでざいんを<ruby>勉強<rt>べんきょう</rt></ruby>しています。

<ruby>以前<rt>いぜん</rt></ruby>どこで<ruby>働<rt>はたら</rt></ruby>いたことがありますか?-<ruby>農家作業員<rt>のうかさぎょういん</rt></ruby>として2<ruby>ヶ月<rt>かげつ</rt></ruby><ruby>働<rt>はたら</rt></ruby>きました。

<ruby>何<rt>なに</rt></ruby>の<ruby>経験<rt>けいけん</rt></ruby>とすきるがありますか?＊-こんぴゅー

Personal information form

You must fill up fields with asterisk *. You can leave other fields blank.

First name* - Robert

Middle name

Last name* - Genscher

Sex* (underline) - <u>Male</u> Female

Age* - Twenty-one years old

Nationality* - German

Family status (underline) - <u>Single</u> Married

Address* - Room 218, student dorms, College Street 36, San Francisco, the USA.

Education - I study computer design in the second year at a college

*Where have you worked before? -
I worked for two months as a farm worker*

What experience and skills have you had?* - I can use a computer

Languages* 0 - no, 10 -

たーが 使えます。

語学*0-なし, 10-流暢-どいつ語-10, 英語-8

運転免許証*(下線)-いいえはい

種類：必要な仕事*(下線)-正社員

あるばいと：毎週１５時間

稼ぎたい額-時給１５どる

namae - roba—to
midorune—mu
myouji - gensha—
seibetsu (kasen) - otoko onna
nenrei - ni juu i ssai
kokuseki - doitsu
kazoku sute—tasu (kasen) - dokushin kikon
juusho - gakusei ryou ni ichi hachi goushitsu, daigaku doori san juu roku ban, sanfuranshisuko, amerika
gakureki - daigaku no ni nen me de, konpyu—ta— dezain wo benkyou shi te i masu. izen doko de hatarai ta koto ga ari masu ka? - nouka sagyou in toshite ni kagetsu hataraki mashi ta.
nan no keiken to sukiru ga ari masu ka? - konpyu—ta— ga tsukae masu.
gogaku zero - nashi, juu - ryuuchou - doitsugo - juu, eigo - hachi
unten menkyo shou (kasen) - iie hai shurui :
hitsuyou na shigoto (kasen) - seishain arubaito :
maishuu juu go jikan
kasegi tai gaku - jikyuu juu go doru

すりむさんは 彼らの個人情報ふぉーむを "さんふらんしすこにゅーす"の編集者へ持って行きました。"編集者は同意をしま

fluently - German - 10, English - 8

Driving license* (underline) - No Yes Kind:

You need a job* (underline) - Full time Part time: 15 hours a week

You want to earn - 15 dollars per hour

Miss Slim took their personal information forms to the editor of "San Francisco News".

"The editor has agreed," Miss

した。"すりむさんは戻ってきて言いました。
"あなたたちは警察ぱとろーるに同伴をして、それから刑事欄のれぽーとを書きます。ぱとかーが明日１７時にあなたたちを迎えにきます。その時間にこちらにこられますか？" "もちろんです。"ろばーとがこたえました。"はい、そうします。"でいびっどは言いました。"さようなら" "さようなら"すりむさんはこたえました。surimu san wa karera no kojin jouhou fo―mu wo "sanfuranshisuko nyu―su" no henshuu sha e mo tte iki mashi ta. "henshuu sha wa doui wo shi mashita," surimu san wa modo tte ki te ii mashi ta. "anata tachi wa keisatsu patoro―ru ni douhan wo shi te, sorekara keiji ran no repo―to wo kaki masu. patoka― ga ashita juu nana ji ni anata tachi wo mukae ni ki masu. sono jikan ni kochira ni korare masu ka?" "mochiron desu." roba―to ga kotae mashi ta. "hai, sou shi masu." deibiddo wa ii mashi ta. "sayounara" "sayounara" surimu san wa kotae mashi ta.

Slim said when she came back, "You will accompany a police patrol and then compose reports for the criminal rubric. A police car will come tomorrow at seventeen o'clock to take you. Be here at this time, will you?"

"Sure," Robert answered.

"Yes, we will," David said, "Goodbye."

"Goodbye," Miss Slim answered.

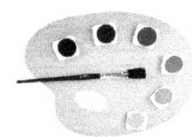

27

Audio

けいさつぱとろ　る　ぱ　と
警察パトロール（パート１）

The police patrol (Part 1)

A

単語
Words

1. １００ [hyaku] - hundred
2. １２ [juu ni] - twelve
3. アラーム、警報機 [ara—mu, keihou ki] - alarm
4. サイレン [sairen] - siren
5. シートベルト [shi—toberuto] - seat belts
6. した、やった、行った [shi ta, ya tta, okona tta] - did
7. しめた、閉じた、閉まっている [shime ta, toji ta, shima tte iru] - closed
8. しめる [shimeru] - fasten
9. スピード違反をする人 [supi—do ihan wo suru hito] - speeder
10. ちくしょう [chikushou] - damn
11. どうしたの？、何があったの？ [dou shi ta no?, nani ga a tta no?] - What is the matter?
12. マイク [maiku] - microphone
13. みんな、全員 [minna, zen'in] - everybody
14. リミット [rimitto] - limit
15. わかった、理解した [waka tta, rikai shi ta] - understood
16. 乾いた；乾かすために [kawaita ; kawakasu tame ni] - dry *(adj)*, to dry

17. 会った、合った [a tta, a tta] - met
18. 値段、価格 [nedan, kakaku] - price
19. 加速、スピード；加速する、スピード違反をする [kasoku, supiーdo ; kasoku suru, supiーdo ihan wo suru] - speed; to speed
20. 同伴した [douhan shi ta] - accompanied
21. 吠えた [hoe ta] - barked
22. 吠える、なりわめく [hoeru, nari wameku] - howling
23. 周りを見る、見て回る、見渡す [mawari wo miru, mi te mawaru, miwatasu] - look around
24. （運転を）始めた [(unten wo) hajime ta] - started (to drive)
25. 巡査部長 [junsa buchou] - sergeant
26. 待った [matta] - waited
27. 恐れる、怖がる [osoreru, kowagaru] - afraid
28. 急いだ [isoi da] - rushed
29. 手錠 [tejou] - handcuffs

30. 泣いた、叫んだ [nai ta, saken da] - cried
31. 泥棒 [dorobou] - robbery
32. 泥棒 [dorobou] - thief
33. 泥棒（複数）[dorobou (fukusuu)] - thieves
34. 疲れた [tsukare ta] - tried
35. 見せた [mise ta] - showed
36. 警察官 [keisatsukan] - officer, policeman
37. 踏んだ [fun da] - stepped
38. 追跡 [tsuiseki] - pursuit
39. 運転した [unten shi ta] - drove
40. 銃 [juu] - gun
41. 鍵 [kagi] - key
42. 開けた、開いた [ake ta, hirai ta] - opened
43. 隠した [kakushi ta] - hid
44. 高い、暑い [takai, atsui] - high

B

警察パトロール（パート１）
けいさつぱとろーる　ぱーと
keisatsu patoroーru （paーto ichi）

翌日、ろばーととでいびっどは"さんふらんしすこにゅーす"の建物に、１７時に到着しました。ぱとかーはすでに彼らを

The police patrol (Part 1)

Robert and David arrived at the building of the newspaper "San Francisco News" at seventeen o'clock next day. The police car was waiting for them

待っていました。"こんにちは。わたしはふらんく・すとりくと巡査部長です。"でいびっどとろばーとが車にくると、彼はそう言いました。yokujitsu, roba―to to deibiddo wa "sanfuranshisuko nyu―su" no tatemono ni, juu nana ji ni touchaku shi mashi ta. patoka― wa sudeni karera wo ma tte i mashi ta. "konnichiwa. watashi wa furanku.sutorikuto junsa buchou desu." deibiddo to roba―to ga kuruma ni kuru to, kare wa sou ii mashi ta.

already. A policeman got out of the car.

"Hello. I am sergeant Frank Strict," he said when David and Robert came to the car.

"こんにちは。お会いできて嬉しいです。ぼくの名前はろばーとです。ぼくたちはあなたに同伴しなくてはなりません。"ろばーとがこたえました。"こんにちは。ぼくはろばーとです。ぼくたちを長い間待っていましたか？"でいびっどが質問しました。"konnichiwa. o ai deki te ureshii desu. boku no namae wa roba―to desu. boku tachi wa anata ni douhan shi naku te wa nari mase n." roba―to ga kotae mashi ta. "konnichiwa. boku wa roba―to desu. boku tachi wo nagai aida ma tte i mashi ta ka?" deibiddo ga shitsumon shi mashi ta.

"Hello. Glad to meet you. My name is Robert. We must accompany you," Robert answered.

"Hello. I am David. Were you waiting long for us?" David asked.

"いいえ。今、着いたところです。さあ、車に乗りましょう。今から街のぱとろーるを始めます。"警察官が言いました。彼らは全員ぱとかーに乗り込みました。"iie. ima, tsui ta tokoro desu. saa, kuruma ni nori masho u. ima kara machi no patoro―ru wo hajime masu." keisatsukan ga ii mashi ta. karera wa zen'in

"No. I have just arrived here. Let us get into the car. We begin city patrolling now," the policeman said. They all got into the police car.

patokā ni no norikomi mashi ta.

"君たちは警察ぱとろーるの同伴は初めてですか？"すとりくと巡査部長がえんじんをかけながら質問しました。
"kimitachi wa keisatsu patorō ru no douhan wa hajimete desu ka?" sutorikuto junsa buchou ga enjin wo kake nagara shitsumon shi mashi ta.

"Are you accompanying a police patrol for the first time?" sergeant Strict asked starting the engine.

"ぼくたちは、今まで警察ぱとろーるに同伴をしたことがありません。"でいびっどがこたえました。このとき、警察の無線がしゃべ喋り始めました："P11とP07、注意して聞いてください！青い車がかれっじ通り沿いをすぴーど違反しています。" "boku tachi wa, ima made keisatsu patorō ru ni douhan wo shi ta koto ga ari mase n." deibiddo ga kotae mashi ta. kono toki, keisatsu no musen ga shaberi hajime mashi ta : "pī juu ichi to pī zero nana, chuui shi te kii te kudasai! aoi kuruma ga karejji doori zoi wo supī do ihan shi te i masu."

"We have never accompanied a police patrol before," David answered.

At this moment the police radio began to talk: "Attention P11 and P07! A blue car is speeding along College street."

"P07、了解です。"すとりくと巡査部長はまいくで言いました。そして彼は男の子たちに言いました："私たちの車はP07番です。"大きな青い車は、とても速いすぴーどで彼らを通り過ぎて行きました。ふらんく巡査部長はまい

"P07 got it," sergeant Strict said in the microphone. Then he said to the boys: "The number of our car is P07." A big blue car rushed past them with very high speed. Frank Strict took the mic again and said: "P07 is speaking. I see

くを再び取って言いました。"こちらP07番です。すぴーど違反をしている青い車を見つけました。追跡を開始します。"その後、彼は男の子たちにいいます。"piー zero nana, ryoukai desu." sutorikuto junsa buchou wa maiku de ii mashi ta. soshite kare wa otokonoko tachi ni ii mashi ta : "watashi tachi no kuruma ha piー zero nana ban desu." ookina aoi kuruma wa, totemo hayai supiーdo de karera wo toorisugi te iki mashi ta. furanku junsa buchou ha maiku wo futatabi to tte ii mashi ta. "kochira piー zero nana ban desu. supiーdo ihan wo shi te iru aoi kuruma wo mitsuke mashi ta. tsuiseki wo kaishi shi masu." sonogo, kare wa otokonoko tachi ni ii masu.

"しーとべるとを閉めてください。"ぱとかーは素早く発進しました。巡査部長は、がすをいっぱいに踏んで、さいれんをつけました。彼らは鳴り渡るさいれんと共に、建物、車そしてばすを急いで抜けます。ふらんく巡査部長は青い車をとめさせました。巡査部長は車から出てすぴーど違反の人のところまで行きました。でいびっどとろばーとは彼の後を行きます。"shi-toberuto wo shime te kudasai." patokaー wa subayaku hasshin shi mashi ta. junsa buchou wa, gasu wo ippai ni fun de, sairen wo tsuke mashi ta. karera wa nariwataru sairen totomoni, tatemono, kuruma soshite basu wo isoi de nuke masu. furanku junsa buchou wa aoi kuruma wo tome sase mashi ta.

the speeding blue car. Begin pursuit," then he said to the boys,

"Fasten your seat belts." The police car started quickly. The sergeant stepped on the gas up to the stop and switched on the siren. They rushed with the howling siren past buildings, cars and buses. Frank Strict made the blue car stop. Sergeant got out of the car and went to the speeder. David and Robert went after him.

junsa buchou wa kuruma kara de te supi─do ihan no hito no tokoro made iki mashi ta. deibiddo to roba─to wa kare no ato wo iki masu.

"わたしはふらんく巡査部長です。運転免許証を見せてください。"警察官がすぴーど違反の人に言いました。"わたしの運転免許証はこれです。"運転手が自分の運転免許証を見せました。"どうしたんですか?"彼は怒りながら言いました。"watashi wa furanku junsa buchou desu. unten menkyo shou wo mise te kudasai." keisatsukan ga supi─do ihan no hito ni ii mashi ta. "watashi no unten menkyo shou wa kore desu." unten shu ga jibun no unten menkyo shou wo mise mashi ta. "dou shi ta n desu ka?" kare wa ikari nagara ii mashi ta.

"あなたは街の中を時速120きろで運転をしていました。すぴーどりみっとは50きろです。"巡査部長が言いました。"ああ、これ。ほら、わたしは車を洗ったばかりなのです。だから、乾かすために少し速く運転していたんですよ。"男はいじわるな笑みで言いました。"車を洗うのには、お金がたくさんかかりますか?"警察官は聞きました。"いいえ、そんなに

"I am police officer Frank Strict. Show your driving license, please," the policeman said to the speeder.

"Here is my driving license," the driver showed his driving license, "What is the matter?" he said angrily.

"You were driving through the city with a speed of one hundred and twenty kilometers an hour. The speed limit is fifty," the sergeant said.

"Ah, this. You see, I have just washed my car. So I was driving a little faster to dry it up," the man said with a sly smile.

"Does it cost much to wash the car?" the policeman asked.

。12どるでしたよ。"すぴーど違反の人は言いました "anata wa machi no naka wo jisoku hyaku ni ju kkiro de unten wo shi te i mashi ta. supi―do rimitto wa go ju kkiro desu." junsa buchou ga ii mashi ta. "aa, kore. hora, watashi wa kuruma wo ara tta bakari na no desu. dakara, kawakasu tame ni sukoshi hayaku unten shi te i ta n desu yo." otoko wa ijiwaru na emi de ii mashi ta. "kuruma wo arau no ni wa, okane ga takusan kakari masu ka?" keisatsukan wa kiki mashi ta. "iie, sonnani. juu ni doru deshi ta yo." supi―do ihan no hito wa ii mashi ta.

"あなたは値段を知らないようですね。"すとりくと巡査部長は言いました。
"本当は212どるなんですよ、なぜならあなたは車を乾かすのに200どる支払うからです。これがすぴーど違反切符です。良い一日を。"警察官は言いました。彼は200どるのすぴーど違反切符と運転免許証をすぴーど違反の人に渡してぱとかーへ戻りました。"anata wa nedan wo shira nai you desu ne." sutorikuto junsa buchou wa ii mashi ta. "hontouwa ni hyaku juu ni doru na n desu yo, nazenara anata wa kuruma wo kawakasu no ni ni hyaku doru shiharau kara desu. kore ga supi―do ihan kippu desu. yoi ichi nichi wo." keisatsukan wa ii mashi ta. kare ha ni zero zero doru no supi―do ihan kippu to unten menkyo shou wo supi―do ihan no hito ni watashi te patoka― e modori mashi ta.

"ふらんく、あなたはたくさんのすぴーど

"Not much. It cost twelve dollars," the speeder said.

"You do not know the prices," sergeant Strict said, "It really costs you two hundred and twelve dollars because you will pay two hundred dollars for drying the car. Here is the ticket. Have a nice day," the policeman said. He gave a speeding ticket for two hundred dollars and the driving license to the speeder and went back to the police car.

"Frank, I think you have lots of

違反者との経験があるんですね、違いますか？" でいびっどが警察官に聞きました。"たくさんありますね。" ふらんくがえんじんをかけながら言いました。"初めは、彼らは怒った虎や、ずる賢い狐のようなのです。でもわたしが話した後には、彼らは怖がる子猫か、間抜けな猿のように見えます。あの青い車の人のように。"

"furanku, anata wa takusan no supīdo ihan sha to no keiken ga aru n desu ne, chigai masu ka?" deibiddo ga keisatsukan ni kiki mashi ta. "takusan ari masu ne." furanku ga enjin wo kake nagara ii mashi ta. "hajime wa, karera wa oko tta tora ya, zuru kashikoi kitsune no you na no desu. demo watashi ga hanashi ta nochi ni wa, karera wa kowagaru koneko ka, manuke na saru no you ni mie masu. ano aoi kuruma no hito no you ni."

その時、小さな白い車が、街の公園から離れていない道沿いを、ゆっくりと走っていました。お店の近くで車は止まりました。男性と女性が車から降りてきて、お店まで行きました。お店は閉まっていました。男は周りを見回しました。そして彼は鍵をいくつか素早く取り出して、どあを開けようとしました。最後に、彼はどあを開け、彼らが中へ入って行きました。

sono toki, chiisana shiroi kuruma ga, machi

"I have met many of them," Frank said starting the engine, "At first they look like angry tigers or sly foxes. But after I speak with them, they look like afraid kittens or silly monkeys. Like that one in the blue car."

Meanwhile a little white car was slowly driving along a street not far from the city park. The car stopped near a shop. A man and a woman got out of the car and went up to the shop. It was closed. The man looked around. Then he quickly took out some keys and tried to open the door. At last he opened it and they went inside.

experiences with speeders, haven't you?" David asked the policeman.

no kouen kara hanare te i nai michi zoi wo, yukkuri to hashi tte i mashi ta. o mise no chikaku de kuruma wa tomari mashi ta. dansei to josei ga kuruma kara ori te ki te, o mise made iki mashita. o mise wa shima tte i mashi ta. otoko wa mawari wo mimawashi mashi ta. soshite kare wa kagi wo ikutsu ka subayaku toridashi te, doa wo akeyo u to shi mashi ta. saigo ni, kare wa doa wo ake, karera ga naka e hai tte iki mashi ta.

"みて！ここには本当にたくさんのどれすがある！" 女性が言いました。彼女は大きなかばんを取り出して、全てをその中に入れ始めました。かばんがいっぱいになると、彼女はそれを車へ持って行き、そして戻ってきました。"急いで全部をつめて！わあ！なんて素敵な帽子なんだ！" 男は言いました。彼はお店のういんどーから大きな黒い帽子を取って、かぶりました。"mi te! koko ni wa hontouni takusan no doresu ga aru!" josei ga ii mashi ta. kanojo wa ookina kaban wo toridashi te, subete wo sono naka ni ire hajime mashi ta. kaban ga ippai ni naru to, kanojo wa sore wo kuruma e mo tte iki, soshite modo tte ki mashi ta. "isoi de zenbu wo tsume te! waa! nante suteki na boushi na n da!" otoko wa ii mashi ta. kare wa o mise no windo— kara ookina kuroi boushi wo to tte, kaburi mashi ta.

"この赤いどれすをみて！すごく気に入った！" 女はそう言い、素早く赤いどれすを着ました。彼女は他のかばんは持っていま

"Look! There are so many dresses here!" the woman said. She took out a big bag and began to put in everything there. When the bag was full, she took it to the car and came back.

"Take everything quickly! Oh! What a wonderful hat!" the man said. He took from the shop window a big black hat and put it on.

"Look at this red dress! I like it so much!" the woman said and quickly put on the red dress. She

せんでした。なので彼女は、他のものも手にとって、外へ走り出てそれらを車に置きました。そして彼女は、他のものを運ぶために中へ走っていきました。"kono akai doresu wo mi te! sugoku kinii tta!" onna wa sou ii, subayaku akai doresu wo ki mashi ta. kanojo wa hoka no kaban wa mo tte i mase n deshi ta. nanode kanojo wa, hoka no mono mo te nitotte, soto e hashiride te sorera wo kuruma ni oki mashi ta. soshite kanojo wa, hoka no mono wo hakobu tame ni naka e hashi tte iki mashi ta.

did not have more bags. So she took more things in her hands, ran outside and put them on the car. Then she ran inside to bring more things.

無線が喋り始めたときに、ぱとかーP07は街の公園沿いをゆっくり運転していました。"全てのぱとろーる隊、注意して聞いてください。街の公園の近くのお店から窃盗警報がなりました。お店の住所はぱーく通り72番です。" musen ga shaberi hajime ta toki ni, patoka—pi— zero nana wa machi no kouen zoi wo yukkuri unten shi te i mashi ta. "subete no patoro—ru tai, chuui shi te kii te kudasai. machi no kouen no chikaku no o mise kara settou keihou ga nari mashi ta. o mise no juusho wa pa—ku doori nana juu ni ban desu."

The police car P07 was slowly driving along the city park when the radio began to talk: "Attention all patrols. We have got a robbery alarm from a shop near the city park. The address of the shop is 72 Park street."

"P07、了解しました。" ふらんくはまいくで言いました。"わたしはこの場所のとても近くにいます。そこへ向かいます。" 彼らはお店をすぐに見つけ、白い車まで

"P07 got it," Frank said in the mic, "I am very close to this place. Drive there." They found the shop very quickly and drove

215

運転して行きました。そして彼らは車から出て行き、その後ろに隠れました。新しい赤いどれすを着た女が、お店から走って出てきます。彼女はいくつかのどれすをぱとかーの上に置いて、走ってお店の中へ戻って行きます。女はとても素早くそれを行いました。彼女はそれがぱとかーだったのに気づかなかったのです！

"pi— zero nana, ryoukai shi mashi ta." furanku wa maiku de ii mashi ta. "watashi wa kono basho no totemo chikaku ni i masu. soko e mukai masu." karera wa o mise wo suguni mitsuke, shiroi kuruma made unten shi te iki mashi ta. soshite karera wa kuruma kara de te iki, sono ushiro ni kakure mashi ta. atarashii akai doresu wo ki ta onna ga, o mise kara hashi tte de te ki masu. kanojo wa ikutsu ka no doresu wo patoka— no ue ni oi te, hashi tte o mise no naka e modo tte iki masu. onna wa totemo subayaku sore wo okonai mashi ta. kanojo wa sore ga patoka— da tta noni kizuka naka tta no desu!

"ちくしょう！警察署に銃を忘れてきた！"ふらんくが言いました。ろばーととでいびっどはすとりくと巡査を見て、そしてお互いに驚きました。警察官はとても混乱していて、でいびっどとろばーとは、彼らが彼を手伝わなければならない、と理解しました。女が店から再び走

up to the white car. Then they got out of the car and hid behind it. The woman in new red dress ran out of the shop. She put some dresses on the police car and ran back in the shop. The woman did it very quickly. She did not see that it was a police car!

"Damn it! I forgot my gun in the police station!" Frank said. Robert and David looked at the sergeant Strict and then surprised at each other. The policeman was so confused that David and Robert understood they must help him. The woman

り出て、ぱとかーの上にどれすをおき、走りもどって行きます。その後、でいびっどがふらんくに言いました："ぼくたち、銃をもっているふりならできますよ。" "chikushou! keisatsu sho ni juu wo wasure te ki ta!" furanku ga ii mashi ta. robaーto to deibiddo wa sutorikuto junsa wo mi te, soshite otagai ni odoroki mashi ta. keisatsukan wa totemo konran shi te i te, deibiddo to robaーto wa, karera ga kare wo tetsudawa nakere ba nara nai, to rikai shi mashi ta. onna ga mise kara futatabi hashiride te, patokaー no ue ni doresu wo oki, hashiri modo tte iki masu. sonogo, deibiddo ga furanku ni ii mashi ta : "boku tachi, juu wo mo tte iru furi nara deki masu yo."

"そうしよう！"ふらんくはこたえました。"でも、立ち上がらないで。泥棒たちは銃を持っているかもしれません。"彼はそう言い、それから叫びました。"こちらは警察です！店の中にいる者は、全員手を上げ、一人ずつゆっくりと店の外へ出てきなさい！"彼らは1分ほど待ちました。誰も出てきませんでした。その後、ろばーとは思いつきました。 "sou shiyo u!" furanku wa kotae mashi ta. "demo, tachiagara nai de. dorobou tachi wa juu wo mo tte iru kamo shire mase n." kare wa sou ii, sore kara sakebi mashi ta. "kochira wa keisatsu desu! mise no naka ni iru mono wa, zen'in te wo age, hitori zutsu yukkuri to mise no soto e de te ki nasai!" karera wa i ppun hodo machi mashi ta. dare mo de te ki mase n deshi ta. sonogo, robaーto wa omoitsuki mashi ta.

ran out of the shop again, put some dresses on the police car and ran back. Then David said to Frank: "We can pretend that we have guns."

"Let's do it," Frank answered, "But you do not get up. The thieves may have guns," he said and then cried, "This is the police speaking! Everybody who is inside the shop put your hands up and come slowly one by one out of the shop!"

They waited for a minute. Nobody came out. Then Robert had an idea.

"もし今出てこないのであれば、警察犬を使います！"彼はそう叫び、怒った大きな犬のように吠えました。泥棒たちは手をあげ、すぐに外へ走って出てきました。ふらんくは急いで彼らに手錠をし、ぱとかーに乗せました。そして彼はろばーとに言いました："犬を持っているふりをしたのは名案でした！わたしはすでに二度も銃を忘れています。忘れたのが3回目だと、もし彼らが知れば、彼らはわたしを解雇するか、もしくはわたしにおふぃすわーくをさせるかもしれません。あなたたちは、このことを誰にもいいませんよね？" "moshi ima de te ko nai no de are ba, keisatsu ken wo tsukai masu!" kare wa sou sakebi, oko tta ookina inu no you ni hoe mashi ta. dorobou tachi wa te wo age, suguni soto e hashi tte de te ki mashi ta. furanku wa isoi de karera ni tejou wo shi, patokaー ni nose mashi ta. soshite kare wa robaーto ni ii mashi ta : "inu wo mo tte iru furi wo shi ta no wa meian deshi ta! watashi wa sudeni ni do mo juu wo wasure te i masu. wasure ta no ga san kai me da to, moshi karera ga shire ba, karera wa watashi wo kaiko suru ka, moshikuha watashi ni ofisu waーku wo sa seru kamo shire mase n. anata tachi wa, kono koto wo dare ni mo ii mase n yo ne?"

"もちろん、言いません！"ろばーとが言いました。"決して言いません。"でいびっどが言います。"わたしを助けてくれて本当にあり

"If you will not come out now, we will set the police dog on you!" he cried and then barked like a big angry dog. The thieves ran out with hands up immediately. Frank quickly put handcuffs on them and got them to the police car. Then he said to Robert: "It was a great idea pretending that we have a dog! You see, I have forgotten my gun two times already. If they learn that I have forgotten it for the third time, they may fire me or make me do office work. You will not tell anybody about it, will you?"

"Sure, not!" Robert said.

"Never," David said.

がとうございます！"ふらんくは彼(かれ)らの手(て)を力強(ちからづよ)く握手(あくしゅ)しました。"mochiron, ii mase n!" roba—to ga ii mashi ta. "kesshite ii mase n." deibiddo ga ii masu. "watashi wo tasuke te kure te hontouni arigatou gozai masu!" furanku wa karera no te wo chikarazuyoku akushu shi mashi ta.

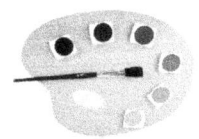

"Thank you very much for helping me, guys!" Frank shook their hands strongly.

28

Audio

<ruby>警察<rt>けいさつ</rt></ruby> パトロール (パート2)

The police patrol (Part 2)

 A

単語
Words

1. かける、なった [kakeru, natta] - rang
2. ガラス [garasu] - glass
3. ショッピングセンター [shoppingu sentaー] - shopping center
4. すいません [suimasen] - Excuse me.
5. なくなる、行く [nakunaru, iku] - gone
6. ポケット [poketto] - pocket
7. ボタン [botan] - button

8. まだ [mada] - yet
9. みた、目撃した [mi ta, mokugeki shi ta] - saw
10. めったにない [mettani nai] - seldom
11. も、同様に、同じく [mo, douyou ni, onajiku] - either, too, also
12. レジ；銀行の支配人、レジ係、テラー [reji ; ginkou no shihainin, reji gakari, teraー] - cash register; cashier, teller
13. わたしの [watashi no] - mine
14. 取られた、盗まれた、 [tora re ta, nusuma re ta,] - taken
15. 向いた、曲がった [mui ta, maga tta] - turned
16. 守る [mamoru] - protect
17. 安全な [anzen na] - safe
18. 密かに、秘密に [hisoka ni, himitsu ni] - secretly
19. 応えた、答えた [kotae ta, kotae ta] - answered
20. 押す [osu] - press
21. 携帯電話、 [keitai denwa,] - mobile
22. 撃つ [utsu] - shot
23. 敬具 [keigu] - yours sincerely
24. 昨日 [kinou] - yesterday
25. 普段の、いつもの [fudan no, itsumo no] - usual
26. 泥棒、強盗、窃盗をする人 [dorobou, goutou, settou wo suru hito] - robber
27. 泥棒、窃盗、強盗 [dorobou, settou, goutou] - robbery
28. 無意識に、意識をなくして [muishiki ni, ishiki wo nakushi te] - unconscious
29. 現金、キャッシュ [genkin, kyasshu] - cash
30. 男性、人（複数） [dansei, hito （fukusuu）] - men
31. 盗まれた [nusuma re ta] - stolen
32. 許す [yurusu] - excuse
33. 誰か [dare ka] - somebody
34. 誰の [dare no] - whose
35. 賢い、頭のいい [kashikoi, atama no ii] - clever
36. 跳飛、跳ね返ること [chouhi, hanekaeru koto] - ricochet
37. 開けた、開いた、開いている [ake ta, hirai ta, hirai te iru] - opened
38. 電話 [denwa] - phone
39. 電話をする [denwa wo suru] - to phone

B

警察パトロール（パート２）

keisatsu patoro—ru (pa—to ni)

翌日、ろばーととでいびっどは、再びふらんくに同伴していました。女性が彼らのほうにやってきた時、彼らは大きなしょっぴんぐせんたーの近くに立っていました。yokujitsu, roba—to to deibiddo wa, futatabi furanku ni douhan shite imashi ta. josei ga karera no hou ni yatteki ta toki, karera wa ookina shoppingu senta— no chikaku ni ta tte i mashi ta.

"お願いします、助けてもらえますか？"彼女は聞きました。"もちろん。何があったんですか？"ふらんくは聞きました。"携帯電話がないんです。盗まれたのだと思います。" "今日、携帯電話は使われていますか？: 警察官は聞きます。"onegai shi masu, tasuke te morae masu ka?" kanojo wa kiki mashi ta. "mochiron. nani ga a tta n desu ka?" furanku wa kiki mashi ta. "keitai denwa ga nai n desu. nusuma re ta no da to omoi masu." "kyou, keitai denwa wa tsukawa re te i masu ka? : keisatsukan wa kiki masu.

"しょっぴんぐせんたーを出る前にわたしが使いました。"彼女は答えました。

The police patrol (Part 2)

Next day Robert and David were accompanying Frank again. They were standing near a big shopping centre when a woman came to them.

"Can you help me please?" she asked.

"Sure, madam. What has happened?" Frank asked.

"My mobile phone is gone. I think it has been stolen."

"Has it been used today?" the policeman asked.

"It had been used by me before I went out of the shopping centre,"

"中へ入りましょう。"ふらんくは言います。彼らはしょっぴんぐせんたーの中に入り、見て回りました。そこには、たくさんの人がいました。"昔ながらの技を使いましょう。"ふらんくは自分の電話を取り出しながら言いました。"shoppingu sentā wo deru mae ni watashi ga tsukai mashi ta." kanojo wa kotae mashi ta. "naka e hairi masho u." furanku wa ii masu. karera wa shoppingu sentā no naka ni hairi, mi te mawari mashi ta. soko ni wa, takusan no hito ga i mashi ta. "mukashinagara no waza wo tsukai masho u." furanku wa jibun no denwa wo toridashi nagara ii mashi ta.

"あなたの電話番号は何ですか？"彼は女性に聞きます。彼女は彼に伝え、彼は彼女の番号に電話をしました。彼らから離れていないところで、携帯電話がなりました。彼らはそれがなったところまで行きました。そこには列がありました。列の中の男が警察官を見て、そして素早く頭の向きを変えました。警察官は近くに行き、注意深く耳を傾けました。電話は男のぽけっとの中でなっています。"anata no denwa bangou wa nan desu ka?" kare wa josei ni kiki masu. kanojo wa kare ni tsutae, kare wa kanojo no bangou

she answered.

"Let's get inside," Frank said. They went into the shopping centre and looked around. There were many people there.

"Let's try an old trick," Frank said taking out his own phone, "What is your telephone number?" he asked the woman. She said and he called her telephone number. A mobile telephone rang not far from them. They went to the place where it was ringing. There was a queue there. A man in the queue looked at the policeman and then quickly turned his head away. The policeman came closer listening carefully. The telephone was ringing in the man's pocket.

ni denwa wo shi mashi ta. karera kara hanare te i nai tokoro de, keitai denwa ga nari mashi ta. karera wa sore ga na tta tokoro made iki mashi ta. soko ni wa retsu ga ari mashi ta. retsu no naka no otoko ga keisatsukan wo mi te, soshite subayaku atama no muki wo kae mashi ta. keisatsukan wa chikaku ni iki, chuuibukaku mimi wo katamuke mashi ta. denwa wa otoko no poketto no naka de na tte i masu.

"すいません。"ふらんくは言いました。男は彼を見ました。"すいません。あなたの電話がなっていますよ。"ふらんくは言いました。"どこですか?"男は言いました。"そこ、あなたのぽけっとの中ですよ。"ふらんくは言いました。"いいえ、違いますよ。"男は言いました。"なっていますよ。"ふらんくは言いました。"わたしのではありません。"男は言いました。"suimasen." furanku wa ii mashi ta. otoko wa kare wo mi mashi ta. "suimasen. anata no denwa ga na tte i masu yo." furanku wa ii mashi ta. "doko desu ka?" otoko wa ii mashi ta. "soko, anata no poketto no naka desu yo." furanku wa ii mashi ta. "iie, chigai masu yo." otoko wa ii mashi ta. "na tte i masu yo." furanku wa ii mashi ta. "watashi no de wa ari mase n." otoko wa ii mashi ta.

"それでは、誰の電話があなたのぽけっとでなっているのですか?"ふらんくが聞きました。"知らないですよ。"男が答えました。"わたしにみせてください。"ふらんくはそう言

"Excuse me," Frank said. The man looked at him.

"Excuse me, your telephone is ringing," Frank said.

"Where?" the man said.

"Here, in your pocket," Frank said.

"No, it is not," the man said.

"Yes, it is," Frank said

"It is not mine," the man said.

"Then whose telephone is ringing in your pocket?" Frank asked.

"I do not know," the man answered.

い、男のぽけっとの中から電話を取り出しました。"ああ、わたしの電話よ！"女性が叫びました。"あなたの電話をうけとってください。"ふらんくはそう言い、彼女に電話を渡します。"soredewa, dare no denwa ga anata no poketto de na tte iru no desu ka?" furanku ga kiki mashi ta. "shira nai desu yo." otoko ga kotae mashi ta. "watashi ni mise te kudasai." furanku wa sou ii, otoko no poketto no naka kara denwa wo toridashi mashi ta. "aa, watashi no denwa yo!" josei ga sakebi mashi ta. "anata no denwa wo uketo tte kudasai." furanku wa sou ii, kanojo ni denwa wo watashi masu.

"いいですか？"ふらんくはそう聞いて、男のぽけっとの中に再び手を入れました。彼は別の電話を取り出しました。そして、またもう一つ。"これらもあなたの電話ではないのですか？"ふらんくは男に聞きました。男は頭を振り、目線を反らしました。"ii desu ka?" furanku wa sou kii te, otoko no poketto no naka ni futatabi te wo ire mashi ta. kare wa betsu no denwa wo toridashi mashi ta. soshite, mata mou hitotsu. "korera mo anata no denwa de wa nai no desu ka?" furanku wa otoko ni kiki mashi ta. otoko wa atama wo furi, mesen wo sorashi mashi ta.

"何ておかしな電話だ！"ふらんくは叫びました。"彼らは持ち主から逃げてきて、この男のぽけっとの中に入り込んだんだ！

"Let me see, please," Frank said and took the telephone out of the man's pocket.

"Oh, it is mine!" the woman cried.

"Take your telephone, madam," Frank said giving it to her.

"May I, sir?" Frank asked and put his hand in the man's pocket again. He took out another telephone, and then one more.

"Are they not yours either?" Frank asked the man.

The man shook his head looking away.

"What strange telephones!" Frank cried, "They ran away from their owners and jump into the pockets of this man! And now

そして彼のぽけっとで今、なっているんですよね？""そうですね。"男は言いました。"わたしの仕事は人々を守ることですよね。なので、わたしはあなたを彼らから守ります。わたしの車にのってください。どんな電話もあなたのぽけっとに入り込めないところへ、わたしがあなたを連れて行きますよ。警察署へいくんですよ。"警察官が言いました。"nani te okashina denwa da!" furanku wa sakebi mashi ta. "karera wa mochinushi kara nige te ki te, kono otoko no poketto no naka ni hairikon da n da! soshite kare no poketto de ima, na tte iru n desu yo ne?" "sou desu ne." otoko wa ii mashi ta. "watashi no shigoto wa hitobito wo mamoru koto desu yo ne. na node, watashi wa anata wo karera kara mamori masu. watashi no kuruma ni no tte kudasai. donna denwa mo anata no poketto ni hairikome nai tokoro e, watashi ga anata wo tsure te iki masu yo. keisatsu sho e iku n desu yo." keisatsukan ga ii mashi ta.

そして、彼は男の腕を掴み、ぱとかーまで連れて行きました。"わたしは、おばかなはんざいしゃ犯罪者たちが好きなんです。"彼らがどろぼう泥棒を警察所へ連れて行ったあとに、ふらんく・すとりくとは笑いました。"賢いのにはあったことがありますか？"でいびっどが聞きました。"はい、ありますよ。でも、ほ

they are ringing in his pockets, aren't they?"

"Yes, they are," the man said.

"You know, my job is to protect people. And I will protect you from them. Get in my car and I will bring you to the place where no telephone can jump in your pocket. We go to the police station," the policeman said.

Then he took the man by the arm and took him to the police car.

"I like silly criminals," Frank Strict smiled after they had taken the thief to the police station.

"Have you met smart ones?" David asked.

とんどありません。" 警察官が答えました。"賢い泥棒を捕まえるのは、大変だからです。" soshite, kare wa otoko no ude wo tsukami, patoka— made tsure te iki mashi ta. "watashi wa, o baka na hanzai sha tachi ga suki na n desu." karera ga dorobou wo keisatsu sho e tsure te i tta ato ni, furanku. sutorikuto wa warai mashi ta. "kashikoi no ni wa a tta koto ga ari masu ka?" deibiddo ga kiki mashi ta. "hai, ari masu yo. demo, hotondo ari mase n." keisatsukan ga kotae mashi ta. "kashikoi dorobou wo tsukamaeru no wa, taihen da kara desu."

その間、二人の男がえくすぷれす銀行の中へ入りました。男の一人が列に並びました。別の男はれじまで行って、れじ係に用紙を渡しました。れじ係は用紙を受け取って、読みます。"拝啓、わたしはえくすぷれす銀行の強盗です。全ての現金をわたしに出してください。もし出さなければ、銃を使います。ありがとうございます。敬具、ぼぶ" sonokan, futari no otoko ga ekusupuresu ginkou no naka e hairi mashi ta. otoko no hitori ga retsu ni narabi mashi ta. betsu no otoko wa reji made i tte, reji gakari ni youshi wo watashi mashi ta. reji gakari ha youshi wo uketo tte, yomi masu. "haikei, watashi wa ekusupuresu ginkou no goutou desu. subete no genkin wo watashi ni dashi te kudasai. moshi dasa nakere ba, juu wo tsukai masu.

"Yes, I have. But very seldom," the policeman answered, "Because it is very hard to catch a smart criminal."

Meanwhile two men came into the Express Bank. One of them took a place in a queue. Another one came up to the cash register and gave a paper to the cashier. The cashier took the paper and read:

"Dear Sir,
this is a robbery of the Express Bank. Give me all the cash. If you do not, then I will use my gun.
Thank you.
Sincerely yours,
Bob"

arigatou gozai masu. keigu, bobu"

"わたしがお手伝いできると思います。"レジ係は、警報ぼたんをこっそり押しながら言いました。"しかし、お金は昨日、わたしが金庫に鍵を閉めて入れてしまったんです。金庫はまだ開けられていません。誰かに金庫を開け、お金を持ってくるように頼みます。大丈夫ですか？" "watashi ga otetsudai dekiru to omoi masu." reji gakari wa, keihou botan wo kossori oshi nagara ii mashi ta. "shikashi, okane wa kinou, watashi ga kinko ni kagi wo shime te ire te shima tta n desu. kinko wa mada ake rare te i mase n. dareka ni kinko wo ake, okane wo mo tte kuru you ni tanomi masu. daijoubu desu ka?"

"わかりました！急いでやってください！"強盗が答えました。"お金をばっぐにつめている間、こーひーを入れましょうか？"レジ係が聞きます。"いいえ、だいじょうぶです。お金だけで。"強盗が答えました。
"wakari mashi ta! isoi de ya tte kudasai!" goutou ga kotae mashi ta. "okane wo baggu ni tsume te iru kan, ko―hi― wo ire masho u ka?" reji gakari ga kiki masu. "iie, daijoubu desu. okane dake de." goutou ga kotae mashi ta.

ぱとかーP07の無線が喋り始めました：全てのぱとろーる隊、注意して聞い

"I think I can help you," the cashier said pressing secretly the alarm button, "But the money had been locked by me in the safe yesterday. The safe has not been opened yet.
I will ask somebody to open the safe and bring the money. Okay?"

"Okay! But do it quickly!" the robber answered.

"Shall I make you a cup of coffee while the money is being put in bags?" the cashier asked.

"No, thank you. Just money," the robber answered.

The radio in the police car P07 began to talk: "Attention all the patrols. We have got a

てください。えくすぷれす銀行の強盗警報がならされました。" "P07、了解しました。"すとりくと巡査部長がこたえました。彼はがすをいっぱいに踏み、車を素早く発進させました。銀行まで運転したときに、他のぱとかーは、まだありませんでした。patokaー piー zero nana no musen ga shaberi hajime mashi ta：subete no patoroーru tai, chuui shi te kii te kudasai. ekusupuresu ginkou no goutou keihou ga narasa re mashi ta." "piー zero nana, ryoukai shi mashi ta." sutorikuto junsa buchou ga kotae mashi ta. kare wa gasu wo ippai ni fumi, kuruma wo subayaku hasshin sa se mashi ta. ginkou made unten shi ta toki ni, ta no patokaー wa, mada ari mase n deshi ta.

"もし中へ入れば、ぼくたちはおもしろい警察れぽーとができるね。"でいびっどが言いました。"あなたたちが必要なことをしてください。わたしは、裏のどあから中へ入ります。"巡査部長が言いました。彼は銃を手に取り、銀行の裏のどあへ素早く行きました。"moshi naka e haire ba, boku tachi wa omoshiroi keisatsu repoーto ga dekiru ne." deibiddo ga ii mashi ta. "anata tachi ga hitsuyou na koto wo shi te kudasai. watashi wa, ura no doa kara naka e hairi masu." junsa buchou ga ii mashi ta. kare wa juu wo te ni tori, ginkou no ura no doa e subayaku iki mashi ta.

robbery alarm from the Express Bank."

"P07 got it," sergeant Strict answered. He stepped on the gas up to the stop and the car started quickly. When they drove up to the bank, there was no other police car yet.

"We will make an interesting report if we go inside," David said.

"You guys do what you need. And I will come inside through the back door," sergeant Strict said. He took out his gun and went quickly to the back door of the bank.

でいびっどとろばーとは、真ん中のどあから銀行の中へ入りました。彼らは、れじの近くに男が立っているのをみつけました。彼はぽけっとの中に片手を入れて辺りを見回しました。彼と一緒に来た男は、列からはなれて彼の方へ来ました。"お金はどこだい？"彼はぼぶに聞きました。"ろじゃー、ばっぐに詰められてるってれじ係が言ってるよ。"別の強盗が答えました。deibiddo to robaーto wa, mannaka no doa kara ginkou no naka e hairi mashi ta. karera wa, reji no chikaku ni otoko ga ta tte iru no wo mitsuke mashi ta. kare wa poketto no naka ni katate wo ire te atari wo mimawashi mashi ta. kare to issho ni ki ta otoko wa, retsu kara hanare te kare no hou e ki mashi ta. "okane wa doko dai?" kare wa bobu ni kiki mashi ta. "rojaー, baggu ni tsume rare teru tte reji gakari ga i tteru yo." betsu no goutou ga kotae mashi ta.

"待ち疲れたよ！"ろじゃーが言いました。彼は銃を取り出して、それをれじ係へ向けました。"今すぐお金を全部もってこい！"強盗はれじ係へそう叫びました。そして彼は、部屋の真ん中まで行き、叫びました。"全員聞け！俺は強盗だ！誰も動くな！"この頃、れじの近く

David and Robert came into the bank through the central door. They saw a man standing near the cash register. He put one hand in his pocket and looked around. The man, who came with him, stepped away from the queue and came up to him.

"Where is the money?" he asked Bob.

"Roger, the cashier has said that it is being put in bags," another robber answered.

"I am tired of waiting!" Roger said. He took out a gun and pointed it to the cashier, "Bring all the money now!" the robber cried at the cashier. Then he went to the middle of the room and cried: "Listen all! This is a robbery! Nobody move!" At this moment somebody near the cash

の誰かが動きました。銃を持った強盗は、それを見もせずに彼を撃ちました。別の強盗が床へ倒れ、叫びました："ろじゃー！ばかものめ！俺を撃ったな！"

"machi zukare ta yo!" rojaー ga ii mashi ta. kare wa juu wo toridashi te, sore wo reji gakari e muke mashi ta. "ima sugu okane wo zenbu mottekoi!" goutou wa reji gakari e sou sakebi mashi ta. soshite kare wa, heya no mannaka made iki, sakebi mashi ta. "zen'in kike! ore wa goutou da! dare mo ugoku na!" kono koro, reji no chikaku no dareka ga ugoki mashi ta. juu wo mo tta goutou wa, sore wo mi mo se zu ni kare wo uchi mashi ta. betsu no goutou ga yuka e taore, sakebi mashi ta : "rojaー! baka mo nome! ore wo u tta na!"

"わあ、ぼびー！君だとは、知らなかったんだ！"ろじゃーが言いました。この瞬間、れじ係は素早く逃げました。"れじ係が逃げて、まだお金が届かないよ！"ろじゃーがぼぶへ叫びました。"警察がすぐ来るかもしれない！どうすればいい？" "waa, bobiー! kimi da to ha, shira naka tta n da!" rojaー ga ii mashi ta. kono shunkan, reji gakari wa subayaku nige mashi ta. "reji gakari ga nige te, mada okane ga todoka nai yo!" rojaー ga bobu e sakebi mashi ta. "keisatsu ga sugu kuru kamo shire nai! dou sure ba ii?"

"何か大きなものを取るんだ！がらすを割って、お金を取るんだ、早く！"ぼぶは叫びました。ろじゃーは金属のいすを取り、れじ

register moved. The robber with the gun without looking shot at him. Another robber fell on the floor and cried: "Roger! You idiot! Damn it! You have shot me!"

"Oh, Bobby! I did not see that it was you!" Roger said. At this moment the cashier quickly ran out.

"The cashier has run away and the money has not been taken here yet!" Roger cried to Bob, "The police may arrive soon! What shall we do?"

"Take something big, break the glass and take the money. Quickly!" Bob cried. Roger took a

のがらすにぶつけました。それはもちろん普通のがらすではないので、割れませんでした。しかし、いすが跳ね返って強盗の頭に当たりました！彼は、意識をなくして床へ倒れました。この瞬間、すとりくと巡査部長は中へ走って行き、強盗にすばやく手錠をかけました。彼はでいびっどとろばーとのほうを向きました。"言ったでしょう！犯罪者のほとんどが、ただのおばかだって！"彼が言いました。"nani ka ookina mono wo toru n da! garasu wo wa tte, okane wo toru n da, hayaku!" bobu wa sakebi mashi ta. roja— wa kinzoku no isu wo tori, reji no garasu ni butsuke mashi ta. sore wa mochiron futsuu no garasu de wa nai node, ware mase n deshi ta. shikashi, isu ga hanekae tte goutou no atama ni atari mashi ta! kare wa, ishiki wo nakushi te yuka e taore mashi ta. kono shunkan, sutorikuto junsa buchou wa naka e hashi tte iki, goutou ni subayaku tejou wo kake mashi ta. kare wa deibiddo to roba—to no hou wo muki mashi ta. "i tta desho u! hanzai sha no hotondo ga, tada no oba ka datte!" kare ga ii mashi ta.

metal chair and hit the glass of the cash register. It was of course not usual glass and it did not break. But the chair went back by ricochet and hit the robber on the head! He fell on the floor unconsciously. At this moment sergeant Strict ran inside and quickly put handcuffs on the robbers. He turned to David and Robert.

"I did say! Most criminals are just silly!" he said.

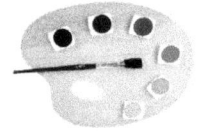

29

Audio

留学生の学校とオペア
School for foreign students (SFS) and au pair

A

単語
Words

1. アメリカ [amerika] - the United States/the USA
2. インターネットのサイト [intaーnetto no saito] - Internet site
3. から [kara] - since *(temporal)*
4. コース [koーsu] - course
5. スタンダードの、普通の [sutandaーdo no, futsuu no] - standard
6. なぜなら、だから [nazenara, dakara] - as, since *(kausal)*

7. ホスト [hosuto] - host
8. ホストファミリー [hosutofamiri一] - the host family
9. また、同じく、同様に [mata, onajiku, douyou ni] - also
10. メール [me一ru] - e-mail
11. 一度 [ichi do] - once
12. 一番近くの [ichiban chikaku no] - nearest
13. 不公平 [fukouhei] - unfair
14. 二度 [ni do] - twice
15. 人 [hito] - person
16. 住んでいた [sun de i ta] - lived
17. 使用人 [shiyounin] - servant
18. 勉強している、習っている [benkyou shi te iru, nara tte iru] - learning
19. 北米とユーラシア [hokubei to yu一rashia] - North America and Eurasia
20. 参加する [sanka suru] - join
21. 参加者 [sanka sha] - participant
22. 可能性 [kanou sei] - possibility
23. 問題 [mondai] - problem
24. 国 [kuni] - country
25. 変える、変わる；変えること、変わること [kaeru, kawaru ; kaeru koto, kawaru koto] - change; to change
26. 契約書 [keiyaku sho] - agreement
27. 娘 [musume] - daughter
28. 希望；願うために [kibou ; negau tame ni] - hope; to hope
29. 年上の [toshiue no] - elder
30. 手紙 [tegami] - letter
31. 支払う、払う [shiharau, harau] - pay
32. 支払った、払った [shihara tta, hara tta] - paid
33. 日付 [hizuke] - date
34. 書いた、手紙を書いた [kai ta, tegami wo kai ta] - wrote
35. 村 [mura] - village
36. コンテスト [contest] - competition
37. 訪問した [houmon shi ta] - visited
38. 送った [oku tta] - sent
39. 通過した、通り過ぎた [tsuuka shi ta, toorisugi ta] - passed
40. 選ぶ、決める [erabu, kimeru] - choose
41. 選んだ、決めた [eran da, kime ta] - chose
42. 電話した [denwa shi ta] - called

B

留学生の学校とオペア
ryuugakusei no gakkou （SFS） to opea

ろばーとの妹、弟、そして両親はどいつに住んでいました。彼らははのーふぁーに住んでいました。妹の名前はがびです。彼女は２０歳でした。彼女は１１歳のときから英語を勉強していました。がびが１５歳のときに、SFSぷろぐらむに参加をしたがりました。SFSは、ゆーらしあの高校生がほすとふぁみりーと一緒に住み、あめりかの学校で勉強をしながら、あめりかで１年間過ごす可能性を与えます。ぷろぐらむは無料です。飛行機代、家族との生活、食べ物、あめりかの学校での勉強は、すべてSFSによって支払われます。しかし、いんたーねっとのさいとからこんてすとの日付を彼女が知ったときにはすでにこんてすとの日は過ぎていました。roba—to no imouto, otouto, soshite

School for foreigner students (SFS) and au pair

Robert's sister, brother and parents lived in Germany. They lived in Hannover. The sister's name was Gabi. She was twenty years old. She had learned English since she was eleven years old. When Gabi was fifteen years old, she wanted to take part in the program SFS. SFS gives the possibility for some high school students from Eurasia to spend a year in the USA, living with a host family and studying in an American school. The program is free. Airplane tickets, living with a family, food, studying at American school are paid by SFS. But by the time when she got the information about the competition date from the Internet site, the competition day had passed.

ryoushin ha doitsu ni sun de i mashi ta. karera wa hano—fa— ni sun de i mashi ta. imouto no namae wa gabi desu. kanojo wa ni ju ssai deshi ta. kanojo wa juu i ssai no toki kara eigo wo benkyou shi te i mashi ta. gabi ga juu go sai no toki ni, SFS puroguramu ni sanka wo shi ta gari mashi ta. SFS wa, yu—rashia no koukousei ga hosutofamiri— to issho ni sumi, amerika no gakkou de benkyou wo shi nagara, amerika de ichi nenkan sugosu kanou sei wo atae masu. puroguramu wa muryou desu. hikouki dai, kazoku to no seikatsu, tabemono, amerika no gakkou de no benkyou wa, subete SFS niyotte shiharawa re masu. shikashi, inta—netto no saito kara kontesuto no hizuke wo kanojo ga shi tta toki ni wa sudeni kontesuto no hi wa sugi te i mashi ta.

その後、彼女はおぺあぷろぐらむについて知りました。このぷろぐらむは、ほすとふぁみりーと一緒に住み、子供のお世話をし、らんげーじこーすで勉強をしながら、別の国で一年か二年間を過ごす可能性を参加者に与えます。ろばーとがさんふらんしすこで勉強をしていたので、がびは彼へめーるを書きました。

sonogo, kanojo wa opeapuroguramu nitsuite shiri mashi ta. kono puroguramu wa, hosutofamiri— to issho ni sumi, kodomo no osewa wo shi, range—ji ko—su de benkyou wo shi nagara, betsu no kuni de ichi nen ka ni nenkan wo sugosu kanou sei wo sanka sha ni atae masu. roba—to ga sanfuranshisuko de benkyou wo shi te i ta node, gabi wa kare e me—ru wo kaki mashi ta.

Then she learned about the program de au pair. This program gives its participants the possibility to spend a year or two in another country living with a host family, looking after children and learning at a language course. Since Robert was studying in San Francisco, Gabi wrote him an e-mail.

あめりかで彼女のためにほすとふぁみりーをみつけてくれるように、彼女は彼に頼みました。ろばーとは新聞と、広告があるいんたーねっとのさいとをみました。彼は、http://www.aupair-world.net/ とhttp://www.placementaupair.com/で、あめりか出身のほすとふぁみりーをいくつか見つけました。そしてろばーとはさんふらんしすこにあるおぺあの紹介所をたずねました。彼は、女性に相談にのってもらいました。彼女の名前はありす・さんふらわーです。amerika de kanojo no tame ni hosutofamiriー wo mitsuke te kureru you ni, kanojo wa kare ni tanomi mashi ta. robaーto wa shinbun to, koukoku ga aru intaーnetto no saito wo mi mashi ta. kare wa, http : / / www. aupair - world. net /
to http : / / www. placementaupair. com / de, amerika shusshin no hosutofamiriー wo ikutsu ka mitsuke mashi ta. soshite robaーto wa sanfuranshisuko ni aru opea no shoukai jo wo tazune mashi ta. kare wa, josei ni soudan ni no tte morai mashi ta. kanojo no namae wa arisu. sanfurawaー desu.

She asked him to find a host family for her in the USA. Robert looked through some newspapers and Internet sites with adverts. He found some host families from the USA on http://www.aupair-world.net/ and on http://www.placementaupair.com/. Then Robert visited an au pair agency in San Francisco. He was consulted by a woman. Her name was Alice Sunflower.

"ぼくの妹はどいつ出身です。彼女はあめりか人の家族のおぺあになりたがっています。この件を、手伝ってもらえますか?"ろばーとはありすに聞きまし

"My sister is from Germany. She would like to be an au pair with an American family. Can you help on this matter?" Robert asked Alice.

た。"喜んでお手伝いします。わたしたちは、あめりか中の家族におぺあを手配しています。おぺあは、ほすとふぁみりーに参加し、家事を手伝って、子供のお世話をする人です。ほすとふぁみりーは、食べ物、部屋、お小遣いをおぺあに与えます。お小遣いは200どるから600どるかもしれません。ほすとふぁみりーは、おぺあのらんげーじこーすの支払いもしなければなりません。"ありすが言いました。"良い家族と、良くない家族がいますよね？"ろばーとが質問します。"boku no imouto wa doitsu shusshin desu. kanojo wa amerika jin no kazoku no opea ni nari ta ga tte i masu. kono ken wo, tetsuda tte morae masu ka?" roba―to wa arisu ni kiki mashi ta. "yorokon de otetsudai shi masu. watashi tachi wa, amerika juu no kazoku ni opea wo tehai shi te i masu. opea wa, hosutofamiri― ni sanka shi, kaji wo tetsuda tte, kodomo no osewa wo suru hito desu. hosutofamiri― wa, tabemono, heya, o kozukai wo opea ni atae masu. o kozukai wa ni hyaku doru kara ro ppyaku doru kamo shire mase n. hosutofamiri― wa, opea no range―ji ko―su no shiharai mo shi nakere ba nari mase n." arisu ga ii mashi ta. "yoi kazoku to, yoku nai kazoku ga i masu yo ne?" roba―to ga shitsumon shi masu.

"家族を選ぶのについては、二つ問題があるんです。まず、家族の中に

"I will be glad to help you. We place au pairs with families all over the USA. An au pair is a person who joins a host family to help around the house and look after children. The host family gives the au pair food, a room and pocket money. Pocket money may be from 200 to 600 dollars. The host family must pay for a language course for the au pair as well," Alice said.

"Are there good and bad families?" Robert asked.

"There are two problems about choosing a family. First some

は、おぺあのことを、家族全員分の料理や掃除、洗濯、庭での仕事などを含む、家の中の全てのことをやらなけらばならない使用人だと思っている人がいるのです。しかし、おぺあは使用人ではありません。おぺあは、年下の子供のことで両親の手伝いをする、家族内の年上のお姉さんや、息子のようなものなのです。彼らの権利を守るために、おぺあはほすとふぁみりーと契約書を作らなければなりません。おぺあ紹介所やほすとふぁみりーが"すたんだーど"な契約書を使うときは、信じないでくださいね。"すたんだーど"な契約書などありません。不公平である場合は、おぺあは契約書のどの部分でも変えることができるんです。おぺあとほすとふぁみりーがする全てのことは、契約書に書かれていなければなりません。"kazoku wo erabu no nitsuite wa, futatsu mondai ga aru n desu. mazu, kazoku no naka ni hwa, opea no koto wo, kazoku zen'in bun no ryouri ya souji, sentaku, niwa de no shigoto nado wo fukumu, ie no naka no subete no koto wo yara na kera ba nara nai shiyounin da to

families think that an au pair is a servant who must do everything in the house including cooking for all family members, cleaning, washing, working in the garden etc. But an au pair is not a servant. An au pair is like an elder daughter or son of the family who helps parents with younger children. To protect their rights au pairs must work out an agreement with the host family. Do not believe it when some au pair agencies or host families say that they use a "standard" agreement. There is no standard agreement. The au pair can change any part of the agreement if it is unfair. Everything that an au pair and host family will do must be written in an agreement.

omo tte iru hito ga iru no desu. shikashi, opea wa shiyounin de wa ari mase n. opea wa, toshishita no kodomo no koto de ryoushin no tetsudai wo suru, kazoku nai no toshiue no o neesan ya, musuko no you na mono na no desu. karera no kenri wo mamoru tame ni, opea wa hosutofamiri— to keiyaku sho wo tsukura nakere ba nari mase n. opea shoukai jo ya hosutofamiri— ga "sutanda—do" na keiyaku sho wo tsukau toki wa, shinji nai de kudasai ne. "sutanda—do" na keiyaku sho nado ari mase n. fukouhei de aru baai wa, opea wa keiyaku sho no dono bubun de mo kaeru koto ga dekiru n desu. opea to hosutofamiri— ga suru subete no koto wa, keiyaku sho ni kaka re te i nakere ba nari mase n.

二つ目の問題はこちらです：家族の中には、らんげーじこーすがなく、空き時間におぺあが行けるところが少ししかない、小さな村に住んでいる家族がいます。この場合には、おぺあが、一番近くの大きな街にいくときのちけっと往復分を、ほすとふぁみりーが支払わなければならない、と契約書の中に含める必要があります。週に一度や二度かもしれません。" futatsu me no mondai wa kochira desu : kazoku no naka ni wa, range—ji ko—su ga naku, aki jikan ni opea ga ikeru tokoro ga sukoshi shika nai, chiisana mura ni sun de iru kazoku ga i masu. kono baai ni wa, opea ga, ichiban chikaku no ookina machi ni iku toki no chiketto oufuku bun wo, hosutofamiri— ga shiharawa nakere ba nara nai, to keiyaku sho no

The second problem is this: Some families live in small villages where there are no language courses and few places where an au pair can go in free time. In this situation it is necessary to include in the agreement that the host family must pay for two way tickets to the nearest big town when the au pair goes there. It may be once or twice a week."

naka ni fukumeru hitsuyou ga ari masu. shuu ni ichi do ya ni do kamo shire mase n."

"なるほど。ぼくの妹はさんふらんしすこの家族を希望しています。この街で、良い家族をみつけてもらえますか？" ろばーとが質問します。"naruhodo. boku no imouto wa sanfuranshisuko no kazoku wo kibou shi te i masu. kono machi de, yoi kazoku wo mitsuke te morae masu ka?" roba―to ga shitsumon shi masu.

"I see. My sister would like a family from San Francisco. Can you find a good family in this city?" Robert asked.

"ええと、さんふらんしすこの家族は現在２０組ほどいます。" ありすは答えました。彼女は、彼らのうちの何人かに電話をかけました。ほすとふぁみりーはどいつからのおぺあに喜びました。ほとんどの家族が、がびからの写真付きの手紙をほしがりました。彼らのうち何人かは、彼女が少しは英語を話すことができるのを確認するために、がびに電話をしたがりました。ですので、ろばーとは彼らに彼女の電話番号を渡しました。何人かのほすとふぁみりーはがびに電話をしました。そして、彼女は彼らに手紙を送りました。最後に彼女

"Well, there are about twenty families from San Francisco now," Alice answered. She telephoned some of them. The host families were glad to have an au pair from Germany. Most of the families wanted to get a letter with a photograph from Gabi. Some of them also wanted to telephone her to be sure that she can speak English a little. So Robert gave them her telephone number.

Some host families called Gabi. Then she sent them letters. At last she chose a suitable family and with the help of Alice worked out an agreement with them. The family

は、ふさわしい家族を選んで、ありすの助けで彼らとの契約書を作りました。家族は、どいつからあめりかまでのちけっとを支払いました。最後には、希望と夢いっぱいに、がびはあめりかへ出発しました。"eeto, sanfuranshisuko no kazoku wa genzai ni ju kkumi hodo i masu." arisu wa kotae mashi ta. kanojo wa, karera no uchi no nan nin ka ni denwa wo kake mashi ta. hosutofamirī wa doitsu kara no opea ni yorokobi mashi ta. hotondo no kazoku ga, gabi kara no shashin tsuki no tegami wo hoshi gari mashi ta. karera no uchi nan nin ka wa, kanojo ga sukoshi wa eigo wo hanasu koto ga dekiru no wo kakunin suru tame ni, gabi ni denwa wo shi ta gari mashi ta. desu node, robāto wa karera ni kanojo no denwa bangou wo watashi mashi ta. nan nin ka no hosutofamirī wa gabi ni denwa wo shi mashi ta. soshite, kanojo wa karera ni tegami wo okuri mashi ta. saigo ni kanojo wa, fusawashii kazoku wo eran de, arisu no tasuke de karera to no keiyaku sho wo tsukuri mashi ta. kazoku wa, doitsu kara amerika made no chiketto wo shiharai mashi ta. saigo ni wa, kibou to yume ippai ni, gabi wa amerika e shuppatsu shi mashi ta.

paid for the ticket from Germany to the USA. At last Gabi started for the USA full of hopes and dreams.

***

にちえいじしょ
日 英 辞 書
Japanese-English dictionary

～に、～で [～ ni, ～ de] - in
１０ [juu] - ten
１００ [hyaku] - hundred
1000 [sen] - thousand
１０億 [juu oku] - billion
１０番目の [juu banme no] - tenth
１１ [juu ichi] - eleven
１２ [juu ni] - twelve
15 [juu go] - fifteen
１７ [juu nana] - seventeen
１年前 [ichi nen mae] - a year ago
１時に [ichi ji ni] - at one o'clock
２０ [ni juu] - twenty
２１ [ni juu ichi] - twenty-one
２５ [ni juu go] - twenty-five
２番目の [ni banme no] - second
3 [san] - three
３０ [san juu] - thirty
３番目の [san banme no] - third
４４ [yon juu yon] - forty-four
4つ [yottsu] - four
4番目の [yon banme no] - fourth
5 [go] - five
5番目の [go banme no] - fifth
6 [roku] - six
60 [roku juu] - sixty
6番目の [roku banme no] - sixth
7 [nana] - seven
7番目の [nana banme no] - seventh
8 [hachi] - eight
8時半に [hachi ji han ni] - at half past eight
8番目の [hachi banme no] - eighth
9 [kyuu] - nine
9番目の [kyuu banme no] - ninth
CD [shi─ di─] - CD
CDプレーヤー [shi─ di─ pure─ya─] - CD player
DVD [DVD] - DVD
TVセット [ti─ bui setto] - TV-set

アーティスト、芸術家 [a─tisuto, geijutsu ka] - artist
アイスクリーム [aisukuri─mu] - ice-cream
アイディア、考え、案 [aidia, kangae, an] - idea
アスピリン（鎮痛剤）[asupirin (chintsuu zai)] - aspirin
あたま、長、リーダー；へ向かう [atama, chou, ri─da─ ; e mukau] - head; to head, to go
あった [a tta] - had
あとで、あとに [atode, ato ni] - after
アドベンチャー、冒険 [adobencha─, bouken] - adventure
あなた [anata] - you
あなたがたのどちらか [anata ga ta no dochira ka] - either of you
あなたの [anata no] - your
あなたの代わりに [anata no kawari ni] - instead of you
あなたは [anata wa] - you
アメリカ [amerika] - the United States/the USA
アメリカ人 [amerika jin] - American
アラーム、警報機 [ara─mu, keihou ki] - alarm
いいえ、ちがいます [iie, chigai masu] - no
いくつか [ikutsu ka] - some
いくつかの [ikutsu ka no] - any
いくつかの、何人かの、いくらかの [ikutsu ka no, nan nin ka no, ikura ka no] - some
いじめる、邪魔をする、困らせる [ijimeru, jama wo suru, komara seru] - bother
いす [isu] - chair
いつ [itsu] - when
いつも [itsumo] - always
いつもの、通常の [itsumo no, tsuujou no] - usual

いつもは、通常は、普段は [itsumo wa, tsuujou wa, fudan wa] - usually
いなくなる、消える、なくなる [i naku naru, kieru, nakunaru] - go away
いやがる、嫌う [iyagaru, kirau] - hate
インターネットのサイト [inta―netto no saito] - Internet site
エアーショー [ea― sho―] - airshow
エイリアン [eirian] - alien
エネルギー、元気 [enerugi―, genki] - energy
エレベーター [erebe―ta―] - lift
エンジニア [enjinia] - engineer
エンジン [enjin] - engine
おい！やあ！ [oi! yaa!] - Hey!
おいしい [oishii] - tasty
オーナー、持ち主 [o―na―, mochinushi] - owner
おかしな、変な [okashina, hen na] - strange
オフィス [ofisu] - office
おもちゃ [omocha] - toy
おやつ、スナック [o yatsu, sunakku] - snack
お互いを知る [otagai wo shiru] - know each other
お客さん、カスタマー [okyaku san, kasutama―] - customer
お店 [o mise] - shop
お店（複数）[o mise （fukusuu）] - shops
お母さん、母親 [okaasan, hahaoya] - mom, mother
お気に入りの、好きな [okiniiri no, suki na] - favourite
お気に入りの映画 [okiniiri no eiga] - favourite film
お皿 [o sara] - plate
お腹がすいている；わたしはお腹がすいています [onaka ga sui te iru ; watashi wa onaka ga sui te i masu] - hungry; I am hungry
お茶 [ocha] - tea
お金 [okane] - money
お願いします [onegai shi masu] - please
お風呂場、お手洗い；お風呂 [o furoba, o tearai ; o furo] - bathroom; bath
お風呂場のテーブル [o furoba no te―buru] - bathroom table
かくれんぼ [kakurenbo] - hide-and-seek
かける、なった [kakeru, na tta] - rang
ガス [gasu] - gas
カップ、コップ [kappu, koppu] - cup
カナダ [kanada] - Canada
カナダ人 [kanada jin] - Canadian
かばん [kaban] - bag
カフェ [kafe] - café
かもしれない [kamo shire nai] - could
かもしれない、許可する・される [kamo shire nai, kyoka suru. sa reru] - may
から [kara] - since (temporal)
から、出身；アメリカ出身 [kara, shusshin ; amerika shusshin] - from; from the USA
ガラス [garasu] - glass
カンガルー [kangaru―] - kangaroo
キーボード [ki―bo―do] - keyboard
キス [kisu] - kiss
キッチン [kicchin] - kitchen
ギフト、贈り物、プレゼント [gifuto, okurimono, purezento] - gift
キャプテン [kyaputen] - captain
キロメートル（km）[kirome―toru (km)] - kilometer
くじら, シャチ [kujira, shachi] - whale; killer whale
クラス、授業 [kurasu, jugyou] - class
クラブ [kurabu] - club
グレイ、灰色 [gurei, haiiro] - grey
ケーブル、電線 [ke―buru, densen] - cable
ゲスト [gesuto] - guest
けれども、しかしながら [keredomo, shikashinagara] - although
コース [ko―su] - course
コーディネーション [ko―dine―shon] - co-ordination
コーヒー [ko―hi―] - coffee
ここ [koko] - here (a place)
ここに、こちらに [koko ni, kochira ni] - here (a direction)
こする [kosuru] - rub

こたえ、解決策 [kotae, kaiketsu saku] - solution, answer
こたえる [kotaeru] - answer
こちらは、これは [kochira wa, kore wa] - here is
こっそり手に入れる、取る、盗む [kossori te ni ireru, toru, nusumu] - steal
ゴム [gomu] - rubber
これ [kore] - this stuff
これ、この；この本 [kore, kono ; kono hon] - this, this book
これは何ですか？ [kore wa nan desu ka?] - What is this?
コンサルタント [konsarutanto] - consultant
コンサルティング [konsarutingu] - consultancy
コンテスト [contest] - competition
コントロールする [kontoro―ru suru] - control
こんにちは [konnichiwa] - hello
コンピューター [konpyu―ta―] - computer
サービスする, 仕える [sa―bisu suru, tsukaeru] - serve
サイレン [sairen] - siren
させる [sa seru] - let
さようなら [sayounara] - goodbye
さようなら、じゃあまた [sayounara, jaa mata] - bye
さらに、もっと、より [sarani, motto, yori] - more
さん、氏 [san, shi] - mister, Mr.
サンドイッチ [sandoicchi] - sandwich
シートベルト [shi―toberuto] - seat belts
した、やった、行った [shi ta, ya tta, okona tta] - did
しっぽ [shippo] - tail
している間、その間 [shi te iru kan, sonokan] - while
してはいけない [shi te ha ike nai] - must not
しなければならない；わたしは行かなければならない [shi nakere ba nara nai ; watashi ha ika nakere ba nara nai] - must; I must go
シマウマ [shimauma] - zebra

しめた、閉じた、閉まっている [shime ta, toji ta, shima tte iru] - closed
しめる [shimeru] - fasten
ジャーナリスト [ja―narisuto] - journalist
ジャンプする、飛び降りる、ジャンプ [janpu suru, tobioriru, janpu] - jump
ショッピングセンター [shoppingu senta―] - shopping center
すいません [suimasen] - Excuse me.
スーパー [su―pa―] - supermarket
スキル、腕前 [sukiru, udemae] - skill
すぐに [suguni] - soon
すごい、大きな [sugoi, ookina] - killer
スタンダードの、普通の [sutanda―do no, futsuu no] - standard
ステータス、事態 ；家族ステータス [sute―tasu, jitai ; kazoku sute―tasu] - status; family status
ストーリー、物語、話 [suto―ri―, monogatari, hanashi] - story
スパニエル [supanieru] - spaniel
スピーチ [supi―chi] - speech
スピード違反をする人 [supi―do ihan wo suru hito] - speeder
スペイン人、スペイン語 [supein jin, supein go] - Spanish
スペイン人の、スペイン語の [supein jin no, supein go no] - Spanish
すべての、全部の [subete no, zenbu no] - all
スポーツ；スポーツ店 [supo―tsu ; supo―tsu ten] - sport; sport shop
スポーツバイク [supo―tsu baiku] - sport bike
ズボン（複数） [zubon（fukusuu）] - trousers
する、やる、行う [suru, yaru, okonau] - do
ずるい、いたずらに [zurui, itazurani] - sly, slyly
ずるい、ずる賢い [zurui, zuru kashikoi] - sly
することができる；わたしは読むことができる [suru koto ga dekiru ; watashi ha yomu koto ga dekiru] - can; I can read

そこ [soko] - there
そして、その後 [soshite, sonogo] - then
その [sono] - its (for neuter)
その後 [sonogo] - after that
それ [sore] - it
それ、あれ [sore, are] - that
それら、あれら（複数） [sorera, are ra (fukusuu)] - these, those
タイヤ [taiya] - wheel
だから、では [dakara, dewa] - so
たくさん、とても [takusan, totemo] - very
たくさん、多くの [takusan, ooku no] - much, many
たくさんの、多くの [takusan no, ooku no] - many, much
タクシー [takushi—] - taxi
タクシードライバー [takushi—doraiba—] - taxi driver
だけ [dake] - just
たたく、あてる [tataku, ateru] - hit, beat
だった [da tta] - was
たどり着く [tadoritsuku] - get (somewhere)
ためす、してみる [tamesu, shi te miru] - try
ために [tame ni] - for
タンカー [tanka—] - tanker
ダンスした, 踊った [dansu shi ta, odo tta] - danced
ダンスしている [dansu shi te iru] - dancing
ダンスする、踊る [dansu suru, odoru] - dance
チーム [chi—mu] - team
ちくしょう [chikushou] - damn
チケット、券 [chiketto, ken] - ticket
チャンス、確率 [chansu, kakuritsu] - chance
つけた [tsuke ta] - switched on
つける [tsukeru] - turn on
で、にて [de, nite] - at
であった [de a tta] - were
デイビッドの本 [deibiddo no hon] - David's book
テーブル、机 [te—buru, tsukue] - table
テーブル、机（複数） [te—buru, tsukue (fukusuu)] - tables
できるだけ頻繁に [dekirudake hinpan ni] - as often as possible
デザイン [dezain] - design
テスト、試験 [tesuto, shiken] - test
テストをするために [tesuto wo suru tame ni] - to test
テストを通過するために [tesuto wo tsuuka suru tame ni] - to pass a test
ではない [de wa nai] - not
でも、しかし [demo, shikashi] - but
テレビ [terebi] - television
と [to] - and
ドア [doa] - door
ドイツ人 [doitsu jin] - German
トイレ [toire] - toilet
どう [dou] - how
どうしたの？、何があったの？ [dou shi ta no?, nani ga a tta no?] - What is the matter?
ときどき、たまに [tokidoki, tamani] - sometimes
どこ、どちら [doko, dochira] - where
ところで [tokorode] - by the way
どの [dono] - which
とめた、やめた、終えた [tome ta, yame ta, oe ta] - stopped
とめる、とまる、終わりにする [tomeru, tomaru, owari ni suru] - stop
とめる、停止する [tomeru, teishi suru] - break, pause
トラック [torakku] - truck
トリック、技 [torikku, waza] - trick
とる、使う、持って行く、食べる、飲む [toru, tsukau, mo tte iku, taberu, nomu] - take
と一緒に、で [to issho ni, de] - with
ない、何も [nai, nani mo] - nothing
なくなる、行く [nakunaru, iku] - gone
なしで、せずに [nashi de, se zu ni] - without
なぜなら、から [nazenara, kara] - since, as
なぜなら、だから [nazenara, dakara] - as, since (kausal)
なぜなら、だって [nazenara, datte] - because
など、等 [nado, tou] - etc.
なに [nani] - what

なる [naru] - be
においのする [nioi no suru] - stinking
について、ほど [nitsuite, hodo] - about
について知った、について学んだ [nitsuite shi tta, nitsuite manan da] - learned about
に対して [nitaishite] - against
に沿って [ni sotte] - along
に注意を払う [ni chuui wo harau] - pay attention to
ねずみ [nezumi] - rat
ノート [no―to] - notebook
ノート（複数）[no―to（fukusuu）] - notebooks
のために [no tame ni] - for
の上に、ついて [no ue ni, tsui te] - on
の下 [no shita] - under
の代わりに [no kawari ni] - instead
の間 [no aida] - between
はい、そうです [hai, sou desu] - yes
ばかげた、ばかな [bakage ta, baka na] - silly
バケツ [baketsu] - pail
はじめた [hajime ta] - began
はじめに、最初に [hajime ni, saisho ni] - at first
バス；バスで行く [basu ; basu de iku] - bus; go by bus
バター [bata―] - butter
パトロール、 [patoro―ru,] - patrol
パニック；パニックするために [panikku ; panikku suru tame ni] - panic; to panic
パパ、お父さん [papa, otousan] – dad, daddy
パラシュート [parashu―to] - parachute
パラシュートをする人 [parashu―to wo suru hito] - parachutist
パン [pan] - bread
ハンドルをきる [handoru wo kiru] - steer
ピーという音 [pi― toiu oto] - beep
ビデオカセット [bideokasetto] - videocassette
ビデオショップ [bideo shoppu] - video-shop
ひどい、命とりの [hidoi, inochitori no] - deadly
ひとつ [hitotsu] - one

ひとりずつ [hitori zutsu] - one by one
ファイナンス、金融 [fainansu, kinyuu] - finance
フォーム [fo―mu] - form
ふたつ [futatsu] - two
ふりをする [furi wo suru] - pretend
ブレーキ [bure―ki] - brake
ブレーキをかけるために [bure―ki wo kakeru tame ni] - to brake
フレーズ、言葉 [fure―zu, kotoba] - phrase
フレンドリーな [furendori― na] - friendly
プログラマー [puroguramu―] - programmer
プログラム [puroguramu] - program
フロント、受付、前、玄関 [furonto, uketsuke, mae, genkan] - front
ベッド [beddo] - bed
ペット [petto] - pet
ベッド（複数）[beddo（fukusuu）] - beds
ペン [pen] - pen
ペン（複数）[pen（fukusuu）] - pens
ポーランド [po―rando] - Poland
ポケット [poketto] - pocket
ポジション、場所 [pojishon, basho] - position
ホスト [hosuto] - host
ホストファミリー [hosutofamiri―] - the host family
ボタン [botan] - button
ホテル [hoteru] - hotel
ホテル（複数）[hoteru（fukusuu）] - hotels
マイク [maiku] - microphone
まだ [mada] - yet
まだ、それでも [mada, soredemo] - still
また、再び、もう一度 [mata, futatabi, mouichido] - again
また、同じく、同様に [mata, onajiku, douyou ni] - also
マットレス [mattoresu] - mattress
まで [made] - until
まわる [mawaru] - round
ミス、さん [misu, san] - Miss
みせる [miseru] - show

みた [mi ta] - looked
みた、目撃した [mi ta, mokugeki shi ta] - saw
ミドルネーム [midoru ne—mu] - middle name
みる [miru] - watch
みる、わかる、理解する [miru, wakaru, rikai suru] - see
みんな、全員 [minna, zen'in] - everybody
メーカー [me—ka—] - maker
メートル [me—toru] - meter
メール [me—ru] - e-mail
めったにない [mettani nai] - seldom
メモ [memo] - note
メンバー [menba—] - member
も、同様に、同じく [mo, douyou ni, onajiku] - either, too, also
もうすでに [mou sudeni] - already
もう一度 [mouichido] - one more
もし [moshi] - if
もちろん [mochiron] - of course
もの、こと [mono, koto] - thing
やあ、こんにちは [yaa, konnichiwa] - hi
やかん [yakan] - kettle
ゆっくりと [yukkuri to] - slowly
よい、おいしい、上手 [yoi, oishii, jouzu] - good, well
より；ジョージはリンダより年上です [yori ; jo—ji wa rinda yori toshiue desu] - than; George is older than Linda.
より大きな [yori ookina] - bigger
より少ない [yori sukunai] - less
より良い [yori yoi] - better
より近い [yori chikai] - closer
より遠く [yori tooku] - further
ライオン [raion] - lion
ラジオ、無線 [rajio, musen] - radio
リーダー [ri—da—] - leader
リスト、リストする [risuto, risuto suru] - list
リハビリ [rihabiri] - rehabilitation
リハビリする [rihabiri suru] - rehabilitate
リミット [rimitto] - limit
ルール、規則 [ru—ru, kisoku] - rule
レーザー [re—za—] - laser
レーダー [re—da—] - radar
レジ；銀行の支配人、レジ係、テラー [reji ; ginkou no shihainin, reji gakari, tera—] - cash register; cashier, teller
レッスン、授業 [ressun, jugyou] - lesson
レポーター [repo—ta—] - reporter
レポート [repo—to] - report
ロット [rotto] - lot
わあ！ああ！ [waa! aa!] - Oh!
わかった、ええと [waka tta, eeto] - okay, well
わかった、理解した [waka tta, rikai shi ta] - understood
わずかに [wazuka ni] - slightly
わたしたちに [watashi tachi ni] - us
わたしたちにさせる、しよう [watashi tachi ni sa seru, shiyo u] - let us
わたしたちの [watashi tachi no] - our
わたしたちは [watashi tachi wa] - we
わたしに [watashi ni] - me
わたしの [watashi no] - mine
わたしの、自分の [watashi no, jibun no] - my
わたしは [watashi wa] - I
わたしは音楽を聞きます。 [watashi wa ongaku wo kiki masu.] - I listen to music.
一定に、定期的に [ittei ni, teiki teki ni] - constant
一度 [ichi do] - once
一方で、その間に [ippou de, sonokan ni] - meanwhile
一番近くの [ichiban chikaku no] - nearest
一瞬、その時、その瞬間 [isshun, sono toki, sono shunkan] - moment
一緒に [issho ni] - together
一部 [ichibu] - part
一部、部品、部分 [ichibu, buhin, bubun] - part
上の、以上の、こえた [ue no, ijou no, koe ta] - over
上着 [uwagi] - jacket
下に [shita ni] - down
下線 [kasen] - underline
不公平 [fukouhei] - unfair

与えた、渡した、あげた [atae ta, watashi ta, age ta] - gave
与える、渡す [ataeru, watasu] - give, hand
世界 [sekai] - world
両親 [ryoushin] - parent
中に、中へ [naka ni, naka e] - inside
中へ、中に [naka e, naka ni] - into
中へ、抜けて、通して [naka e, nuke te, tooshi te] - through
中心；中心街 [chuushin ; chuushin gai] - centre; city centre
中心の、真ん中の [chuushin no, mannaka no] - central
乗った、取った、使った、食べた、飲んだ [no tta, to tta, tsuka tta, tabe ta, non da] - took
乾いた；乾かすために [kawaita ; kawakasu tame ni] - dry (adj), to dry
予定、計画 [yotei, keikaku] - plan
予測する、予想する [yosoku suru, yosou suru] - estimate
事故 [jiko] - accident
二度 [ni do] - twice
人々 [hitobito] - people
人 [hito] - person
人事部 [jinji bu] - personnel department
人命救助のトリック [jinmei kyuujo no torikku] - life-saving trick
人形 [ningyou] - doll
人形（パラシュートをする人） [ningyou(parashu―to wo suru hito)] - stuffed parachutist
人間 [ningen] - human
今、現在 [ima, genzai] - now
今すぐに [ima suguni] - immediately
今日、本日 [kyou, honjitsu] - today
仕事；職業紹介所 [shigoto ; shokugyou shoukai jo] - job; job agency
仕事がたくさんある [shigoto ga takusan aru] - have a lot of work
他の、別の [ta no, betsu no] - other, else
代わりに [kawari ni] - instead of
企業、会社 [kigyou, kaisha] - firm
企業、会社（複数） [kigyou, kaisha （fukusuu）] - firms
会う [au] - meet
会った、合った [a tta, a tta] - met
会社 [kaisha] - company
住んでいた [sun de i ta] - lived
住んでいる [sun de iru] - live, living
住所 [juusho] - address
何か [nani ka] - something
何でも [nani demo] - anything
何のテーブルですか？ [nan no te―buru desu ka?] - What table?
何も言わずに [nani mo iwa zu ni] - without a word
作る、料理をする [tsukuru, ryouri wo suru] - make
作る、構成する、文章を作る [tsukuru, kousei suru, bunshou wo tsukuru] - compose
作家、ライター [sakka, raita―] - writer
使う [tsukau] - use
使用人 [shiyounin] - servant
例 [rei] - example
例えば [tatoeba] - for example
信じる；の目を信じない [shinjiru ; no me wo shinji nai] - believe; to not believe one's eyes
個人的な、個人の、自分の [kojin teki na, kojin no, jibun no] - personal
個別に、別々に [kobetsu ni, betsubetsu ni] - individually
値段、価格 [nedan, kakaku] - price
健康 [kenkou] - health
働いた、 [hatarai ta,] - worked
兄、弟 [ani, otouto] - brother
先生 [sensei] - teacher
全て、全部 [subete, zenbu] - everything
全ての、それぞれの [subete no, sorezore no] - every
全ての、全部 [subete no, zenbu] - all
公園 [kouen] - park
公園（複数） [kouen （fukusuu）] - parks
写真 [shashin] - picture

写真; カメラマン [shashin ; kameraman] - photograph; photographer
冷たい [tsumetai] - cold (adj)
冷たさ [tsumeta sa] - coldness
出版 [shuppan] - publishing
分 [fun] - minute
刑事上の、犯罪の [keiji jou no, hanzai no] - criminal
列 [retsu] - queue
別の、違う [betsu no, chigau] - another
到着した、ついた [touchaku shi ta, tsui ta] - arrived
到着する [touchaku suru] - arrive
前 [mae] - ago
前に、前は [mae ni, mae wa] - before
前輪 [zenrin] - front wheels
創造的な [souzou teki na] - creative
力、強さ [chikara, tsuyo sa] - strength
加速、スピード；加速する、スピード違反をする [kasoku, supi―do ; kasoku suru, supi―do ihan wo suru] - speed; to speed
助ける、手伝う；助けるために、手伝うために [tasukeru, tetsudau ; tasukeru tame ni, tetsudau tame ni] - help; to help
助ける、救助する [tasukeru, kyuujo suru] - rescue
助手 [joshu] - helper
勉強している、習っている [benkyou shi te iru, nara tte iru] - learning
勉強する [benkyou suru] - study
動いた、動かした [ugoi ta, ugokashi ta] - moved
動いている、働いている [ugoi te iru, hatarai te iru] - working
動物 [doubutsu] - animal
動物園 [doubutsu en] - zoo
勧めた、推薦した [susume ta, suisen shi ta] - recommended
化学 [kagaku] - chemistry
化学の、化学的な [kagaku no, kagaku teki na] - chemical(adj)
化学物質（複数） [kagaku busshitsu （fukusuu）] - chemicals

北米とユーラシア [hokubei to yu―rashia] - North America and Eurasia
医療の [iryou no] - medical
医者 [isha] - doctor
半分 [hanbun] - half
半分の [hanbun no] - half
単語、言葉 [tango, kotoba] - word
単語、言葉（複数） [tango, kotoba （fukusuu）] - words
単調な [tanchou na] - monotonous
去った、いなくなった [sa tta, i naku na tta] - went away
去って、離れて [sa tte, hanare te] - away
去る、なくなる、出る [saru, nakunaru, deru] - leave
参加する [sanka suru] - join
参加者 [sanka sha] - participant
友達 [tomodachi] - friend
取られた、盗まれた、 [tora re ta, nusuma re ta,] - taken
取る、手に入れる、得る [toru, te ni ireru, eru] - get (something)
受話器 [juwaki] - phone handset
可能である [kanou de aru] - possible
可能性 [kanou sei] - possibility
右 [migi] - right
合っている、ぴったりの、ふさわしい [a tte iru, pittari no, fusawashii] - suitable
同じ [onaji] - the same
同じく、〜も [onajiku, 〜 mo] - too
同じように、同じ程度 [onaji you ni, onaji teido] - as
同伴した [douhan shi ta] - accompanied
同伴する [douhan suru] - accompany
同僚 [douryou] - colleague
同意する [doui suru] - agree
同時に [douji ni] - at the same time
同様に、同じく [douyou ni, onajiku] - as well
名前、名前を挙げる、教える [namae, namae wo ageru, oshieru] - name
向いた、曲がった [mui ta, maga tta] - turned
向ける [mukeru] - pointed

向こうの、渡った [mukou no, wata tta] - over, across
吠えた [hoe ta] - barked
吠える、なりわめく [hoeru, nari wameku] - howling
周りを見る、見て回る、見渡す [mawari wo miru, mi te mawaru, miwatasu] - look around
命 [inochi] - life
命令する、言いつける [meirei suru, ii tsukeru] - order
唯一の [yuiitsu no] - only
問題 [mondai] - problem
喜んでいる、幸せ [yorokon de iru, shiawase] - happy
噛む [kamu] - bite
固まる、凍える、凍る [katamaru, kogoeru, kooru] - freeze
国 [kuni] - country
国籍 [kokuseki] - nationality
土曜日 [doyoubi] - Saturday
地図 [chizu] - map
地球 [chikyuu] - earth
声 [koe] - voice
声に出して [koe ni dashi te] - aloud
売る [uru] - sell
変える、変わる；変えること、変わること [kaeru, kawaru ; kaeru koto, kawaru koto] - change; to change
夕方 [yuugata] - evening
外で [soto de] - outdoors
夜 [yoru] - night
夢 [yume] - dream
夢を見るために [yume wo miru tame ni] - to dream
大きい／より大きな／一番大きい [ookii ／ yori ookina ／ ichiban ookii] - big / bigger / the biggest
大きな、大きい [ookina, ookii] - big
大丈夫、平気、わかる [daijoubu, heiki, wakaru] - OK, well
大事な [daiji na] - important
大変な [taihen na] - hard
大学 [daigaku] - college
天気 [tenki] - weather
失う、なくす [ushinau, nakusu] - loose
契約書 [keiyaku sho] - agreement
女の子 [onnanoko] - girl
女性 [josei] - female, woman
好き；わたしはそれが好きです [suki ; watashi wa sore ga suki desu] - like; I like that.
好き、大好き [suki, daisuki] - like, love
姉、妹 [ane, imouto] - sister
始める、始まる [hajimeru, hajimaru] - begin, start
娘 [musume] - daughter
嬉しい [ureshii] - glad
子供 [kodomo] - child
子供たち [kodomo tachi] - children
子犬 [koinu] - puppy
子猫 [koneko] - kitten
季節 [kisetsu] - season
学ぶ、習う [manabu, narau] - learn
学校 [gakkou] - school
学歴、教育 [gakureki, kyouiku] - education
宇宙、スペース [uchuu, supe—su] - space
宇宙船 [uchuusen] - spaceship
守る [mamoru] - protect
安全な [anzen na] - safe
宣伝、広告 [senden, koukoku] - advert
家 [ie] - house
家、家庭；帰宅する、家に帰る [ie, katei ; kitaku suru, ie ni kaeru] - home; go home
家具 [kagu] - furniture
家族 [kazoku] - family
宿題 [shukudai] - homework
密かに、秘密に [hisoka ni, himitsu ni] - secretly
寮 [ryou] - dorms
将来 [shourai] - future
小さい、少ない [chiisai, sukunai] - small
少しの、小さな [sukoshi no, chiisana] - little
少ない；いくつかの少ない [sukunai ; ikutsu ka no sukunai] - few; a few
少なくとも [sukunakutomo] - at least

屋根 [yane] - roof
岸 [kishi] - shore
巡査部長 [junsa buchou] - sergeant
左 [hidari] - left
希望；願うために [kibou ; negau tame ni] - hope; to hope
帽子 [boushi] - hat
年 [toshi] - year
年、年齢 [toshi, nenrei] - age
年上の [toshiue no] - elder
幸せ [shiawase] - happiness
幼稚園 [youchien] - kindergarten
広く [hiroku] - wide, widely
広める、広げる [hiromeru, hirogeru] - spread
広告 [koukoku] - ad, advert
広場 [hiroba] - square
床 [yuka] - floor
店員 [ten'in] - shop assistant
座る ; 席に座る [suwaru ; seki ni suwaru] - seat; take a seat
座る [suwaru] - sit, sit down
庭 [niwa] - garden
庭、場 [niwa, ba] - yard
式典 [shikiten] - ceremony
引っ張る、引く [hipparu, hiku] - pull
強い、強く [tsuyoi, tsuyoku] - strong, strongly
強く [tsuyoku] - strong, strongly
彼に [kare ni] - him
彼の ; 彼のベッド [kare no ; kare no beddo] - his, his bed
彼は [kare wa] - he
彼らの [karera no] - their
彼らは [karera wa] - they
彼女、女の子の友達 [kanojo, onnanoko no tomodachi] - girlfriend
彼女の ; 彼女の本 [kanojo no ; kanojo no hon] - her; her book
彼女は [kanojo wa] - she
彼氏、男の子の友達 [kareshi, otokonoko no tomodachi] - boyfriend
待つ [matsu] - wait

待った [matta] - waited
後で [atode] - after
後ろ、あと [ushiro, ato] - behind
従業員、労働者 [juugyou in, roudou sha] - worker
得る、着く、なる [eru, tsuku, naru] - get
微笑みかけるために [hohoemikakeru tame ni] - to smile
微笑む、笑いかける [hohoemu, waraikakeru] - smile
心配しないで！ [shinpai shi nai de!] - Do not worry!
心配する [shinpai suru] - worry
必要である、必要とする [hitsuyou de aru, hitsuyou to suru] - need
忘れる [wasureru] - forget
応えた、答えた [kotae ta, kotae ta] - answered
応募する [oubo suru] - apply
怒って [oko tte] - angrily
怒っている [oko tte iru] - angry
思い出した、覚えていた [omoidashi ta, oboe te i ta] - remembered
急いだ [isoi da] - rushed
性別 [seibetsu] - sex
恐れる、怖がる [osoreru, kowagaru] - afraid
恥じる ; 彼は恥ずかしがっている [hajiru ; kare wa hazukashi ga tte iru] - be ashamed; he is ashamed
息子 [musuko] - son
悪い、良くない [warui, yoku nai] - bad
悲しい [kanashii] - sad
情報 [jouhou] - information
惑星 [wakusei] - planet
愛 [ai] - love
愛した [aishi ta] - loved
愛するために [aisuru tame ni] - to love
感謝する ; ありがとうございます、ありがとう [kansha suru ; arigatou gozai masu, arigatou] - thank; thank you, thanks
戦争 [sensou] - war
戻る [modoru] - back
手作業 [tesagyou] - manual work

手紙 [tegami] - letter
手錠 [tejou] - handcuffs
押す [osu] - press, push
持っている、飼っている、ある；彼／彼女／それは持っている；彼は本を持っている [motte iru, ka tte iru, aru ; kare ／ kanojo ／ sore wa mo tte iru ; kare wa hon wo mo tte iru] - have, he/she/it has, he has a book.
振った [fu tta] - shook
振る、揺れる [furu, yureru] - shake
捕まえる、掴む、引っかかる [tsukamaeru, tsukamu, hikkakaru] - catch
接続詞なので訳さない [setsuzokushi na node yakusa nai] - that *(conj)*
接続詞なので訳さない；わたしはこの本が面白いことを知っています [setsuzokushi na node yakusa nai ; watashi wa kono hon ga omoshiroi koto wo shi tte i masu] - that; I know that this book is interesting.
推薦、おすすめ [suisen, osusume] - recommendation
推薦する、すすめる [suisen suru, susumeru] - recommend
揺れる [yureru] - pitch
搬入する、積む；搬入作業員 [hannyuu suru, tsumu ; hannyuu sagyou in] - load; loader
携帯電話、 [keitai denwa,] - mobile
撃つ [utsu] - shot
操縦席、パイロット [soujuu seki, pairotto] - pilot
支払う、払う [shiharau, harau] - pay
支払った、払った [shihara tta, hara tta] - paid
放す、自由にする [hanasu, jiyuu ni suru] - set free
故障中 [koshou chuu] - out of order
救う、助ける [sukuu, tasukeru] - save
救助サービス [kyuujo saーbisu] - rescue service
教える [oshieru] - teach
教室 [kyoushitsu] - classroom
教科書 [kyoukasho] - textbook
教科書、本文 [kyoukasho, honbun] - text

敬具 [keigu] - yours sincerely
数字 [suuji] - number
文章、原稿、コンポジション（文章構成法）[bunshou, genkou, konpojishon （bunshou kousei hou）] - composition
料理をする [ryouri wo suru] - cooking
断る、拒否する [kotowaru, kyohi suru] - refuse
新しい [atarashii] - new
新聞 [shinbun] - newspaper
新聞、新聞社 [shinbun, shinbun sha] - newspaper
方法、やりかた [houhou, yari kata] - method
旅行 [ryokou] - travel
日；毎日、日常的に [nichi ; mainichi, nichijou teki ni] - day; daily
日付 [hizuke] - date
明日 [ashita] - tomorrow
星 [hoshi] - star
星印（＊）[hoshi jirushi （＊）] - asterisk
映画 [eiga] - film
昨日 [kinou] - yesterday
時；2時です [ji ; ni ji desu] - o'clock; It is two o'clock.
時間；毎時 [jikan ; maiji] - hour; hourly
時間 [jikan] - hour, time
普段の、いつもの [fudan no, itsumo no] - usual
暖かい [atatakai] - warm
暖める [atatameru] - warm up
暗い、黒い [kurai, kuroi] - dark
曲がる、曲げる、向ける、向く [magaru, mageru, mukeru, muku] - turn
書いた、手紙を書いた [kai ta, tegami wo kai ta] - wrote
書く [kaku] - write
最後に [saigo ni] - at last
月曜日 [getsuyoubi] - Monday
服 [fuku] - clothes
服を着ている [fuku wo ki te iru] - dressed
朝 [asa] - morning
朝食 [choushoku] - breakfast

朝食をとる [choushoku wo toru] - have breakfast
本 [hon] - book
本当に [hontouni] - really
本当の、実際の [hontou no, jissai no] - real
本文、文章、原稿、メッセージ [honbun, bunshou, genkou, messe―ji] - text
本棚 [hondana] - bookcase
机、デスク [tsukue, desuku] - desk
村 [mura] - village
来た、行った [ki ta, okona tta] - came
来る / 行く [kuru / iku] - come / go
楽しい [tanoshii] - fun
楽しむ [tanoshimu] - enjoy
橋 [hashi] - bridge
機械 [kikai] - machine
欄、題目 [ran, daimoku] - rubric
欲しい、欲しがる [hoshii, hoshi garu] - want
欲しがられる [hoshi gara reru] - wanted
歌う；歌手 [utau ; kashu] - sing; singer
正しく、正確に；直すために [tadashiku, seikaku ni ; naosu tame ni] - correct, correctly; to correct
歩いて [arui te] - on foot
歩いている [arui te iru] - walking
歩く [aruku] - walk
死ぬ、亡くなる [shinu, nakunaru] - die
死んだ、亡くなった [shin da, nakuna tta] - died
残る、とどまる [nokoru, todomaru] - remain
殺した [koroshi ta] - killed
母、お母さん [haha, okaasan] - mother
母国語 [bokoku go] - native language
毎時、1時間ごと [maiji, ichi jikan goto] - per hour
気にする [ki ni suru] - care
気をつける、注意深い [ki wo tsukeru, chuuibukai] - careful
気持ち、感じる、思う [kimochi, kanjiru, omou] - feeling
水 [mizu] - water
汚い、汚れた [kitanai, yogore ta] - dirty
決してない、二度とない [kesshite nai, nidoto nai] - never
波 [nami] - wave
泣いた、叫んだ [nai ta, saken da] - cried
泣く、叫ぶ [naku, sakebu] - cry
泥棒（複数）[dorobou（fukusuu）] - robbery, thief, thieves
泥棒、強盗、窃盗をする人 [dorobou, goutou, settou wo suru hito] - robber, robbery
注ぐ [sosogu] - pour
注意 [chuui] - attention
注意してきく、注意深くきく [chuui shi te kiku, chuuibukaku kiku] - listen carefully
注意深く [chuuibukaku] - carefully
泳ぐ [oyogu] - swim
洗う [arau] - wash
洗濯機 [sentakuki] - washer
流れる [nagareru] - flow
流暢に、上手に [ryuuchou ni, jouzu ni] - fluently
浅い [asai] - swallow
浮いている [ui te iru] - floating
浮く [uku] - float
海 [umi] - sea
海岸 [kaigan] - seashore
消す [kesu] - turn off
混乱する [konran suru] - confused
湖 [mizuumi] - lake
満たす、いっぱいにする [mitasu, ippai ni suru] - fill up
満ちている、いっぱいの [michi te iru, ippai no] - full
濡れている [nure te iru] - wet
火 [hi] - fire
無意識に、意識をなくして [muishiki ni, ishiki wo nakushi te] - unconscious
物語、ストーリー [monogatari, suto―ri―] - story
特に [tokuni] - especially
犬 [inu] - dog
状況、シチュエーション [joukyou, shichue―shon] - situation

独身 [dokushin] - single
猫 [neko] - cat, pussycat
猿 [saru] - monkey
獣医 [juui] - vet
現金、キャッシュ [genkin, kyasshu] - cash
理由 [riyuu] - reason
理解する、わかる [rikai suru, wakaru] - understand
瓶 [bin] - jar
生徒、学生 [seito, gakusei] - student
生徒達、学生達（複数）[seito tachi, gakusei tachi（fukusuu）] - students
生産する、作る [seisan suru, tsukuru] - produce
用意する、準備する [youi suru, junbi suru] - prepare
用意できている、準備できている [youi deki te iru, junbi deki te iru] - ready
用紙、シート [youshi, shi―to] - sheet (of paper)
申し訳ない、悪いと思う；ごめんなさい [moushiwake nai, warui to omou ; gomennasai] - be sorry; I am sorry.
男の人、男性 [otoko no hito, dansei] - guy
男の子 [otokonoko] - boy
男性 [dansei] - male
男性、人 [dansei, hito] - man
男性、人（複数）[dansei, hito（fukusuu）] - men
町 [machi] - town
畑、フィールド [hatake, fi―rudo] - field
留守番電話 [rusuban denwa] - answering machine
異なる、違う [kotonaru, chigau] - different
疲れた [tsukare ta] - tried
疲れている [tsukare te iru] - tired
白い [shiroi] - white
白髪の [hakuhatsu no] - grey - headed
盗まれた [nusuma re ta] - stolen
目 [me] - eye
目（複数）[me（fukusuu）] - eyes
相談する [soudan suru] - consult
真剣に [shinken ni] - seriously

眠っている [nemu tte iru] - sleeping
眠る、寝る [nemuru, neru] - sleep
着る、身に着ける [kiru, mi ni tsukeru] - put on
知っていた、知った [shi tte i ta, shi tta] - knew
知らせた [shirase ta] - informed
知らせる [shiraseru] - inform
知る [shiru] - know
短い [mijikai] - short
石 [ishi] - stone
石油 [sekiyu] - oil
砂 [suna] - sand
破壊する、壊す [hakai suru, kowasu] - destroy
確信している [kakushin shi te iru] - sure
確認する [kakunin suru] - check
秘密 [himitsu] - secret
秘書 [hisho] - secretary
種 [tane] - seed
種類 [shurui] - kind, type
稼ぐ；わたしは時給１０ドルを稼ぎます [kasegu ; watashi wa jikyuu juu doru wo kasegi masu] - earn; I earn 10 dollars per hour.
積極的に参加する [sekkyoku teki ni sanka suru] - take part
空いている [ai te iru] - free
空き時間 [aki jikan] - free time
空の、空いている [kara no, ai te iru] - empty
空中、空気、エアー [kuuchuu, kuuki, ea―] - air
空欄、空白 [kuuran, kuuhaku] - blank, empty
突然 [totsuzen] - suddenly
窓 [mado] - window
窓（複数）[mado（fukusuu）] - windows
立つ [tatsu] - stand
笑う [warau] - laugh
笑った、微笑んだ [wara tta, hohoen da] - smiled
箱、ダンボール [hako, danbo―ru] - box

簡単な、単純な [kantan na, tanjun na] - simple
精神作業 [seishin sagyou] - mental work
紙 [kami] - paper
素敵な、優しい、素晴らしい [suteki na, yasashii, subarashii] - nice
素早く、速く、急いで [subayaku, hayaku, isoi de] - quick, quickly
素晴らしい [subarashii] - wonderful
素晴らしい、偉大な [subarashii, idai na] - great
素晴らしい、良い [subarashii, yoi] - fine
紹介所、代理店 [shoukai jo, dairi ten] - agency
終わった、終えた [owa tta, oe ta] - finished
終わる、終える ; 終えるために [owaru, oeru ; oeru tame ni] - finish; to finish
経験 [keiken] - experience
続く [tsuzuku] - be continued
続く、かかる ; 映画は3時間以上かかります [tsuzuku, kakaru ; eiga wa san jikan ijou kakari masu] - last, take; The movie lasts more than three hours.
続ける [tsuzukeru] - continue
綺麗、清潔 [kirei, seiketsu] - clean
綺麗な [kirei na] - cleaned
緑の [midori no] - green
編集者 [henshuu sha] - editor
置く、場所 [oku, basho] - place
美しい、綺麗な [utsukushii, kirei na] - beautiful
考えている [kangae te iru] - thinking
考える [kangaeru] - think
耳 [mimi] - ear
聞いた [kii ta] - heard
聞く、聴く [kiku, kiku] - listen
職業 [shokugyou] - profession
腕相撲する、腕 [udezumou suru, ude] - arm
自動車免許証 [jidousha menkyo shou] - driving license
自然 [shizen] - nature
自身の [jishin no] - own

自転車 [jitensha] - bike
自転車で行く [jitensha de iku] - go by bike, ride a bike
興味深い、おもしろい [kyoumibukai, omoshiroi] - interesting
船 [fune] - ship
花 [hana] - flower
芸術、アート [geijutsu, a—to] - art
若い、年下の [wakai, toshishita no] - young
落ちた [ochi ta] - fallen, fell
落ちる [ochiru] - fall, falling
落ちるために [ochiru tame ni] - to fall
薬局 [yakkyoku] - pharmacy
虎 [tora] - tiger
蚊 [ka] - mosquito
蛇口 [jaguchi] - tap
行く ; 銀行へ行く [iku ; ginkou e iku] - go; I go to the bank
街、市 [machi, shi] - city
見せた [mise ta] - showed
見せる [miseru] - show
見つけた、見つかった、わかった [mitsuke ta, mitsuka tta, waka tta] - found
見つける、探す [mitsukeru, sagasu] - find
見る、理解する [miru, rikai suru] - look, see
見続ける [mi tsuzukeru] - continued to watch
親愛なる [shinai naru] - dear
観客 [kankyaku] - audience
解雇する [kaiko suru] - fire
言う、伝える [iu, tsutaeru] - tell, say
言った、発言した [i tta, hatsugen shi ta] - said
言語 [gengo] - language
計画するために [keikaku suru tame ni] - to plan
訓練する、鍛える ; 訓練されている、鍛えられている [kunren suru, kitaeru ; kunren sa re te iru, kitae rare te iru] - train; trained
記録 [kiroku] - record
訪問した [houmon shi ta] - visited
許す [yurusu] - excuse
評価した、予想した [hyouka shi ta, yosou shi ta] - estimated

話す [hanasu] - speak
話す、喋る [hanasu, shaberu] - talk
誤って [ayama tte] - incorrectly
説明する [setsumei suru] - explain
読む [yomu] - read
読んでいる [yon de iru] - reading
誰 [dare] - who
誰か [dare ka] - somebody
誰の [dare no] - whose
誰も、一人も〜ない [dare mo, hitori mo 〜 nai] - nobody
課題、タスク [kadai, tasuku] - task
調理道具、コンロ [chouri dougu, konro] - cooker
謎、ミステリー [nazo, misuteriー] - mystery
警察 [keisatsu] - police
警察官 [keisatsukan] - officer, policeman
貧しい [mazushii] - poor
買う [kau] - buy
費やす、かける、過ごす [tsuiyasu, kakeru, sugosu] - spend
費用がかかる [hiyou ga kakaru] - cost
賢い、頭のいい [kashikoi, atama no ii] - clever
質問した、聞いた、頼んだ [shitsumon shi ta, kii ta, tanon da] - asked
質問する、頼む、お願いする [shitsumon suru, tanomu, onegai suru] - ask
質問表 [shitsumon hyou] - questionnaire
赤い [akai] - red
走り去る、逃げる [hashirisaru, nigeru] - run away
走る、動かす [hashiru, ugokasu] - run, running
起きた、起こった [oki ta, oko tta] - happened
起きる、起こる [okiru, okoru] - happen
起き上がる；起きて！ [okiagaru ; oki te!] - get up; Get up!
足 [ashi] - foot, leg
跳飛、跳ね返ること [chouhi, hanekaeru koto] - ricochet
踏む [fumu] - step

踏む；踏むために [fumu ; fumu tame ni] - step; to step
踏んだ [fun da] - stepped
車 [kuruma] - car
辞める、とめる [yameru, tomeru] - quite
農場 [noujou] - farm
農家 [nouka] - farmer
近い [chikai] - close
近いこと [chikai koto] - nearness
近くに、近くの、隣の [chikaku ni, chikaku no, tonari no] - near, nearby, next
近所の人 [kinjo no hito] - neighbour
追跡 [tsuiseki] - pursuit
送った [oku tta] - sent
透明の、クリスタルの [toumei no, kurisutaru no] - crystal
通り、道 [toori, michi] - street
通り、道（複数） [toori, michi （fukusuu）] - streets
通り過ぎる、過ぎた [toorisugiru, sugi ta] - past
通訳、翻訳家 [tsuuyaku, hon'yaku ka] - translator
通過した、通り過ぎた [tsuuka shi ta, toorisugi ta] - passed
連続ドラマ（読み方） [renzoku dorama （yomikata）] - serial
週 [shuu] - week
遊ぶ、する [asobu, suru] - play
遊んでいる、プレイしている [ason de iru, purei shi te iru] - playing
運ぶ、持ってくる、 [hakobu, mo tte kuru,] - bring
運転した [unten shi ta] - drove
運転する [unten suru] - drive
運転手 [unten shu] - driver
運送する、運ぶ [unsou suru, hakobu] - transport
道 [michi] - way
道路 [douro] - road
遠い、離れた [tooi, hanare ta] - far
選ぶ、決める [erabu, kimeru] - choose
選んだ、決めた [eran da, kime ta] - chose

部屋 [heya] - room
部屋（複数）[heya (fukusuu)] - rooms
金属 [kinzoku] - metal
銀行 [ginkou] - bank
銃 [juu] - gun
錠剤、ピル [jouzai, piru] - pill
鍵 [kagi] - key
長い [nagai] - long
閉じる、閉める、近い [tojiru, shimeru, chikai] - close
開けた、開いた、開いている [ake ta, hirai ta, hirai te iru] - opened
開ける、開く [akeru, hiraku] - open
開発する、育てる [kaihatsu suru, sodateru] - develop
降りる [oriru] - get off
降ろす、荷おろしをする [orosu, ni oroshi wo suru] - unload
陸上、着陸する [rikujou, chakuriku suru] - land
階段（複数）[kaidan (fukusuu)] - stairs
隠した [kakushi ta] - hid
隠れる [kakureru] - hide
雇い主 [yatoinushi] – employer
雑誌 [zasshi] - magazine
難しい、困難な [muzukashii, konnan na] - difficult
雨 [ame] - rain
電気の [denki no] - electric
電流 [denryuu] - current
電話 [denwa] - phone
電話した [denwa shi ta] - called
電話する；コールセンター [denwa suru ; ko―ru senta―] - call; call centre
電話する [denwa suru] - call on the phone
電話をかける、呼ぶ [denwa wo kakeru, yobu] - call
電話をする、鳴らす；電話をするために [denwa wo suru, narasu ; denwa wo suru tame ni] - ring; to ring, to phone
電話機；電話をする [denwaki ; denwa wo suru] - telephone; to telephone
電車 [densha] - train
電車の駅 [densha no eki] - railway station
青い [aoi] - blue
青白い [aojiroi] - pale
静かに、黙って [shizuka ni, dama tte] - quietly; silent, silently
面白い [omoshiroi] - funny
音楽 [ongaku] - music
項目 [koumoku] - field
頭の良い、賢い [atama no yoi, kashikoi] - smart
頻繁に、よく [hinpan ni, yoku] - often
顔 [kao] - face
風 [kaze] - wind
飛び去った [tobi sa tta] - flew away
飛行機 [hikouki] - airplane
食べる [taberu] - eat
食べ物 [tabemono] - food
飲む [nomu] - drink
餌付けする [ezuke suru] - feed
驚いている [odoroi te iru] - surprised
驚かせる [odoroka seru] - surprise
驚かせるために [odoroka seru tame ni] - to surprise
高い、暑い [takai, atsui] - high
髪の毛 [kaminoke] - hair
鳥 [tori] - bird
黄色い [kiiroi] - yellow
黒い [kuroi] - black
鼻 [hana] - nose

えいにちじしょ
英 日 辞 書
English-Japanese dictionary

a year ago - 1年前 [ichi nen mae]
about - について、ほど [nitsuite, hodo]
accident - 事故 [jiko]
accompanied - 同伴した [douhan shi ta]
accompany - 同伴する [douhan suru]
ad - 広告 [koukoku]
address - 住所 [juusho]
adventure - アドベンチャー、冒険 [adobenchaー, bouken]
advert - 宣伝、広告 [senden, koukoku]
afraid - 恐れる、怖がる [osoreru, kowagaru]
after - あとで、あとに [atode, ato ni]
after that - その後 [sonogo]
again - また、再び、もう一度 [mata, futatabi, mouichido]
against - に対して [nitaishite]
age - 年、年齢 [toshi, nenrei]
agency - 紹介所、代理店 [shoukai jo, dairi ten]
ago - 前 [mae]
agree - 同意する [doui suru]
agreement - 契約書 [keiyaku sho]
air - 空中、空気、エアー [kuuchuu, kuuki, eaー]
airplane - 飛行機 [hikouki]
airshow - エアーショー [eaー shoー]
alarm - アラーム、警報機 [araーmu, keihou ki]
alien - エイリアン [eirian]
all - すべての、全部の [subete no, zenbu no]; 全ての、全部 [subete no, zenbu]
along - に沿って [ni sotte]
aloud - 声に出して [koe ni dashi te]
already - もうすでに [mou sudeni]
also - また、同じく、同様に [mata, onajiku, douyou ni]
although - けれども、しかしながら [keredomo, shikashinagara]
always - いつも [itsumo]

American - アメリカ人 [amerika jin]
and - と [to]
angrily - 怒って [oko tte]
angry - 怒っている [oko tte iru]
animal - 動物 [doubutsu]
another - 別の、違う [betsu no, chigau]
answer - こたえる [kotaeru]
answered - 応えた、答えた [kotae ta, kotae ta]
answering machine - 留守番電話 [rusuban denwa]
any - いくつかの [ikutsu ka no]
anything - 何でも [nani demo]
apply - 応募する [oubo suru]
arm - 腕相撲する、腕 [udezumou suru, ude]
arrive - 到着する [touchaku suru]
arrived - 到着した、ついた [touchaku shi ta, tsui ta]
art - 芸術、アート [geijutsu, aーto]
artist - アーティスト、芸術家 [aーtisuto, geijutsu ka]
as - 同じように、同じ程度 [onaji you ni, onaji teido]
as often as possible - できるだけ頻繁に [dekirudake hinpan ni]
as well - 同様に、同じく [douyou ni, onajiku]
as, since *(kausal)* - なぜなら、だから [nazenara, dakara]
ask - 質問する、頼む、お願いする [shitsumon suru, tanomu, onegai suru]
asked - 質問した、聞いた、頼んだ [shitsumon shi ta, kii ta, tanon da]
aspirin - アスピリン（鎮痛剤）[asupirin（chintsuu zai）]
asterisk - 星印(＊) [hoshi jirushi (＊)]
at - で、にて [de, nite]
at first - はじめに、最初に [hajime ni, saisho ni]
at half past eight - 8時半に [hachi ji han ni]

at last - 最後に [saigo ni]
at least - 少なくとも [sukunakutomo]
at one o'clock - １時に [ichi ji ni]
at the same time - 同時に [douji ni]
attention - 注意 [chuui]
audience - 観客 [kankyaku]
away - 去って、離れて [sa tte, hanare te]
back - 戻る [modoru]
bad - 悪い、良くない [warui, yoku nai]
bag - かばん [kaban]
bank - 銀行 [ginkou]
barked - 吠えた [hoe ta]
bathroom table - お風呂場のテーブル [o furoba no te－buru]
bathroom; bath - お風呂場、お手洗い；お風呂 [o furoba, o tearai ; o furo]
be - なる [naru]
be ashamed; he is ashamed - 恥じる；彼は恥ずかしがっている [hajiru ; kare wa hazukashi ga tte iru]
be continued - 続く [tsuzuku]
be sorry; I am sorry. - 申し訳ない、悪いと思う；ごめんなさい [moushiwake nai, warui to omou ; gomennasai]
beautiful - 美しい、綺麗な [utsukushii, kirei na]
because - なぜなら、だって [nazenara, datte]
bed - ベッド [beddo]
beds - ベッド（複数）[beddo（fukusuu）]
beep - ピーという音 [pi－ toiu oto]
before - 前に、前は [mae ni, mae wa]
began - はじめた [hajime ta]
begin - 始める、始まる [hajimeru, hajimaru]
behind - 後ろ、あと [ushiro, ato]
believe; to not believe one's eyes - 信じる；の目を信じない [shinjiru ; no me wo shinji nai]
better - より良い [yori yoi]
between - の間 [no aida]

big / bigger / the biggest - 大きい／より大きな／一番大きい [ookii ／ yori ookina ／ ichiban ookii]
bike - 自転車 [jitensha]
billion - １０億 [juu oku]
bird - 鳥 [tori]
bite - 噛む [kamu]
black - 黒い [kuroi]
blank, empty - 空欄、空白 [kuuran, kuuhaku]
blue - 青い [aoi]
book - 本 [hon]
bookcase - 本棚 [hondana]
bother - いじめる、邪魔をする、困らせる [ijimeru, jama wo suru, komara seru]
box - 箱、ダンボール [hako, danbo－ru]
boy - 男の子 [otokonoko]
boyfriend - 彼氏、男の子の友達 [kareshi, otokonoko no tomodachi]
brake - ブレーキ [bure－ki]
bread - パン [pan]
break, pause - とめる、停止する [tomeru, teishi suru]
breakfast - 朝食 [choushoku]
bridge - 橋 [hashi]
bring - 運ぶ、持ってくる、[hakobu, mo tte kuru,]
brother - 兄、弟 [ani, otouto]
bus; go by bus - バス；バスで行く [basu ; basu de iku]
but - でも、しかし [demo, shikashi]
butter - バター [bata－]
button - ボタン [botan]
buy - 買う [kau]
by the way - ところで [tokorode]
bye - さようなら、じゃあまた [sayounara, jaa mata]
cable - ケーブル、電線 [ke－buru, densen]
café - カフェ [kafe]
call - 電話をかける、呼ぶ [denwa wo kakeru, yobu]
call on the phone - 電話する [denwa suru]
call; call centre - 電話する；コールセンター [denwa suru ; ko－ru senta－]

called - 電話した [denwa shi ta]
came - 来た、行った [ki ta, okona tta]
can; I can read - することができる ; わたしは読むことができる [suru koto ga dekiru ; watashi ha yomu koto ga dekiru]
Canada - カナダ [kanada]
Canadian - カナダ人 [kanada jin]
captain - キャプテン [kyaputen]
car - 車 [kuruma]
care - 気にする [ki ni suru]
careful - 気をつける、注意深い [ki wo tsukeru, chuuibukai]
carefully - 注意深く [chuuibukaku]
cash - 現金、キャッシュ [genkin, kyasshu]
cash register; cashier, teller - レジ ; 銀行の支配人、レジ係、テラー [reji ; ginkou no shihainin, reji gakari, teraー]
cat - 猫 [neko]
catch - 捕まえる、掴む、引っかかる [tsukamaeru, tsukamu, hikkakaru]
CD - CD [shiー diー]
CD player - CDプレーヤー [shiー diー pureーyaー]
central - 中心の、真ん中の [chuushin no, mannaka no]
centre; city centre - 中心 ; 中心街 [chuushin ; chuushin gai]
ceremony - 式典 [shikiten]
chair - いす [isu]
chance - チャンス、確率 [chansu, kakuritsu]
change; to change - 変える、変わる ; 変えること、変わること [kaeru, kawaru ; kaeru koto, kawaru koto]
check - 確認する [kakunin suru]
chemical(adj) - 化学の、化学的な [kagaku no, kagaku teki na]
chemicals - 化学物質（複数） [kagaku busshitsu（fukusuu）]
chemistry - 化学 [kagaku]
child - 子供 [kodomo]
children - 子供たち [kodomo tachi]
choose - 選ぶ、決める [erabu, kimeru]
chose - 選んだ、決めた [eran da, kime ta]

city - 街、市 [machi, shi]
class - クラス、授業 [kurasu, jugyou]
classroom - 教室 [kyoushitsu]
clean - 綺麗、清潔 [kirei, seiketsu]
cleaned - 綺麗な [kirei na]
clever - 賢い、頭のいい [kashikoi, atama no ii]
close - 閉じる、閉める、近い [tojiru, shimeru, chikai]
closed - しめた、閉じた、閉まっている [shime ta, toji ta, shima tte iru]
closer - より近い [yori chikai]
clothes - 服 [fuku]
club - クラブ [kurabu]
coffee - コーヒー [koーhiー]
cold (adj) - 冷たい [tsumetai]
coldness - 冷たさ [tsumeta sa]
colleague - 同僚 [douryou]
college - 大学 [daigaku]
come / go - 来る / 行く [kuru / iku]
company - 会社 [kaisha]
competition - コンテスト [contest]
compose - 作る、構成する、文章を作る [tsukuru, kousei suru, bunshou wo tsukuru]
composition - 文章、原稿、コンポジション（文章構成法） [bunshou, genkou, konpojishon（bunshou kousei hou）]
computer - コンピューター [konpyuーtaー]
confused - 混乱する [konran suru]
constant - 一定に、定期的に [ittei ni, teiki teki ni]
consult - 相談する [soudan suru]
consultancy - コンサルティング [konsarutingu]
consultant - コンサルタント [konsarutanto]
continue - 続ける [tsuzukeru]
continued to watch - 見続ける [mi tsuzukeru]
control - コントロールする [kontoroーru suru]
cooker - 調理道具、コンロ [chouri dougu, konro]
cooking - 料理をする [ryouri wo suru]

261

co-ordination - コーディネーション [koーdineーshon]
correct, correctly; to correct - 正しく、正確に ; 直すために [tadashiku, seikaku ni ; naosu tame ni]
cost - 費用がかかる [hiyou ga kakaru]
could - かもしれない [kamo shire nai]
country - 国 [kuni]
course - コース [koーsu]
creative - 創造的な [souzou teki na]
cried - 泣いた、叫んだ [nai ta, saken da]
criminal - 刑事上の、犯罪の [keiji jou no, hanzai no]
cry - 泣く、叫ぶ [naku, sakebu]
crystal - 透明の、クリスタルの [toumei no, kurisutaru no]
cup - カップ、コップ [kappu, koppu]
current - 電流 [denryuu]
customer - お客さん、カスタマー [okyaku san, kasutamaー]
dad - パパ、お父さん [papa, otousan]
daddy - パパ、お父さん [papa, otousan]
damn - ちくしょう [chikushou]
dance - ダンスする、踊る [dansu suru, odoru]
danced - ダンスした, 踊った [dansu shi ta, odo tta]
dancing - ダンスしている [dansu shi te iru]
dark - 暗い、黒い [kurai, kuroi]
date - 日付 [hizuke]
daughter - 娘 [musume]
David's book - デイビッドの本 [deibiddo no hon]
day - 日 [nichi]
day; daily - 日 ; 毎日、日常的に [nichi ; mainichi, nichijou teki ni]
deadly - ひどい、命とりの [hidoi, inochitori no]
dear - 親愛なる [shinai naru]
design - デザイン [dezain]
desk - 机、デスク [tsukue, desuku]
destroy - 破壊する、壊す [hakai suru, kowasu]
develop - 開発する、育てる [kaihatsu suru, sodateru]
did - した、やった、行った [shi ta, ya tta, okona tta]
die - 死ぬ、亡くなる [shinu, nakunaru]
died - 死んだ、亡くなった [shin da, nakuna tta]
different - 異なる、違う [kotonaru, chigau]
difficult - 難しい、困難な [muzukashii, konnan na]
dirty - 汚い、汚れた [kitanai, yogore ta]
do - する、やる、行う [suru, yaru, okonau]
Do not worry! - 心配しないで！ [shinpai shi nai de!]
doctor - 医者 [isha]
dog - 犬 [inu]
doll - 人形 [ningyou]
door - ドア [doa]
dorms - 寮 [ryou]
down - 下に [shita ni]
dream - 夢 [yume]
dressed - 服を着ている [fuku wo ki te iru]
drink - 飲む [nomu]
drive - 運転する [unten suru]
driver - 運転手 [unten shu]
driving license - 自動車免許証 [jidousha menkyo shou]
drove - 運転した [unten shi ta]
dry (adj), to dry - 乾いた ; 乾かすために [kawaita ; kawakasu tame ni]
DVD - DVD [DVD]
ear - 耳 [mimi]
earn; I earn 10 dollars per hour. - 稼ぐ ; わたしは時給１０ドルを稼ぎます [kasegu ; watashi wa jikyuu juu doru wo kasegi masu]
earth - 地球 [chikyuu]
eat - 食べる [taberu]
editor - 編集者 [henshuu sha]
education - 学歴、教育 [gakureki, kyouiku]
eight - 8 [hachi]
eighth - ８番目の [hachi banme no]
either of you - あなたがたのどちらか [anata ga ta no dochira ka]

either, too, also - も、同様に、同じく [mo, douyou ni, onajiku]
elder - 年上の [toshiue no]
electric - 電気の [denki no]
eleven - 11 [juu ichi]
else - 他の、別の [taj no, betsu no]
e-mail - メール [me一ru]
employer - 雇い主 [yatoinushi]
empty - 空の、空いている [kara no, ai te iru]
energy - エネルギー、元気 [enerugi一, genki]
engine - エンジン [enjin]
engineer - エンジニア [enjinia]
enjoy - 楽しむ [tanoshimu]
especially - 特に [tokuni]
estimate - 予測する、予想する [yosoku suru, yosou suru]
estimated - 評価した、予想した [hyouka shi ta, yosou shi ta]
etc. - など、等 [nado, tou]
evening - 夕方 [yuugata]
every - 全ての、それぞれの [subete no, sorezore no]
everybody - みんな、全員 [minna, zen'in]
everything - 全て、全部 [subete, zenbu]
example - 例 [rei]
excuse - 許す [yurusu]
Excuse me. - すいません [suimasen]
experience - 経験 [keiken]
explain - 説明する [setsumei suru]
eye - 目 [me]
eyes - 目（複数）[me （fukusuu）]
face - 顔 [kao]
fall - 落ちる [ochiru]
fallen - 落ちた [ochi ta]
falling - 落ちる [ochiru]
family - 家族 [kazoku]
far - 遠い、離れた [tooi, hanare ta]
farm - 農場 [noujou]
farmer - 農家 [nouka]
fasten - しめる [shimeru]
favourite - お気に入りの、好きな [okiniiri no, suki na]

favourite film - お気に入りの映画 [okiniiri no eiga]
feed - 餌付けする [ezuke suru]
feeling - 気持ち、感じる、思う [kimochi, kanjiru, omou]
fell - 落ちた [ochi ta]
female - 女性 [josei]
few; a few - 少ない；いくつかの少ない [sukunai ; ikutsu ka no sukunai]
field - 畑、フィールド [hatake, fi一rudo]; 項目 [koumoku]
fifteen - 15 [juu go]
fifth - 5番目の [go banme no]
fill up - 満たす、いっぱいにする [mitasu, ippai ni suru]
film - 映画 [eiga]
finance - ファイナンス、金融 [fainansu, kinyuu]
find - 見つける、探す [mitsukeru, sagasu]
fine - 素晴らしい、良い [subarashii, yoi]
finish; to finish - 終わる、終える；終えるために [owaru, oeru ; oeru tame ni]
finished - 終わった、終えた [owa tta, oe ta]
fire - 火 [hi]; 解雇する [kaiko suru
firm, firms - 企業、会社（複数）[kigyou, kaisha （fukusuu）]
five - 5 [go]
flew away - 飛び去った [tobi sa tta]
float - 浮く [uku]
floating - 浮いている [ui te iru]
floor - 床 [yuka]
flow - 流れる [nagareru]
flower - 花 [hana]
fluently - 流暢に、上手に [ryuuchou ni, jouzu ni]
food - 食べ物 [tabemono]
foot - 足 [ashi]
for - ために [tame ni]; のために [no tame ni]
for example - 例えば [tatoeba]
forget - 忘れる [wasureru]
form - フォーム [fo一mu]
forty-four - 44 [yon juu yon]

263

found - 見つけた、見つかった、わかった [mitsuke ta, mitsuka tta, waka tta]
four - 4つ [yottsu]
fourth - 4番目の [yon banme no]
free - 空いている [ai te iru]
free time - 空き時間 [aki jikan]
freeze - 固まる、凍える、凍る [katamaru, kogoeru, kooru]
friend - 友達 [tomodachi]
friendly - フレンドリーな [furendorī na]
from; from the USA - から、出身;アメリカ出身 [kara, shusshin ; amerika shusshin]
front - フロント、受付、前、玄関 [furonto, uketsuke, mae, genkan]
front wheels - 前輪 [zenrin]
full - 満ちている、いっぱいの [michi te iru, ippai no]
fun - 楽しい [tanoshii]
funny - 面白い [omoshiroi]
furniture - 家具 [kagu]
further - より遠く [yori tooku]
future - 将来 [shourai]
garden - 庭 [niwa]
gas - ガス [gasu]
gave - 与えた、渡した、あげた [atae ta, watashi ta, age ta]
German - ドイツ人 [doitsu jin]
get - 得る、着く、なる [eru, tsuku, naru]
get (something) - 取る、手に入れる、得る [toru, te ni ireru, eru]
get (somewhere) - たどり着く [tadoritsuku]
get off - 降りる [oriru]
get up; Get up! - 起き上がる;起きて！ [okiagaru ; oki te!]
gift - ギフト、贈り物、プレゼント [gifuto, okurimono, purezento]
girl - 女の子 [onnanoko]
girlfriend - 彼女、女の子の友達 [kanojo, onnanoko no tomodachi]
give, hand - 与える、渡す [ataeru, watasu]
glad - 嬉しい [ureshii]
glass - ガラス [garasu]
go away - いなくなる、消える、なくなる [i naku naru, kieru, nakunaru]
go by bike, ride a bike - 自転車で行く [jitensha de iku]
go; I go to the bank - 行く;銀行へ行く [iku ; ginkou e iku]
gone - なくなる、行く [nakunaru, iku]
good, well - よい、おいしい、上手 [yoi, oishii, jouzu]
goodbye - さようなら [sayounara]
great - 素晴らしい、偉大な [subarashii, idai na]
green - 緑の [midori no]
grey - グレイ、灰色 [gurei, haiiro]
grey-headed - 白髪の [hakuhatsu no]
guest - ゲスト [gesuto]
gun - 銃 [juu]
guy - 男の人、男性 [otoko no hito, dansei]
had - あった [a tta]
hair - 髪の毛 [kaminoke]
half - 半分 [hanbun]; 半分の [hanbun no]
handcuffs - 手錠 [tejou]
happen - 起きる、起こる [okiru, okoru]
happened - 起きた、起こった [oki ta, oko tta]
happiness - 幸せ [shiawase]
happy - 喜んでいる、幸せ [yorokon de iru, shiawase]
hard - 大変な [taihen na]
hat - 帽子 [boushi]
hate - いやがる、嫌う [iyagaru, kirau]
have a lot of work - 仕事がたくさんある [shigoto ga takusan aru]
have breakfast - 朝食をとる [choushoku wo toru]
have, he/she/it has, he has a book. - 持っている、飼っている、ある;彼／彼女／それは持っている;彼は本を持っている [mo tte iru, ka tte iru, aru ; kare ／ kanojo ／ sore wa mo tte iru ; kare wa hon wo mo tte iru]
he - 彼は [kare wa]
head; to head, to go - あたま、長、リーダー;へ向かう [atama, chou, rīdā ; e mukau]

health - 健康 [kenkou]
heard - 聞いた [kii ta]
hello - こんにちは [konnichiwa]
help; to help - 助ける、手伝う；助けるために、手伝うために [tasukeru, tetsudau ; tasukeru tame ni, tetsudau tame ni]
helper - 助手 [joshu]
her; her book - 彼女の；彼女の本 [kanojo no ; kanojo no hon]
here (a direction) - ここに、こちらに [koko ni, kochira ni]
here (a place) - ここ [koko]
here is - こちらは、これは [kochira wa, kore wa]
Hey! - おい！やあ！ [oi! yaa!]
hi - やあ、こんにちは [yaa, konnichiwa]
hid - 隠した [kakushi ta]
hide - かくれんぼ [kakurenbo]; 隠れる [kakureru]
high - 高い、暑い [takai, atsui]
him - 彼に [kare ni]
his, his bed - 彼の；彼のベッド [kare no ; kare no beddo]
hit, beat - たたく、あてる [tataku, ateru]
home; go home - 家、家庭；帰宅する、家に帰る [ie, katei ; kitaku suru, ie ni kaeru]
homework - 宿題 [shukudai]
hope; to hope - 希望；願うために [kibou ; negau tame ni]
host - ホスト [hosuto]
hotel - ホテル [hoteru]
hotels - ホテル（複数）[hoteru（fukusuu）]
hour - 時間 [jikan]
hour; hourly - 時間；毎時 [jikan ; maiji]
house - 家 [ie]
how - どう [dou]
howling - 吠える、なりわめく [hoeru, nari wameku]
human - 人間 [ningen]
hundred - １００ [hyaku]

hungry; I am hungry - お腹がすいている；わたしはお腹がすいています [onaka ga sui te iru ; watashi wa onaka ga sui te i masu]
I - わたしは [watashi wa]
I listen to music. - わたしは音楽を聞きます。 [watashi wa ongaku wo kiki masu.]
ice-cream - アイスクリーム [aisukuriーmu]
idea - アイディア、考え、案 [aidia, kangae, an]
if - もし [moshi]
immediately - 今すぐに [ima suguni]
important - 大事な [daiji na]
in - 〜に、〜で [〜 ni, 〜 de]
incorrectly - 誤って [ayama tte]
individually - 個別に、別々に [kobetsu ni, betsubetsu ni]
inform - 知らせる [shiraseru]
information - 情報 [jouhou]
informed - 知らせた [shirase ta]
inside - 中に、中へ [naka ni, naka e]
instead - の代わりに [no kawari ni]
instead of - 代わりに [kawari ni]
instead of you - あなたの代わりに [anata no kawari ni]
interesting - 興味深い、おもしろい [kyoumibukai, omoshiroi]
Internet site - インターネットのサイト [intaーnetto no saito]
into - 中へ、中に [naka e, naka ni]
it - それ [sore]
its *(for neuter)* - その [sono]
jacket - 上着 [uwagi]
jar - 瓶 [bin]
job; job agency - 仕事；職業紹介所 [shigoto ; shokugyou shoukai jo]
join - 参加する [sanka suru]
journalist - ジャーナリスト [jaーnarisuto]
jump - ジャンプする、飛び降りる、ジャンプ [janpu suru, tobioriru, janpu]
just - だけ [dake]
kangaroo - カンガルー [kangaruー]
kettle - やかん [yakan]
key - 鍵 [kagi]

keyboard - キーボード [kiーboーdo]
killed - 殺した [koroshi ta]
killer - すごい、大きな [sugoi, ookina]
kilometer - キロメートル(km) [kiromeーtoru (km)]
kind, type - 種類 [shurui]
kindergarten - 幼稚園 [youchien]
kiss - キス [kisu]
kitchen - キッチン [kicchin]
kitten - 子猫 [koneko]
knew - 知っていた、知った [shi tte i ta, shi tta]
know - 知る [shiru]
know each other - お互いを知る [otagai wo shiru]
lake - 湖 [mizuumi]
land - 陸上、着陸する [rikujou, chakuriku suru]
language - 言語 [gengo]
laser - レーザー [reーzaー]
last, take; The movie lasts more than three hours. - 続く、かかる; 映画は3時間以上かかります [tsuzuku, kakaru ; eiga wa san jikan ijou kakari masu]
laugh - 笑う [warau]
leader - リーダー [riーdaー]
learn - 学ぶ、習う [manabu, narau]
learned about - について知った、について学んだ [nitsuite shi tta, nitsuite manan da]
learning - 勉強している、習っている [benkyou shi te iru, nara tte iru]
leave - 去る、なくなる、出る [saru, nakunaru, deru]
left - 左 [hidari]
leg - 足 [ashi]
less - より少ない [yori sukunai]
lesson - レッスン、授業 [ressun, jugyou]
let - させる [sa seru]
let us - わたしたちにさせる、しよう [watashi tachi ni sa seru, shiyo u]
letter - 手紙 [tegami]
life - 命 [inochi]

life-saving trick - 人命救助のトリック [jinmei kyuujo no torikku]
lift - エレベーター [erebeーtaー]
like, love - 好き、大好き [suki, daisuki]
like; I like that. - 好き; わたしはそれが好きです [suki ; watashi wa sore ga suki desu]
limit - リミット [rimitto]
lion - ライオン [raion]
list - リスト、リストする [risuto, risuto suru]
listen - 聞く、聴く [kiku, kiku]
listen carefully - 注意してきく、注意深くきく [chuui shi te kiku, chuuibukaku kiku]
little - 少しの、小さな [sukoshi no, chiisana]
live - 住んでいる [sun de iru]
lived - 住んでいた [sun de i ta]
living - 住んでいる [sun de iru]
load - 搬入する、積む [hannyuu suru, tsumu]
load; loader - 搬入する、積む; 搬入作業員 [hannyuu suru, tsumu ; hannyuu sagyou in]
long - 長い [nagai]
look - 見る [miru]
look around - 周りを見る、見て回る、見渡す [mawari wo miru, mi te mawaru, miwatasu]
looked - みた [mi ta]
loose - 失う、なくす [ushinau, nakusu]
lot - ロット [rotto]
love - 愛 [ai]
loved - 愛した [aishi ta]
machine - 機械 [kikai]
magazine - 雑誌 [zasshi]
make - 作る、料理をする [tsukuru, ryouri wo suru]
maker - メーカー [meーkaー]
male - 男性 [dansei]
man - 男性、人 [dansei, hito]
manual work - 手作業 [tesagyou]
many, much - たくさんの、多くの [takusan no, ooku no]
map - 地図 [chizu]
mattress - マットレス [mattoresu]

may - かもしれない、許可する・される [kamo shire nai, kyoka suru. sa reru]
me - わたしに [watashi ni]
meanwhile - 一方で、その間に [ippou de, sonokan ni]
medical - 医療の [iryou no]
meet - 会う [au]
member - メンバー [menbaー]
men - 男性、人（複数）[dansei, hito（fukusuu）]
mental work - 精神作業 [seishin sagyou]
met - 会った、合った [a tta, a tta]
metal - 金属 [kinzoku]
meter - メートル [meーtoru]
method - 方法、やりかた [houhou, yari kata]
microphone - マイク [maiku]
middle name - ミドルネーム [midoru neーmu]
mine - わたしの [watashi no]
minute - 分 [fun]
Miss - ミス、さん [misu, san]
mister, Mr. - さん、氏 [san, shi]
mobile - 携帯電話、[keitai denwa,]
mom, mother - お母さん、母親 [okaasan, hahaoya]
moment - 一瞬、その時、その瞬間 [isshun, sono toki, sono shunkan]
Monday - 月曜日 [getsuyoubi]
money - お金 [okane]
monkey - 猿 [saru]
monotonous - 単調な [tanchou na]
more - さらに、もっと、より [sarani, motto, yori]
morning - 朝 [asa]
mosquito - 蚊 [ka]
mother - 母、お母さん [haha, okaasan]
moved - 動いた、動かした [ugoi ta, ugokashi ta]
much, many - たくさん、多くの [takusan, ooku no]
music - 音楽 [ongaku]
must not - してはいけない [shi te ha ike nai]

must; I must go - しなければならない；わたしは行かなければならない [shi nakere ba nara nai ; watashi ha ika nakere ba nara nai]
my - わたしの、自分の [watashi no, jibun no]
mystery - 謎、ミステリー [nazo, misuteriー]
name - 名前、名前を挙げる、教える [namae, namae wo ageru, oshieru]
nationality - 国籍 [kokuseki]
native language - 母国語 [bokoku go]
nature - 自然 [shizen]
near, nearby, next - 近くに、近くの、隣の [chikaku ni, chikaku no, tonari no]
nearest - 一番近くの [ichiban chikaku no]
nearness - 近いこと [chikai koto]
need - 必要である、必要とする [hitsuyou de aru, hitsuyou to suru]
neighbour - 近所の人 [kinjo no hito]
never - 決してない、二度とない [kesshite nai, nidoto nai]
new - 新しい [atarashii]
newspaper - 新聞、新聞社 [shinbun, shinbun sha]
nice - 素敵な、優しい、素晴らしい [suteki na, yasashii, subarashii]
night - 夜 [yoru]
nine - 9 [kyuu]
ninth - 9番目の [kyuu banme no]
no - いいえ、ちがいます [iie, chigai masu]
nobody - 誰も、一人も〜ない [dare mo, hitori mo 〜 nai]
North America and Eurasia - 北米とユーラシア [hokubei to yuーrashia]
nose - 鼻 [hana]
not - ではない [de wa nai]
note - メモ [memo]
notebook - ノート [noーto]
notebooks - ノート（複数）[noーto（fukusuu）]
nothing - ない、何も [nai, nani mo]
now - 今、現在 [ima, genzai]
number - 数字 [suuji]

o'clock; It is two o'clock. - 時 ； 2 時です [ji ; ni ji desu]
of course - もちろん [mochiron]
office - オフィス [ofisu]
officer, policeman - 警察官 [keisatsukan]
often - 頻繁に、よく [hinpan ni, yoku]
Oh! - わあ！ああ！ [waa! aa!]
oil - 石油 [sekiyu]
OK, well - 大丈夫、平気、わかる [daijoubu, heiki, wakaru]
okay, well - わかった、ええと [waka tta, eeto]
on - の上に、ついて [no ue ni, tsui te]
on foot - 歩いて [arui te]
once - 一度 [ichi do]
one - ひとつ [hitotsu]
one by one - ひとりずつ [hitori zutsu]
one more - もう一度 [mouichido]
only - 唯一の [yuiitsu no]
open - 開ける、開く [akeru, hiraku]
opened - 開けた、開いた、開いている [ake ta, hirai ta, hirai te iru]
order - 命令する、言いつける [meirei suru, ii tsukeru]
other - 他の、別の [ta no, betsu no]
our - わたしたちの [watashi tachi no]
out of order - 故障中 [koshou chuu]
outdoors - 外で [soto de]
over - 上の、以上の、こえた [ue no, ijou no, koe ta]
over, across - 向こうの、渡った [mukou no, wata tta]
own - 自身の [jishin no]
owner - オーナー、持ち主 [o—na—, mochinushi]
paid - 支払った、払った [shihara tta, hara tta]
pail - バケツ [baketsu]
pale - 青白い [aojiroi]
panic; to panic - パニック；パニックするために [panikku ; panikku suru tame ni]
paper - 紙 [kami]
parachute - パラシュート [parashu—to]
parachutist - パラシュートをする人 [parashu—to wo suru hito]
parent - 両親 [ryoushin]
park - 公園 [kouen]
parks - 公園（複数） [kouen（fukusuu）]
part - 一部、部品、部分 [ichibu, buhin, bubun]
participant - 参加者 [sanka sha]
passed - 通過した、通り過ぎた [tsuuka shi ta, toorisugi ta]
past - 通り過ぎる、過ぎた [toorisugiru, sugi ta]
patrol - パトロール、 [patoro—ru,]
pay - 支払う、払う [shiharau, harau]
pay attention to - に注意を払う [ni chuui wo harau]
pen - ペン [pen]
pens - ペン（複数） [pen（fukusuu）]
people - 人々 [hitobito]
per hour - 毎時、1時間ごと [maiji, ichi jikan goto]
person - 人 [hito]
personal - 個人的な、個人の、自分の [kojin teki na, kojin no, jibun no]
personnel department - 人事部 [jinji bu]
pet - ペット [petto]
pharmacy - 薬局 [yakkyoku]
phone - 電話 [denwa]
phone handset - 受話器 [juwaki]
photograph; photographer - 写真；カメラマン [shashin ; kameraman]
phrase - フレーズ、言葉 [fure—zu, kotoba]
picture - 写真 [shashin]
pill - 錠剤、ピル [jouzai, piru]
pilot - 操縦席、パイロット [soujuu seki, pairotto]
pitch - 揺れる [yureru]
place - 置く、場所 [oku, basho]
plan - 予定、計画 [yotei, keikaku]
planet - 惑星 [wakusei]
plate - お皿 [o sara]

play - 遊ぶ、する [asobu, suru]
playing - 遊んでいる、プレイしている [ason de iru, purei shi te iru]
please - お願いします [onegai shi masu]
pocket - ポケット [poketto]
pointed - 向ける [mukeru]
Poland - ポーランド [po―rando]
police - 警察 [keisatsu]
poor - 貧しい [mazushii]
position - ポジション、場所 [pojishon, basho]
possibility - 可能性 [kanou sei]
possible - 可能である [kanou de aru]
pour - 注ぐ [sosogu]
prepare - 用意する、準備する [youi suru, junbi suru]
press - 押す [osu]
pretend - ふりをする [furi wo suru]
price - 値段、価格 [nedan, kakaku]
problem - 問題 [mondai]
produce - 生産する、作る [seisan suru, tsukuru]
profession - 職業 [shokugyou]
program - プログラム [puroguramu]
programmer - プログラマー [purogurama―]
protect - 守る [mamoru]
publishing - 出版 [shuppan]
pull - 引っ張る、引く [hipparu, hiku]
puppy - 子犬 [koinu]
pursuit - 追跡 [tsuiseki]
push - 押す [osu]
pussycat - 猫 [neko]
put on - 着る、身に着ける [kiru, mi ni tsukeru]
questionnaire - 質問表 [shitsumon hyou]
queue - 列 [retsu]
quick, quickly - 素早く、速く、急いで [subayaku, hayaku, isoi de]
quietly - 静かに [shizuka ni]
quite - 辞める、とめる [yameru, tomeru]
radar - レーダー [re―da―]
radio - ラジオ、無線 [rajio, musen]
railway station - 電車の駅 [densha no eki]

rain - 雨 [ame]
rang - かける、なった [kakeru, na tta]
rat - ねずみ [nezumi]
read - 読む [yomu]
reading - 読んでいる [yon de iru]
ready - 用意できている、準備できている [youi deki te iru, junbi deki te iru]
real - 本当の、実際の [hontou no, jissai no]
really - 本当に [hontouni]
reason - 理由 [riyuu]
recommend - 推薦する、すすめる [suisen suru, susumeru]
recommendation - 推薦、おすすめ [suisen, osusume]
recommended - 勧めた、推薦した [susume ta, suisen shi ta]
record - 記録 [kiroku]
red - 赤い [akai]
refuse - 断る、拒否する [kotowaru, kyohi suru]
rehabilitate - リハビリする [rihabiri suru]
rehabilitation - リハビリ [rihabiri]
remain - 残る、とどまる [nokoru, todomaru]
remembered - 思い出した、覚えていた [omoidashi ta, oboe te i ta]
report - レポート [repo―to]
reporter - レポーター [repo―ta―]
rescue - 助ける、救助する [tasukeru, kyuujo suru]
rescue service - 救助サービス [kyuujo sa―bisu]
ricochet - 跳飛、跳ね返ること [chouhi, hanekaeru koto]
right - 右 [migi]
ring; to ring - 電話をする、鳴らす ; 電話をするために [denwa wo suru, narasu ; denwa wo suru tame ni]
road - 道路 [douro]
robber - 泥棒、強盗、窃盗をする人 [dorobou, goutou, settou wo suru hito]
robbery - 泥棒、窃盗、強盗 [dorobou, settou, goutou]
roof - 屋根 [yane]

room - 部屋 [heya]
rooms - 部屋（複数）[heya（fukusuu）]
round - まわる [mawaru]
rub - こする [kosuru]
rubber - ゴム [gomu]
rubric - 欄、題目 [ran, daimoku]
rule - ルール、規則 [ruーru, kisoku]
run - 走る、動かす [hashiru, ugokasu]
run away - 走り去る、逃げる [hashirisaru, nigeru]
running - 走る、動かす [hashiru, ugokasu]
rushed - 急いだ [isoi da]
sad - 悲しい [kanashii]
safe - 安全な [anzen na]
said - 言った、発言した [i tta, hatsugen shi ta]
same - 同じ [onaji]
sand - 砂 [suna]
sandwich - サンドイッチ [sandoicchi]
Saturday - 土曜日 [doyoubi]
save - 救う、助ける [sukuu, tasukeru]
saw - みた、目撃した [mi ta, mokugeki shi ta]
say - 言う [iu]
school - 学校 [gakkou]
sea - 海 [umi]
seashore - 海岸 [kaigan]
season - 季節 [kisetsu]
seat belts - シートベルト [shiーtoberuto]
seat; take a seat - 座る；席に座る [suwaru ; seki ni suwaru]
second - ２番目の [ni banme no]
secret - 秘密 [himitsu]
secretary - 秘書 [hisho]
secretly - 密かに、秘密に [hisoka ni, himitsu ni]
see - みる、わかる、理解する [miru, wakaru, rikai suru]
seed - 種 [tane]
seek - and
seldom - めったにない [mettani nai]
sell - 売る [uru]

sent - 送った [oku tta]
sergeant - 巡査部長 [junsa buchou]
serial - 連続ドラマ（読み方）[renzoku dorama（yomikata）]
seriously - 真剣に [shinken ni]
servant - 使用人 [shiyounin]
serve - サービスする, 仕える [saーbisu suru, tsukaeru]
set free - 放す、自由にする [hanasu, jiyuu ni suru]
seven - ７ [nana]
seventeen - １７ [juu nana]
seventh - ７番目の [nana banme no]
sex - 性別 [seibetsu]
shake - 振る、揺れる [furu, yureru]
she - 彼女は [kanojo wa]
sheet (of paper) - 用紙、シート [youshi, shiーto]
ship - 船 [fune]
shook - 振った [fu tta]
shop - お店 [o mise]
shop assistant - 店員 [ten'in]
shopping center - ショッピングセンター [shoppingu sentaー]
shops - お店（複数）[o mise（fukusuu）]
shore - 岸 [kishi]
short - 短い [mijikai]
shot - 撃つ [utsu]
show - みせる [miseru]
showed - 見せた [mise ta]
silent, silently - 静かに、黙って [shizuka ni, dama tte]
silly - ばかげた、ばかな [bakage ta, baka na]
simple - 簡単な、単純な [kantan na, tanjun na]
since (temporal) - から [kara]
since, as - なぜなら、から [nazenara, kara]
sing; singer - 歌う；歌手 [utau ; kashu]
single - 独身 [dokushin]
siren - サイレン [sairen]
sister - 姉、妹 [ane, imouto]

sit - 座る [suwaru]
sit down - 座る [suwaru]
situation - 状況、シチュエーション [joukyou, shichue―shon]
six - 6 [roku]
sixth - 6番目の [roku banme no]
sixty - 60 [roku juu]
skill - スキル、腕前 [sukiru, udemae]
sleep - 眠る、寝る [nemuru, neru]
sleeping - 眠っている [nemu tte iru]
slightly - わずかに [wazuka ni]
slowly - ゆっくりと [yukkuri to]
sly - ずるい、ずる賢い [zurui, zuru kashikoi]
sly, slyly - ずるい、いたずらに [zurui, itazurani]
small - 小さい、少ない [chiisai, sukunai]
smart - 頭の良い、賢い [atama no yoi, kashikoi]
smile - 微笑む、笑いかける [hohoemu, waraikakeru]
smiled - 笑った、微笑んだ [wara tta, hohoen da]
snack - おやつ、スナック [o yatsu, sunakku]
so - だから、では [dakara, dewa]
solution, answer - こたえ、解決策 [kotae, kaiketsu saku]
some - いくつか [ikutsu ka]; いくつかの、何人かの、いくらかの [ikutsu ka no, nan nin ka no, ikura ka no]
somebody - 誰か [dare ka]
something - 何か [nani ka]
sometimes - ときどき、たまに [tokidoki, tamani]
son - 息子 [musuko]
soon - すぐに [suguni]
space - 宇宙、スペース [uchuu, supe―su]
spaceship - 宇宙船 [uchuusen]
spaniel - スパニエル [supanieru]
Spanish - スペイン人、スペイン語 [supein jin, supein go]; スペイン人の、スペイン語の [supein jin no, supein go no]
speak - 話す [hanasu]
speech - スピーチ [supi―chi]

speed; to speed - 加速、スピード；加速する、スピード違反をする [kasoku, supi―do ; kasoku suru, supi―do ihan wo suru]
speeder - スピード違反をする人 [supi―do ihan wo suru hito]
spend - 費やす、かける、過ごす [tsuiyasu, kakeru, sugosu]
sport bike - スポーツバイク [supo―tsu baiku]
sport; sport shop - スポーツ；スポーツ店 [supo―tsu ; supo―tsu ten]
spread - 広める、広げる [hiromeru, hirogeru]
square - 広場 [hiroba]
stairs - 階段（複数）[kaidan（fukusuu）]
stand - 立つ [tatsu]
standard - スタンダードの、普通の [sutanda―do no, futsuu no]
star - 星 [hoshi]
start - 始める、始まる [hajimeru, hajimaru]
started (to drive) - （運転を）始めた [(unten wo) hajime ta]
status; family status - ステータス、事態 ; 家族ステータス [sute―tasu, jitai ; kazoku sute―tasu]
steal - こっそり手に入れる、取る、盗む [kossori te ni ireru, toru, nusumu]
steer - ハンドルをきる [handoru wo kiru]
step - 踏む [fumu]
step; to step - 踏む; 踏むために [fumu ; fumu tame ni]
stepped - 踏んだ [fun da]
still - まだ、それでも [mada, soredemo]
stinking - においのする [nioi no suru]
stolen - 盗まれた [nusuma re ta]
stone - 石 [ishi]
stop - とめる、とまる、終わりにする [tomeru, tomaru, owari ni suru]
stopped - とめた、やめた、終えた [tome ta, yame ta, oe ta]

story - ストーリー、物語、話 [suto―ri―, monogatari, hanashi]; 物語、ストーリー [monogatari, suto―ri―]
strange - おかしな、変な [okashina, hen na]
street - 通り、道 [toori, michi]
streets - 通り、道（複数） [toori, michi （fukusuu）]
strength - 力、強さ [chikara, tsuyo sa]
strong, strongly - 強い、強く [tsuyoi, tsuyoku]
student - 生徒、学生 [seito, gakusei]
students - 生徒達、学生達（複数） [seito tachi, gakusei tachi （fukusuu）]
study - 勉強する [benkyou suru]
stuffed parachutist - 人形（パラシュートをする人） [ningyou(parashu―to wo suru hito)]
suddenly - 突然 [totsuzen]
suitable - 合っている、ぴったりの、ふさわしい [a tte iru, pittari no, fusawashii]
supermarket - スーパー [su―pa―]
sure - 確信している [kakushin shi te iru]
surprise - 驚かせる [odoroka seru]
surprised - 驚いている [odoroi te iru]
swallow - 浅い [asai]
swim - 泳ぐ [oyogu]
switched on - つけた [tsuke ta]
table - テーブル、机 [te―buru, tsukue]
tables - テーブル、机（複数） [te―buru, tsukue （fukusuu）]
tail - しっぽ [shippo]
take - とる、使う、持って行く、食べる、飲む [toru, tsukau, mo tte iku, taberu, nomu]
take part - 積極的に参加する [sekkyoku teki ni sanka suru]
taken - 取られた、盗まれた、 [tora re ta, nusuma re ta,]
talk - 話す、喋る [hanasu, shaberu]
tanker - タンカー [tanka―]
tap - 蛇口 [jaguchi]
task - 課題、タスク [kadai, tasuku]
tasty - おいしい [oishii]

taxi - タクシー [takushi―]
taxi driver - タクシードライバー [takushi― doraiba―]
tea - お茶 [ocha]
teach - 教える [oshieru]
teacher - 先生 [sensei]
team - チーム [chi―mu]
telephone; to telephone - 電話機；電話をする [denwaki ; denwa wo suru]
television - テレビ [terebi]
tell, say - 言う、伝える [iu, tsutaeru]
ten - 10 [juu]
tenth - １０番目の [juu banme no]
test - テスト、試験 [tesuto, shiken]
text - 本文、文章、原稿、メッセージ [honbun, bunshou, genkou, messe―ji]
textbook, text - 教科書 [kyoukasho]
than; George is older than Linda. - より；ジョージはリンダより年上です [yori ; jo―ji wa rinda yori toshiue desu]
thank; thank you, thanks - 感謝する；ありがとうございます、ありがとう [kansha suru ; arigatou gozai masu, arigatou]
that - それ、あれ [sore, are]
that (conj) - 接続詞なので訳さない [setsuzokushi na node yakusa nai]
that; I know that this book is interesting. - 接続詞なので訳さない；わたしはこの本が面白いことを知っています [setsuzokushi na node yakusa nai ; watashi wa kono hon ga omoshiroi koto wo shi tte i masu]
the host family - ホストファミリー [hosutofamiri―]
their - 彼らの [karera no]
then - そして、その後 [soshite, sonogo]
there - そこ [soko]
these, those - それら、あれら（複数） [sorera, are ra （fukusuu）]
they - 彼らは [karera wa]
thief - 泥棒 [dorobou]
thieves - 泥棒（複数） [dorobou （fukusuu）]

thing - もの、こと [mono, koto]
think - 考える [kangaeru]
thinking - 考えている [kangae te iru]
third - 3番目の [san banme no]
thirty - 30 [san juu]
this stuff - これ [kore]
this, this book - これ、この；この本 [kore, kono ; kono hon]
thousand - 1000 [sen]
three - 3 [san]
through - 中へ、抜けて、通して [naka e, nuke te, tooshi te]
ticket - チケット、券 [chiketto, ken]
tiger - 虎 [tora]
time - 時間 [jikan]
tired - 疲れている [tsukare te iru]
today - 今日、本日 [kyou, honjitsu]
together - 一緒に [issho ni]
toilet - トイレ [toire]
tomorrow - 明日 [ashita]
too - 同じく、〜も [onajiku, 〜 mo]
took - 乗った、取った、使った、食べた、飲んだ [no tta, to tta, tsuka tta, tabe ta, non da]
town - 町 [machi]
toy - おもちゃ [omocha]
train - 電車 [densha]
train; trained - 訓練する、鍛える；訓練されている、鍛えられている [kunren suru, kitaeru ; kunren sa re te iru, kitae rare te iru]
translator - 通訳、翻訳家 [tsuuyaku, hon'yaku ka]
transport - 運送する、運ぶ [unsou suru, hakobu]
travel - 旅行 [ryokou]
trick - トリック、技 [torikku, waza]
tried - 疲れた [tsukare ta]
trousers - ズボン（複数）[zubon（fukusuu）]
truck - トラック [torakku]
try - ためす、してみる [tamesu, shi te miru]

turn - 曲がる、曲げる、向ける、向く [magaru, mageru, mukeru, muku]
turn off - 消す [kesu]
turn on - つける [tsukeru]
turned - 向いた、曲がった [mui ta, maga tta]
TV-set - TVセット [tiー bui setto]
twelve - 12 [juu ni]
twenty - 20 [ni juu]
twenty-five - 25 [ni juu go]
twenty-one - 21 [ni juu ichi]
twice - 二度 [ni do]
two - ふたつ [futatsu]
unconscious - 無意識に、意識をなくして [muishiki ni, ishiki wo nakushi te]
under - の下 [no shita]
underline - 下線 [kasen]
understand - 理解する、わかる [rikai suru, wakaru]
understood - わかった、理解した [waka tta, rikai shi ta]
unfair - 不公平 [fukouhei]
United States/the USA - アメリカ [amerika]
unload - 降ろす、荷おろしをする [orosu, ni oroshi wo suru]
until - まで [made]
us - わたしたちに [watashi tachi ni]
USA - アメリカ [amerika]
use - 使う [tsukau]
usual - 普段の、いつもの、通常の [fudan no, itsumo no, tsuujou no]
usually - いつもは、通常は、普段は [itsumo wa, tsuujou wa, fudan wa]
very - たくさん、とても [takusan, totemo]
vet - 獣医 [juui]
videocassette - ビデオカセット [bideokasetto]
video-shop - ビデオショップ [bideo shoppu]
village - 村 [mura]
visited - 訪問した [houmon shi ta]
voice - 声 [koe]
wait - 待つ [matsu]
waited - 待った [matta]
walk - 歩く [aruku]

walking - 歩いている [arui te iru]
want - 欲しい、欲しがる [hoshii, hoshi garu]
wanted - 欲しがられる [hoshi gara reru]
war - 戦争 [sensou]
warm - 暖かい [atatakai]
warm up - 暖める [atatameru]
was - だった [da tta]
wash - 洗う [arau]
washer - 洗濯機 [sentakuki]
watch - みる [miru]
water - 水 [mizu]
wave - 波 [nami]
way - 道 [michi]
we - わたしたちは [watashi tachi wa]
weather - 天気 [tenki]
week - 週 [shuu]
went away - 去った、いなくなった [sa tta, i naku na tta]
were - であった [de a tta]
wet - 濡れている [nure te iru]
whale; killer whale - くじら, シャチ [kujira, shachi]
what - なに [nani]
What is the matter? - どうしたの？、何があったの？ [dou shi ta no?, nani ga a tta no?]
What is this? - これは何ですか？ [kore wa nan desu ka?]
What table? - 何のテーブルですか？ [nan no te－buru desu ka?]
wheel - タイヤ [taiya]
when - いつ [itsu]
where - どこ、どちら [doko, dochira]
which - どの [dono]
while - している間、その間 [shi te iru kan, sonokan]
white - 白い [shiroi]
who - 誰 [dare]
whose - 誰の [dare no]
wide, widely - 広く [hiroku]

will - （これから）する [（korekara） suru]
wind - 風 [kaze]
window - 窓 [mado]
windows - 窓（複数） [mado （fukusuu）]
with - と一緒に、で [to issho ni, de]
without - なしで、せずに [nashi de, se zu ni]
without a word - 何も言わずに [nani mo iwa zu ni]
woman - 女性 [josei]
wonderful - 素晴らしい [subarashii]
word - 単語、言葉 [tango, kotoba]
words - 単語、言葉（複数） [tango, kotoba （fukusuu）]
worked - 働いた、 [hatarai ta,]
worker - 従業員、労働者 [juugyou in, roudou sha]
working - 動いている、働いている [ugoi te iru, hatarai te iru]
world - 世界 [sekai]
worry - 心配する [shinpai suru]
write - 書く [kaku]
writer - 作家、ライター [sakka, raita－]
wrote - 書いた、手紙を書いた [kai ta, tegami wo kai ta]
yard - 庭、場 [niwa, ba]
year - 年 [toshi]
yellow - 黄色い [kiiroi]
yes - はい、そうです [hai, sou desu]
yesterday - 昨日 [kinou]
yet - まだ [mada]
you - あなた [anata]; あなたは [anata wa]
young - 若い、年下の [wakai, toshishita no]
your - あなたの [anata no]
yours sincerely - 敬具 [keigu]
zebra - シマウマ [shimauma]
zoo - 動物園 [doubutsu en]

Recommended reading

First Japanese Reader for Beginners
Bilingual for Speakers of English
Beginner and Elementary (A1 A2)

The book consists of Beginner and Elementary courses with parallel Japanese-English texts. The author maintains learners' motivation with funny stories about real life situations such as meeting people, studying, job searches, working etc. The method utilizes the natural human ability to remember words used in texts repeatedly and systematically. The second and the following chapters of the Beginner course have only about thirty new words each. The audio tracks are available inclusive on www.lppbooks.com/Japanese/

First Japanese Reader for Students
Bilingual for Speakers of English
Beginner Elementary (A1 A2)

Each chapter is filled with words that are organized by topic, then used in a story in Japanese. Questions and answers rephrase information and text is repeated in English to aid comprehension. The quick and easy-to-use format organizes many of life's situations from knowing your way around the house, studying at university, or getting a job. The method utilizes the natural human ability to remember words used in texts repeatedly and systematically. The audio tracks are available inclusive on www.lppbooks.com/Japanese/

Learn Japanese Language Through Dialogue
Bilingual for Speakers of English
Beginner Elementary (A1 A2)

The textbook gives you a lot of examples on how questions in Japanese should be formed. It is easy to see the difference between Japanese and English using parallel translation. Common questions and answers used in everyday situations are explained simply enough even for beginners. The audio tracks are available inclusive on www.lppbooks.com/Japanese/

First Japanese Reader for Business
Bilingual for Speakers of English
Beginner Elementary (A1 A2)

First Japanese Reader for Business is a resource that guides readers with the Japanese vocabulary, phrases, and questions that are relevant to many situations in the workplace. With twenty-five chapters on topics from the office to software and supplementary resources including the Japanese/English and English/Japanese dictionaries, it is the book to help the businessperson take their Japanese language knowledge to the professional level. The audio tracks are available inclusive on www.lppbooks.com/Japanese/

First Japanese Medical Reader for Health Professions and Nursing
Bilingual for Speakers of English
Beginner Elementary (A1 A2)

First Japanese Medical Reader for Health Professions and Nursing will give you the words and phrases necessary for helping patients making appointments, informing them of their diagnosis, and their treatment options. Medical specialties range from ENT to dentistry. Supplementary resources include the Japanese/English and English/Japanese dictionaries. Use this book to take your Japanese knowledge to the health professional's level. The audio tracks are available inclusive on www.lppbooks.com/Japanese/

www.ingramcontent.com/pod-product-compliance
Lightning Source LLC
Chambersburg PA
CBHW080911170426
43201CB00017B/2292